Ready to Test

SKILLS & STRATEGIES

GRADE **5**

D0521583

AMERICAN EDUCATION PUBLISHING™

An imprint of Carson-Dellosa Publishing
Greensboro, NC

American Education Publishing™
An imprint of Carson-Dellosa Publishing LLC
P.O. Box 35665
Greensboro, NC 27425 USA

ISBN 978-1-60996-537-2

Table of Contents

Language Arts
Reading

Chapter 1: Vocabulary

Chapter 2: Reading Comprehension

Language Arts
Language

Chapter 3: Mechanics

Chapter 4: Usage

Chapter 5: Writing

Math

Chapter 6: Concepts

Chapter 7: Computation

Chapter 8: Geometry

Chapter 9: Measurement

Chapter 10: Applications

Letter to Parents

Dear Parents and Guardians:

The *Ready to Test* series will prepare your child for standardized tests by providing him or her with test-taking tips and strategies for success. The sample questions and tests in this book will allow your child to gain familiarity with standardized tests, making him or her more comfortable on test day and, therefore, more likely to do well.

You can help your child with this important part of learning. Allow your child to become familiar with the testing strategies presented in this book. If your child gets stuck at any point when completing the book, encourage him or her to think of those tips to help determine what to do.

Time your child to help him or her learn time management when taking tests. On average, a lesson page in this book should take about 10 minutes to complete. A Practice Test should take about 45–60 minutes to complete. Keep in mind, however, that the goal is not how fast your child can complete each page. Instead, the goal is to provide practice and strategies for success on test day.

Below are some additional suggestions that will help your child make the most of *Ready to Test*.

- Provide a quiet place to work.
- Go over the work with your child.
- Tell your child he or she is doing a good job.
- Remind him or her to use the tips that are included throughout the book.

By preparing your child with test-taking tips and strategies, *Ready to Test* can help take the fear out of standardized tests and help your child achieve the best scores possible.

Introduction

About the Common Core State Standards

The Common Core State Standards Initiative is a state-led effort developed in collaboration with teachers, school administrators, and experts to provide a clear and consistent framework to prepare children for college and the workforce. The standards are based on the most effective models from states across the country. They provide teachers and parents with a common understanding of what students are expected to learn. Consistent standards will provide appropriate benchmarks for all students, regardless of where they live.

The Common Core State Standards provide a consistent, clear understanding of what students are expected to learn, so teachers and parents know how to help them. The standards are designed to be relevant to the real world, reflecting the knowledge and skills that children need for success in college and their future careers. With students fully prepared for the future, our communities and our country will be best positioned to compete successfully in the global economy.

These standards define the knowledge and skills students should have within their education so that they will graduate high school able to succeed in college and in workforce training programs. The standards:

- are aligned with college and work expectations.
- are clear, understandable, and consistent.
- include rigorous content and application of knowledge through high-order skills.
- build upon strengths and lessons of current state standards.
- are informed by other top-performing countries, so that all students are prepared to succeed in our global economy and society.
- are evidence-based.

Common Core Standards: Language Arts

The Language Arts standards focus on five key areas. Students who are proficient in these areas are able to demonstrate independence, build strong content knowledge, comprehend as well as critique, respond to the varying demands of the task, value evidence, use technology strategically and effectively, and understand other perspectives and cultures.

Reading

The Common Core Standards establish increasing complexity in what students must be able to read, so that all students are ready for the demands of college- and career-level reading. The standards also require the progressive development of reading comprehension, so that students are able to gain more from what they read.

Writing

The ability to write logical arguments based on substantive claims, sound reasoning, and relevant evidence is a cornerstone of the writing standards. Research is emphasized throughout the standards but most prominently in the writing strand, since a written analysis and presentation of findings is often critical.

Speaking and Listening

The standards require that students gain, evaluate, and present increasingly complex information, ideas, and evidence through listening and speaking, as well as through media.

Language

The standards expect that students will grow their vocabularies through a mix of conversations, direct instruction, and reading. The standards will help students determine word meanings, appreciate the nuances of words, and steadily expand their vocabulary of words and phrases.

Media and Technology

Skills related to media use are integrated throughout the standards, just as media and technology are integrated in school curriculum for life in the 21st century.

Common Core Standards: Math

The mathematically proficient student must be able to:

Make sense of problems and persevere in solving them. Mathematically proficient students start by thinking about the meaning of a problem and deciding upon the best way to find the solution. They think the problem through while solving it, and they continually ask themselves, "Does this make sense?"

Reason abstractly and quantitatively. Mathematically proficient students make sense of quantities and their relationships in problem situations. Quantitative reasoning entails an understanding of the problem at hand; paying attention to the units involved; considering the meaning of quantities, not just how to compute them; and knowing and using different properties of operations and objects.

Construct viable arguments and critique the reasoning of others. Mathematically proficient students understand and use stated assumptions, definitions, and previously established results in constructing arguments. Students at all grades can listen or read the arguments of others, decide whether they make sense, and ask useful questions to clarify or improve the arguments.

Model with mathematics. Mathematically proficient students can apply the math they've learned to solve problems arising in everyday life.

Use appropriate tools strategically. Mathematically proficient students consider the available tools when solving a mathematical problem and make appropriate decisions about when each of these tools might be helpful.

Attend to precision. Mathematically proficient students try to communicate precisely to others and in their own reasoning. They state the meaning of the symbols they choose. They calculate accurately and express answers efficiently.

Look for and make use of structure. Mathematically proficient students look closely to discern a pattern or structure. Students can also step back for an overview and shift perspective.

Look for and express regularity in repeated reasoning. Mathematically proficient students look for patterns and shortcuts. As they work to solve a problem, students continue to keep the big picture in mind while attending to the details. They continually evaluate whether or not their results make logical sense.

To learn more about the Common Core State Standards, visit corestandards.org.

Synonyms

Directions: Read each item. Fill in the circle next to the word that means the same, or about the same, as the underlined word.

Example

a small <u>dwelling</u>

Ⓐ school

Ⓑ home

Ⓒ suburb

Ⓓ tribe

Answer: (B)

1. a successful <u>corporation</u>

Ⓐ business

Ⓑ team

Ⓒ person

Ⓓ country

2. a skilled <u>laborer</u>

Ⓕ musician

Ⓖ professor

Ⓗ worker

Ⓙ relative

3. a tiny <u>particle</u>

Ⓐ animal

Ⓑ package

Ⓒ piece

Ⓓ gift

4. a desert <u>region</u>

Ⓕ area

Ⓖ culture

Ⓗ religion

Ⓙ plant

5. An <u>imaginary</u> story is _____.

Ⓐ biographical

Ⓑ fictional

Ⓒ actual

Ⓓ humorous

6. To <u>interpret</u> is to _____.

Ⓕ organize

Ⓖ adjust

Ⓗ catch

Ⓙ explain

7. To <u>pave</u> is to _____.

Ⓐ cover

Ⓑ hide

Ⓒ recycle

Ⓓ fly

8. An <u>affectionate</u> person is _____.

Ⓕ hostile

Ⓖ adorable

Ⓗ loving

Ⓙ ill

Choose only one answer. Be sure to fill in the circle completely.

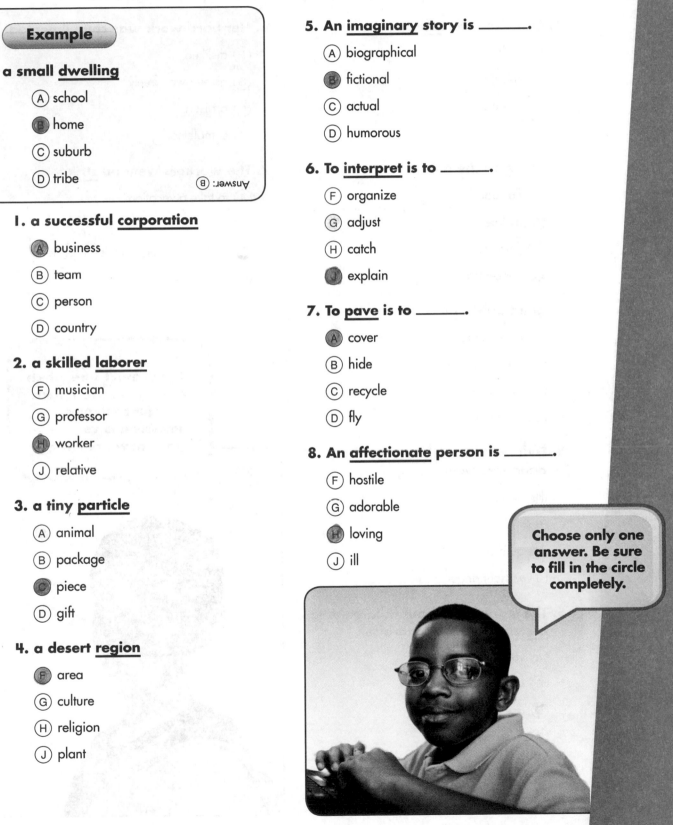

Synonyms

Directions: Read each item. Fill in the circle next to the word that means the same, or about the same, as the underlined word.

1. Complete the <u>assignment</u>.

- Ⓐ task
- Ⓑ assistant
- Ⓒ design
- Ⓓ office

2. <u>Focus</u> on the object.

- Ⓕ fluctuate
- Ⓖ irritate
- Ⓗ compile
- Ⓙ concentrate

3. good <u>publicity</u>

- Ⓐ appreciation
- Ⓑ public attention
- Ⓒ publisher
- Ⓓ celebrity

4. Tom waited <u>anxiously</u> for the announcement.

- Ⓕ nervously
- Ⓖ without concern
- Ⓗ quickly
- Ⓙ without anger

5. The story was about children who <u>benefit</u> from the fundraiser.

- Ⓐ volunteer
- Ⓑ serve
- Ⓒ receive help
- Ⓓ raise money

6. Her hard work was <u>complimented</u>.

- Ⓕ disliked
- Ⓖ given away freely
- Ⓗ praised
- Ⓙ completed

7. The workers went on <u>strike</u>.

- Ⓐ to take a vacation
- Ⓑ to hit
- Ⓒ to stop working in order to protest
- Ⓓ to throw a ball

If you aren't sure which answer is correct, take your best guess. Eliminate answer choices you know are wrong.

Antonyms

Directions: Read each item. Fill in the circle next to the word that means the opposite of the underlined word.

Example

The guests departed.

- (A) honored
- (B) excited
- (C) gathered
- (D) neglected

Answer: C

---

1. Accept the truth.

- (A) deny
- (B) understand
- (C) illustrate
- (D) respect

2. attentive people

- (F) beautiful
- (G) prosperous
- (H) messy
- (J) careless

3. an absurd story

- (A) logical
- (B) exciting
- (C) rewarding
- (D) fanciful

4. generous servings

- (F) large
- (G) grateful
- (H) small
- (J) general

5. a brief description

- (A) important
- (B) lengthy
- (C) short
- (D) casual

6. confident in your abilities

- (F) uncertain
- (G) assured
- (H) proud
- (J) neglectful

7. employ the workers

- (A) befriend
- (B) manage
- (C) argue with
- (D) dismiss

Remember, you are looking for the answer that means the opposite.

Name _____   Date _____

Antonyms

Directions: Read each item. Fill in the circle next to the word that means the opposite of the underlined word.

1. **Joseph has a <u>superior</u> attitude that no one really <u>likes</u>.**

   Ⓐ extreme

   🅑 inferior

   Ⓒ great

   Ⓓ focused

2. **Mr. Howard made a <u>rare</u> appearance at the jazz club.**

   🅕 frequent

   Ⓖ old

   Ⓗ uncommon

   Ⓙ distant

3. **Will Selena <u>admit</u> that she broke the vase?**

   Ⓐ pretend

   Ⓑ agree

   🅒 deny

   Ⓓ ignore

4. **Please <u>combine</u> the ingredients.**

   Ⓕ display

   Ⓖ put together

   Ⓗ mix

   🅙 separate

5. **Aunt Marian bought <u>imitation</u> vanilla.**

   🅐 genuine

   Ⓑ expired

   Ⓒ unusual

   Ⓓ fake

6. **The dentist put a <u>temporary</u> crown on Dad's tooth.**

   Ⓕ gold

   🅖 permanent

   Ⓗ short-lived

   Ⓙ brand-new

7. **The football team celebrated after their <u>victory</u>.**

   Ⓐ win

   🅑 defeat

   Ⓒ game

   Ⓓ excitement

8. **I'll <u>increase</u> the volume on my phone.**

   Ⓕ remove

   Ⓖ change

   Ⓗ turn up

   🅙 decrease

Multiple-Meaning Words

Directions: Read each item. Fill in the circle next to the best answer.

Example

Set the package _____ to the side.
We had the day _____.

- (A) over
- (B) off
- (C) apart
- (D) away

Answer: (B)

---

1. The train is _____ for Seattle.
Mr. Lachhey tightly _____ the
mattress to the roof of the car.

- (A) headed
- (B) tied
- (C) secured
- (D) bound

2. Bess put a clean _____ on the
bed.
Jason washed the cookie _____
after he finished baking.

- (F) pillow
- (G) tray
- (H) sheet
- (J) cover

3. We _____ nearer to the warmth
of the campfire.
He _____ the wrong conclusion
from the facts that were presented.

- (A) drew
- (B) moved
- (C) identified
- (D) illustrated

4. When the twins are frustrated,
they _____ their feet and cry.
Did you put a _____ on the letter
before you mailed it?

- (F) kick
- (G) stamp
- (H) label
- (J) stomp

**Use the meaning
of the sentence to
help you choose the
correct answer.**

Name _____ Date _____

Multiple-Meaning Words

Directions: Choose the answer in which the underlined word is used in the same way as it is in the boldface sentence.

1. Unemployment is <u>running</u> high here since the factory closed.

- (A) Tracy saw the horse <u>running</u> through the field.
- (B) Katrina was <u>running</u> the lawnmower.
- (C) Club attendance was <u>running</u> low due to heavy snow.
- (D) Parker is <u>running</u> for class president.

2. Kieran could <u>picture</u> the beach in his mind.

- (F) I took a <u>picture</u> with my new camera.
- (G) Piper drew a lovely <u>picture</u> for her grandma.
- (H) The <u>picture</u> in the catalog is on page 7.
- (J) <u>Picture</u> yourself doing something you love.

3. Groaning, he rolled over and <u>planted</u> his feet firmly on the floor.

- (A) Liza <u>planted</u> four rows of cucumbers.
- (B) The lawyer claimed that the evidence had been <u>planted</u>.
- (C) The settlers <u>planted</u> new crops.
- (D) Anya <u>planted</u> her feet in the dirt before swinging the bat.

4. My grandmother had to <u>raise</u> 11 children all on her own.

- (F) Next summer, we will <u>raise</u> chickens and goats.
- (G) Ms. Khan asked her boss for a <u>raise</u>.
- (H) <u>Raise</u> your hands, and then touch your toes.
- (J) We can <u>raise</u> the board if we work together.

5. Jack has a <u>degree</u> in zoology.

- (A) My little brother got a third-<u>degree</u> burn on his arm.
- (B) Shilpy will graduate in June with a <u>degree</u> in English.
- (C) The temperature today is only one <u>degree</u> warmer than yesterday.
- (D) Please turn down the thermostat a <u>degree</u> or two.

6. He plans to <u>store</u> the corn in his barn.

- (F) She went to the grocery <u>store</u>.
- (G) My dad will <u>store</u> the lawnmower in the shed.
- (H) There is a lot of fun in <u>store</u> when you visit the zoo.
- (J) My favorite <u>store</u> is in the mall.

7. Will you <u>brush</u> my hair?

- (A) She bought a new <u>brush</u>.
- (B) After the storm, the yard was littered with <u>brush</u>.
- (C) I need to <u>brush</u> the dog.
- (D) She felt the kitten <u>brush</u> against her leg.

Words in Context

Directions: Read the paragraph. Find the word that best fits in each numbered blank.

Example

The United States Capitol is well known for its _____ **(A)**, or round room. The room has a large dome. A bronze Statue of Freedom _____ **(B)** on top of the dome.

A. (A) parlor

(B) library

(C) rotunda

(D) media center

Answer: C

B. (F) stands

(G) centered

(H) flies

(J) bends

Answer: F

The Montgolfier brothers _____ **(1)** the hot-air balloon in 1783. However, they _____ **(2)** never guessed how high or how far one of these balloons could go. In the brothers' first _____ **(3)**, they used a huge bag made of paper and _____ **(4)**. They held its open end over a _____ **(5)**. The bag filled with smoke and hot air. Then, it rose into the air and _____ **(6)** for a mile and a half.

---

1. (A) discovered

(B) invented

(C) explored

(D) arranged

2. (F) probably

(G) randomly

(H) rarely

(J) frequently

3. (A) grade

(B) demonstration

(C) hope

(D) suggestion

4. (F) steel

(G) bricks

(H) mortar

(J) fabric

5. (A) pool

(B) puddle

(C) fire

(D) engine

6. (F) dropped

(G) recorded

(H) sank

(J) floated

> **Look carefully at each answer choice. Choose the word that sounds best in the sentence.**

Words in Context

Directions: Read the paragraph. Find the word that best fits in each numbered blank.

Cells are the smallest and most basic units of _____ **(1)** matter. They are the small _____ **(2)** that, when put together, make organs, plants, and even people. All living things are made of cells, though not all cells are exactly _____ **(3)**.

Both animal and plant cells have a cell membrane, which _____ **(4)** all the cell parts together. The nucleus is one of the largest parts of the cell. It is the command center of the cell and controls the _____ **(5)** in the cell. Chromosomes inside this command center control what an organism will be like. For instance, your chromosomes _____ **(6)** the information that makes you have blue or brown eyes and black or red hair. Cytoplasm is the thick _____ **(7)** that all the parts of the cell float in. It's mostly water but also has some important _____ **(8)** inside.

1. Ⓐ stone
   Ⓑ important
   Ⓒ living
   Ⓓ educational

2. Ⓕ pieces
   Ⓖ organs
   Ⓗ fluids
   Ⓙ bones

3. Ⓐ growing
   Ⓑ large
   Ⓒ separate
   Ⓓ alike

4. Ⓕ creates
   Ⓖ divides
   Ⓗ reverses
   Ⓙ holds

5. Ⓐ outside
   Ⓑ activities
   Ⓒ immobility
   Ⓓ surviving

6. Ⓕ carry
   Ⓖ reflect
   Ⓗ follow
   Ⓙ escalate

7. Ⓐ covering
   Ⓑ metal
   Ⓒ liquid
   Ⓓ transparency

8. Ⓕ information
   Ⓖ cells
   Ⓗ chemicals
   Ⓙ patterns

Word Study

Directions: Read each item. Fill in the circle next to the best answer.

Example

Which of these words probably comes from the Latin word *albus* meaning *white*?

- Ⓐ albino
- Ⓑ album
- Ⓒ algebra
- Ⓓ alchemy

Answer: Ⓐ

---

1. Which of these words probably comes from the Greek word *demos kratos*, meaning *rule of the people*?

- Ⓐ demolish
- Ⓑ democracy
- Ⓒ demote
- Ⓓ demonstration

2. Which of these words probably comes from the Latin word *audire*, meaning *to hear*?

- Ⓕ audit
- Ⓖ auburn
- Ⓗ auction
- Ⓙ audio

3. The stadium was filled with _____.
   Which of these words would indicate that there was an audience at the stadium?

- Ⓐ spectators
- Ⓑ performers
- Ⓒ soldiers
- Ⓓ employees

4. Ramon's grandfather stored family _____ in the attic.
   Which of these words means there were heirlooms in the attic?

- Ⓕ relics
- Ⓖ trophies
- Ⓗ documents
- Ⓙ rubbish

5. Maggy was _____ that her team lost the game.
   Which of these words would indicate that Maggy felt sad?

- Ⓐ related
- Ⓑ frustrated
- Ⓒ disappointed
- Ⓓ angry

Look for key words in the question. They will help you choose the correct answer!

Name _____   Date _____

Word Study

Directions: Choose the answer that best defines the underlined part of the word.

1. <u>pre</u>cede   <u>pre</u>dict

- Ⓐ after
- Ⓑ around
- Ⓒ before
- Ⓓ between

2. <u>dis</u>appear   <u>dis</u>able

- Ⓕ without
- Ⓖ opposite of
- Ⓗ unseen
- Ⓙ broken

3. <u>re</u>wind   <u>re</u>member

- Ⓐ again
- Ⓑ before
- Ⓒ around
- Ⓓ memory

4. <u>anti</u>bacterial   <u>anti</u>perspirant

- Ⓕ clean
- Ⓖ soap
- Ⓗ germ
- Ⓙ against

5. <u>bi</u>cycle   <u>bin</u>oculars

- Ⓐ round
- Ⓑ through
- Ⓒ to see
- Ⓓ two

6 <u>trans</u>portation   <u>trans</u>fer

- Ⓕ across
- Ⓖ above
- Ⓗ under
- Ⓙ round

7. <u>non</u>fiction   <u>non</u>sense

- Ⓐ true
- Ⓑ empty
- Ⓒ humorous
- Ⓓ not

8. <u>over</u>used   <u>over</u>whelming

- Ⓕ strong
- Ⓖ above
- Ⓗ too much
- Ⓙ tired

9. <u>cour</u>ier   <u>cour</u>ser

- Ⓐ running
- Ⓑ ruling
- Ⓒ coursing
- Ⓓ turning

10. <u>prim</u>er   <u>prim</u>eval

- Ⓕ elementary
- Ⓖ original
- Ⓗ first
- Ⓙ former

Word Study

Directions: Choose the answer that best defines the underlined part of the word.

1. bio**logy**   geo**logy**
   - (A) person who
   - (B) study of
   - (C) quality of being
   - (D) full of

2. break**able**   bend**able**
   - (F) quality of
   - (G) lacking
   - (H) can be
   - (J) in the manner of

3. tele**phone**   **phon**ics
   - (A) words
   - (B) writing
   - (C) sound
   - (D) mobile

4. shy**ness**   hopeful**ness**
   - (F) quality of
   - (G) lacking
   - (H) quiet
   - (J) in the manner of

5. inter**rupt**   e**rupt**
   - (A) break
   - (B) loud
   - (C) fall
   - (D) fire

6. con**struct**   **structure**
   - (F) wooden
   - (G) climb
   - (H) connect
   - (J) build

7. **port**able   trans**port**ing
   - (A) vehicle
   - (B) boat
   - (C) carry
   - (D) water

8. bio**graphy**   auto**graph**
   - (F) story
   - (G) write
   - (H) name
   - (J) page

9. **mis**judge   **mis**pronounce
   - (A) correctly
   - (B) before
   - (C) to do after
   - (D) wrongly

10. **sub**zero   **sub**urban
   - (F) under
   - (G) without
   - (H) apart
   - (J) backward

Sample Test 1: Vocabulary

Directions: Read each item. Fill in the circle next to the word that means the same, or about the same, as the underlined word.

Example

spoiled fruit

- (A) citrus
- (B) bruised
- (C) fresh
- (D) rotten

Answer: D

1. Do it now.
- (A) immediately
- (B) later
- (C) soon
- (D) slowly

2. artistic film
- (F) play
- (G) drama
- (H) movie
- (J) episode

3. in the cellar
- (A) attic
- (B) basement
- (C) garage
- (D) workshop

4. newspaper article
- (F) story
- (G) novel
- (H) journal
- (J) book

5. Something that has concluded is
- (A) in progress.
- (B) continuing.
- (C) beginning.
- (D) finished.

6. An irregular shape is
- (F) symmetrical.
- (G) uneven.
- (H) balanced.
- (J) broken.

7. A career is
- (A) a hobby.
- (B) a university.
- (C) an occupation.
- (D) a library.

8. To take a brisk walk means to walk
- (F) quickly.
- (G) leisurely.
- (H) by yourself.
- (J) with others.

GO

Sample Test 1: Vocabulary

Directions: Read each item. Fill in the circle next to the word that means the same, or about the same, as the underlined word.

**9. The <u>association</u> works to help animals.
<u>Association</u> means**

(A) occupation.

(B) college.

(C) friendship.

(D) organization.

**10. You can see the sunlight through the <u>sheer</u> curtains.
<u>Sheer</u> means**

(F) white.

(G) thick.

(H) transparent.

(J) open.

**11. Helga is a <u>loyal</u> friend.
<u>Loyal</u> means**

(A) devoted.

(B) dangerous.

(C) good.

(D) dishonest.

**12. The time line marked the <u>milestones</u> of the Civil War.
<u>Milestones</u> means**

(F) speeches.

(G) roads.

(H) events.

(J) conditions.

Directions: Fill in the circle next to the word that means the opposite of the underlined word.

13. <u>express</u> your thoughts

(A) yell

(B) withhold

(C) summarize

(D) tell

14. <u>obvious</u> signs

(F) unclear

(G) apparent

(H) momentary

(J) secondary

15. <u>ignore</u> the noise

(A) contribute to

(B) notice

(C) overlook

(D) behave

16. <u>respect</u> for the law

(F) obedience

(G) trust

(H) honor

(J) contempt

17. with <u>regret</u>

(A) happiness

(B) sorrow

(C) fear

(D) bravery

18. a great <u>achievement</u>

(F) victory

(G) failure

(H) mistake

(J) accomplishment

GO

Sample Test 1: Vocabulary

Directions: Choose the word that best completes both sentences.

19. Please _____ my coat to the bus.
    An actor's voice must _____ to the last row of seats.

    (A) deliver

    (B) reach

    (C) take

    (D) carry

20. Throw the _____ to me.
    Sheila wore a formal dress to the _____.

    (F) party

    (G) ball

    (H) coat

    (J) dance

21. Reach out with your _____.
    The soldiers gathered _____ for the battle.

    (A) arms

    (B) legs

    (C) supplies

    (D) muskets

22. The class visited a _____ art museum.
    He had to pay a _____ for speeding.

    (F) modern

    (G) charge

    (H) quality

    (J) fine

Directions: Read each item, and mark the best answer.

23. I tied the <u>key</u> on a string.
    In which sentence does the word *key* mean the same thing as in the sentence above?

    (A) The <u>key</u> to a riddle provides the answer.

    (B) I sailed around the <u>key</u>.

    (C) I opened the door with my <u>key</u>.

    (D) The choir sang in <u>key</u>.

24. I opened a savings account at the <u>bank</u>.
    In which sentence does the word *bank* mean the same thing as in the sentence above?

    (F) The pilot flew through a <u>bank</u> of clouds.

    (G) My mom is a manager at the <u>bank</u>.

    (H) Harry's house sits on the <u>bank</u> of a river.

    (J) <u>Bank</u> to the left at the intersection.

Directions: Choose the answer that best defines the underlined part of the words.

25. <u>sub</u>way <u>sub</u>marine

    (A) under

    (B) over

    (C) apart

    (D) backward

26. care<u>less</u> thought<u>less</u>

    (F) less than one

    (G) full of

    (H) without

    (J) forward

Name _____ Date _____

LANGUAGE ARTS

23

Sample Test 1: Vocabulary

Directions: Read each item, and mark the best answer.

27. Which of these words probably comes from the Latin word *barba*, meaning *beard*?

- (A) barb
- (B) barbarian
- (C) barber
- (D) bargain

28. Which of these words probably comes from the Greek word *kolla*, meaning *glue*?

- (F) college
- (G) collage
- (H) collide
- (J) collar

29. The pioneers moved west to settle the _____.
Which of these words means the settlers moved to the border of their country?

- (A) soil
- (B) state
- (C) suburb
- (D) frontier

30. The police officer inspected the accident _____.
Which of these words means the officer inspected the location of the accident?

- (F) site
- (G) situation
- (H) victims
- (J) problem

Directions: Read the paragraph. Find the word that best fits in each numbered blank.

Wang Yani was born in a small town in southern China. Her father, an art teacher, recognized her interest and _____ **(31)** in art very early in her life. Her first art _____ **(32)** was held in Shanghai when Yani was only four years old. Yani paints using traditional Chinese _____ **(33)**, but her style of broad brush strokes, say her critics, is refreshingly _____ **(34)**.

31. (A) disgust
- (B) personality
- (C) talent
- (D) charm

32. (F) exhibition
- (G) experience
- (H) school
- (J) project

33. (A) containers
- (B) wood
- (C) homes
- (D) materials

34. (F) stale
- (G) unique
- (H) menacing
- (J) undeveloped

STOP

Sample Test 1: Vocabulary

Ready to Test • Fifth Grade

Name _____   Date _____

Main Idea

Directions: Read the paragraph, and answer the questions that follow.

Example

In school, veterinarians learn about animals' bodies, animal diseases, and the medicines used to treat them. They also learn how to perform surgeries

What is this paragraph about?

Ⓐ how veterinarians are trained

Ⓑ the duties of a veterinarian

Ⓒ equipment that veterinarians use

Ⓓ the clothing that veterinarians wear

Answer: (A)

> Look for the topic sentence in the passage. It will help you understand the main idea.

An urban habitat is home to many animals. Birds like pigeons and starlings nest on tall buildings. Mice and rats build their nests in or near buildings. Squirrels, rabbits, and opossums make their homes in the wide-open spaces of city parks. Timid animals, like foxes and raccoons, search for food in neighborhood garbage cans at night. Perhaps the favorite city animals, though, are the ones that live in the homes of people—cats, dogs, and the other animal friends we call *pets*.

1. What would be a good title for this passage?

Ⓐ "Pests Among Us"

Ⓑ "City Critters"

Ⓒ "A Nocturnal Nuisance"

Ⓓ "An Urban Legend"

2. What is the main idea of this passage?

Ⓕ People should protect city animals.

Ⓖ Urban animals cause many problems.

Ⓗ Many animals live in the city.

Ⓙ People who live in cities should not have pets.

3. If the author wanted to continue describing urban habitats, what would be a good topic for the next paragraph?

Ⓐ career opportunities in cities

Ⓑ urban crime

Ⓒ city schools

Ⓓ plants that can be found in cities

4. What is the author's purpose for writing this passage?

Ⓕ to tell people about animals that live in urban habitats

Ⓖ to warn people about urban animals

Ⓗ to present a plan to city officials about protecting animals

Ⓙ to explain how people and animals work together

Main Idea

Directions: Read the passages, and answer the questions that follow.

> Skyler had never been as scared as he was the first time he tried to go inline skating. His legs felt like jelly. The skates kept slipping out from under him. He had thought it would be a snap to soar through the air in jumps and spins, but he found out that skating isn't as easy as it looks. Skyler wasn't going to give up. He practiced and practiced until he started to improve. Finally, he was able to skate without falling down. Skyler knew that if he kept practicing, someday he'd be able to do jumps and spins, too.

1. What is the main idea of this passage?

- (A) Skyler gets hurt skating and decides to quit.
- (B) Skyler doesn't like inline skating.
- (C) Skyler learns that if he practices, he can become good at inline skating.
- (D) Skyler learns how to do jumps and spins while inline skating.

2. Which word describes Skyler's mood at the beginning of the passage?

- (F) bored
- (G) confident
- (H) angry
- (J) nervous

> "London Bridge" is often sung today as young children play a simple game. The rhyme has many verses. Some verses tell about things that did not happen, but the first verse is different. It tells about when the real London Bridge of the 1100s was destroyed by Norse warriors. The other verses tell about efforts to build the bridge again.

3. What is the main idea of this paragraph?

- (A) The children's rhyme "London Bridge" is based on some real events in history.
- (B) "London Bridge" is a children's song.
- (C) The real London Bridge was rebuilt.
- (D) "London Bridge" has many verses.

4. Which of the following is not a fact?

- (F) The first verse is the best part of "London Bridge."
- (G) Norse warriors destroyed the real London Bridge.
- (H) "London Bridge" is a popular children's nursery rhyme.
- (J) "London Bridge" has more than one verse.

Name _____ Date _____

Recalling Details

Directions: Read the paragraph, and answer the questions that follow.

Example

People laugh when I tell them what kind of farm we have. My family raises catfish! The fish live in ponds on our farm. We feed them pellets that look almost like the food you feed cats or dogs.

What does catfish food look like?

(A) bird seed

(B) dog food

(C) pebbles

(D) sand

Read the questions first. Then, while you read the passage, you can look for the information that you will be asked about.

Answer: (B)

Today was very busy. Jane, Cal, and I went out around 8:00 to fill our buckets with blackberries. It was hard work, and we didn't get back until it was time for lunch. This afternoon, Aunt Mara showed us how to wash and sort the berries. When it was time to make jam, Aunt Mara did the cooking. Then, she let us fill the jars and decorate the labels. Aunt Mara is letting me take a jar of jam home for Mom. She'll be surprised that I helped make it. I hope the rest of my stay here is as much fun as today was.

1. What was the first thing the narrator did?

(A) picked blackberries

(B) ate lunch

(C) decorated labels

(D) washed berries

2. Who cooked the berries?

(F) the narrator

(G) Jane

(H) Cal

(J) Aunt Mara

3. How does the narrator feel about this experience?

(A) frustrated

(B) surprised

(C) happy

(D) angry

4. When did the children pick the berries?

(F) at night

(G) in the afternoon

(H) in the evening

(J) in the morning

Name _____ Date _____

Recalling Details

Directions: Read each passage. Fill in the circle next to the best answer to each question.

> Ice hockey originated in the mid-1800s when British troops played games of field hockey on the frozen lakes and ponds of Canada's provinces of Ontario and Nova Scotia. It became Canada's national sport by the early 1900s. Since then, the sport has become popular in European countries such as Russia and Sweden, as well as in the United States.

1. Ontario and Nova Scotia are _____ in Canada.

- (A) towns
- (B) provinces ✓
- (C) cities
- (D) counties

2. Ice hockey was first played

- (F) in Europe.
- (G) on fields in Ontario and Nova Scotia. ✓
- (H) in Russia.
- (J) by British troops.

3. Ice hockey has been played for

- (A) 100 years.
- (B) more than 150 years.
- (C) 50 years.
- (D) more than 200 years.

> People from each part of the United States have special foods that help make that region unique. For example, in the Great Plains region, lefse is a popular favorite. Lefse is a soft flatbread made from potatoes, milk, and flour. It looks a little like a tortilla. Scandinavian immigrants to the Great Plains brought the recipe with them to America.

4. In which region of the United States is lefse popular?

- (F) the South
- (G) the Southwest
- (H) the Great Plains
- (J) Scandinavia

5. Where did lefse originate?

- (A) America
- (B) the American Southwest
- (C) the Great Plains
- (D) Scandinavia

6. Which of the following foods is most similar to lefse?

- (F) a biscuit
- (G) a tortilla
- (H) a cracker
- (J) a birthday cake

Determining Meaning Using Content

Directions: Read the passage. Then, define the terms that follow using information in the passage.

Always running out of money? Have no idea where your money goes? Saving for a special trip, activity, or object? If you answered *yes* to any of these questions, it is time to plan a budget and stick to it. Budgets have a bad rap as being too restrictive or too hard to follow. In reality, a budget can be very simple, and understanding how to use one can help you save for special things. There are three easy steps to follow.

The first step in building a livable budget is to record your spending habits. Look at your expenditures. Do you buy your lunch? Do you buy a soft drink or even water from a machine? You may discover you spend money foolishly. Buying a snack for $0.50 every day may seem insignificant, but by the end of the month, it adds up to $15.00. Instead, put a snack from home in your backpack.

The next step is determining your debits and credits. Look at what money comes in and what goes out. If you have determined your spending habits, you know what your debits are. Credits might be harder to figure out if you do not have a job. Think about all the ways you get money. How much each week do you have available to spend? What are your sources of income? If you do not have a regular source of income, you need to find ways to make money. Do you have an allowance? Can you negotiate with your parents to raise your allowance? Offer to do more chores or special jobs that will increase your income. Check out the neighborhood. Lawn work and babysitting are two jobs that you might like. Remember, your debits should not be more than your credits.

The last step is determining your cash flow and savings goals. How much money do you have available each week to spend? You might budget a small cash flow for yourself because you want to save for a new pair of skis. You might earn $10.00 a week, but only allow yourself to spend $3.00. Look at three important categories. How much money do you wish to save? How much money do you need for essentials? How much money do you want for frivolous activities? Determining the balance between savings goals and cash flow is an important decision for any budget.

1. expenditures

The act of spending money.

2. debit

a business record showing money paid out or owed

3. credit

the balance in an account in a person's favor

4. cash flow

The sum of the after-tax profit

Determining Meaning Using Content

Directions: Read each passage. Then, for each word that follows, fill in the circle next to the meaning that best describes how the word is used in the passage.

People who travel or cross the Amazon and Orinoco Rivers of South America are careful never to <u>dangle</u> a foot or hand from the side of their boat. Just below the surface of these waters <u>lurks</u> a small fish feared throughout the <u>continent</u>. That fish is the flesh-eating piranha. Although smaller fish make up most of its diet, the piranha will attack both humans and other animals.

1. dangle

- (A) lose
- (B) hang
- (C) brush
- (D) leave

2. lurks

- (F) swims dangerously
- (G) waits in hiding
- (H) floats
- (J) appears

3. continent

- (A) landmass
- (B) lake
- (C) canoe
- (D) story

In 3000 B.C., early Egyptian boats were <u>constructed</u> from the papyrus plant. With the Egyptians' limited knowledge of navigation, they could only sail with the wind. These <u>reeds</u>, from which early paper was made, could grow to be 20 feet high. The reeds were cut, <u>bundled</u>, and tied together to form the boat.

4. constructed

- (F) chopped
- (G) floated
- (H) designed
- (J) built

5. reeds

- (A) fish
- (B) paper
- (C) plants
- (D) instruments

6. bundled

- (F) gathered
- (G) twisted
- (H) packed
- (J) stacked

Name _____   Date _____

Making Inferences

Directions: Read the paragraph, and answer the questions that follow.

Example

Leo wrote an article called "Lizards" for the school paper. He didn't expect anyone to get excited about it, but they did. His teacher was pleased that Leo had done such a good job. "This was the best story you ever wrote," she said. "I'm going to enter it in the state writing competition for you. Maybe you'll win a prize!"

How do you think Leo felt about his teacher's reaction to his article?

(A) afraid

(B) unhappy

(C) embarrassed

(D) xsurprised

Answer: (D)

I was so nervous. I hadn't seen Tasha in three years, not since my mom got that new job. I remember the day we moved away. Tasha brought me our photograph in a frame. I gave her a necklace with a friendship charm on it. We promised to stay friends forever. Now that I was finally going to see her again, I wondered if we would still like the same kinds of things and laugh at the same kinds of jokes. I rubbed my sweaty palms on my jeans as we pulled into Tasha's driveway.

1. Why hasn't the narrator seen Tasha for three years?

(A) because they were best friends

(B) because they didn't like each other's gifts

(C) because they had a fight

(D) because the narrator had to move away

2. Why are the narrator's palms sweaty?

(F) because she is nervous

(G) because she has a fever

(H) because she feels sick

(J) because she doesn't want to move

3. The passage gives you enough information to believe that the narrator

(A) was angry at her mom for making her move.

(B) had a special friendship with Tasha.

(C) liked her new school.

(D) doesn't keep her promises.

4. The narrator will feel happy if

(F) Tasha is not home.

(G) Tasha has changed a lot.

(H) she gets to move again.

(J) she and Tasha still get along.

Name _____ Date _____

Making Inferences

Directions: Read the story, and answer the questions that follow.

Lauren entered the science fair. For her project, she wanted to see which brand of batteries lasted longest: Everglo, Glomore, or Everlasting. She decided to place new batteries into identical new flashlights, turn on the flashlights, and then wait for the batteries to run down. She wrote down the following results: Everglo—lasted 19 hours; Glomore—lasted 17 hours; Everlasting—lasted 25 hours.

She then decided to redo the experiment to confirm the results. For her second experiment, she placed new batteries into the old flashlights that her parents kept in the garage, the kitchen, and their bedroom. She then turned on the flashlights and waited for the batteries to run down. This time, she wrote down the following results: Everglo—lasted 13 hours; Glomore—lasted 16 hours; Everlasting—lasted 9 hours.

Lauren was puzzled by the results of her second experiment. Because it was so similar to her first experiment, she thought she would get the same results.

1. What is the best explanation for why Lauren's second experiment had different results than her first experiment?

(A) Lauren used different brands of batteries in the second experiment.

(B) The second experiment used old flashlights, while the first experiment used new flashlights.

(C) The second experiment was too much like the first experiment.

(D) There is no good explanation; sometimes things just happen.

2. How was Lauren sure that the results of the second experiment were different from the results of the first experiment?

(F) She read on the side of the battery packages how long each brand would last before it ran down.

(G) She simply remembered how long it took each brand of battery to run down.

(H) She recorded exactly how long it took each brand of battery to run down for each experiment.

(J) She cannot be sure; her experiment was faulty.

3. If Lauren tries the experiment a third time, which of the following should she do to confirm the results of her first attempt?

(A) make sure the batteries are brand new

(B) clean the old flashlights before putting new batteries in them

(C) use only two old flashlights and two brands of batteries

(D) use three identical, new flashlights

4. Which of the following can be inferred about Lauren from the story?

(F) She is not a good student.

(G) She will be a scientist someday.

(H) She is interested in science.

(J) She likes to go camping.

Story Elements

Directions: Read the passage, and answer the questions that follow.

Example

It was Saturday morning. All the world was smiling and bright—all that is, except Tom Sawyer. With his pail of whitewash and a large brush, Tom stared sadly at the long fence. He dipped his brush into the white glop and began the job of whitewashing the fence.

This passage tells about a boy named *Tom Sawyer*. How does Tom feel about whitewashing the fence?

(A) glum

(B) joyful

(C) excited

(D) cheerful

Answer: (A)

> Skim the passage, and then read the questions. Go back to the passage to find the answers to the questions.

One day, just as the leaves were beginning to change color, Rip Van Winkle walked through the woods and up the mountains. By early afternoon, he found himself on one of the highest points of the Catskill Mountains. By late afternoon, Rip was tired and panting, so he found a spot with a beautiful view where he could lie down and rest. Through an opening in the trees, Rip could see miles and miles of lower country and rich woodland. In the distance, he could view the mighty Hudson River. It was moving calmly along its course, showing reflections of the soft white clouds in the sky.

1. What part of a story does this passage tell about?

(A) the setting

(B) the plot

(C) the conflict

(D) the characters

2. How do you think Rip feels about where he is?

(F) He thinks it is exciting.

(G) He thinks it is annoying.

(H) He thinks it is peaceful.

(J) He thinks it is dangerous.

3. Where in a story would you most likely find this passage?

(A) near the beginning

(B) in the middle

(C) near the end

(D) in the table of contents

4. At what time of year does this passage take place?

(F) winter

(G) spring

(H) summer

(J) fall

Story Elements

Directions: Read the passage, and answer the questions that follow.

"What do you think that one is?" Lela asked her sister, pointing up into the large fir. Sofia squinted, trying to locate the bird. A moment later, she could see the black-and-white speckled feathers through the branches.

"Wow, Lela," said Sofia, "I think that's a downy woodpecker! Be really quiet for a second. I'm going to go get Mom's camera and see if I can get a few pictures." Sofia quietly opened the back door and returned a moment later with her mother's digital camera.

"Don't move, okay, Lela?" Sofia zoomed in and began snapping pictures. Someone slammed a car door across the street, and the woodpecker zoomed off in a flurry of feathers.

"Is it gone? Did you get any?" asked Lela.

Sofia shrugged. "I got a few," she said, showing her sister the images on the tiny screen. "That last one shows his markings pretty well." She set down the camera on the patio table, and turned to her sister. "Do you feel like jumping on the trampoline?"

"Yeah!" exclaimed Lela. Jumping on the trampoline was still her favorite thing to do, even though they'd had it for almost a year.

That evening, Mrs. Morales was setting the table while the girls helped their dad chop vegetables. "Oh, I almost forgot. Has anyone seen my camera?" she asked. "I can't find it, and I wanted to take some pictures of Lela's art project to send to Nana."

Sofia stopped chopping. She looked outside at the dark sky and the splatters of raindrops on the pavement. She felt her stomach muscles tighten as she remembered where she had left the camera.

1. Who is the main character in this passage?

Ⓐ Lela

~~Ⓑ~~ Sofia

Ⓒ Mrs. Morales

Ⓓ Nana

2. What is the conflict in the story?

Ⓕ The girls see a downy woodpecker in the fir tree.

Ⓖ Sofia and Lela get into an argument.

~~Ⓗ~~ Sofia has left her mother's camera out in the rain.

Ⓙ Mr. Morales does not want the girls to help him make dinner.

3. Which of the following is not a setting for this story?

Ⓐ the Morales's house

Ⓑ the kitchen

Ⓒ the backyard

~~Ⓓ~~ Sofia's school

4. Describe what you think the resolution to this story might be.

Getting the camera, take out the memory chip. If the camera is broken, buy a new one.

Identifying Literature Genres

Directions: Read each story below, and write the kind of story it is on the line.

The following list tells you about four types of stories, called *genres*.

Science Fiction—a make-believe story based on scientific possibilities. Science fiction may describe future settings, aliens, or space travel, but it can also include scientific facts.

Myth—a make-believe story that explains how something came to be. Myths often describe how the world was created.

Nonfiction—factual information. Nonfiction stories are true. They include actual details and facts.

Realistic Fiction—a make-believe story that could actually happen. These stories aren't true, but it's easy to believe they are.

1. **Juniper trees grow in Arizona. Tiny fairies live in their trunks. During the full moon, the fairies come out and dance at night. While dancing, they place blue berries on each tree for decoration. That's how the juniper gets its berries.**

   Myth

2. **"It's a bird!" Farid shouted. "It's a plane!" Audrey said. But it was a spaceship! It landed next to a juniper tree. Little green men got off the spaceship. They clipped off several branches of the tree. "They're collecting tree samples to study on Mars," Audrey whispered. They watched, amazed, as the spaceship disappeared into the sky.**

   Science Fiction

3. **Jason and Patrick went for a hike. Because they were in the high desert, they carried water with them. When they got tired, the two boys sat in the shade of a juniper tree to rest and drink their water. That's when the rattlesnake appeared. "Don't move!" Patrick said to Jason. The boys sat still until the snake moved away. "What an adventure!" Jason said as the two boys returned home.**

   Realistic Fiction

4. **Juniper trees are small, gnarly trees that grow in many parts of the world. Members of the evergreen family, they remain green year round. Juniper trees can be easily identified by their tiny blue or red berries. There are 13 different kinds of juniper trees in the United States. One kind of juniper tree is called the *alligator juniper* because its bark looks similar to the skin of an alligator. It grows in the Southwest.**

   Nonfiction

Identifying Literature Genres

Directions: Read the passages. Then, follow the directions on the next page.

Hibernation

Have you ever wondered why some animals hibernate? Hibernation is when animals sleep through the winter. Animals get their warmth and energy from food. Some animals cannot find enough food in the winter, so they must eat large amounts of food in the fall. Their bodies store this food as fat. Then, in winter, they hibernate and their bodies live on the stored fat. Since their bodies need much less food during hibernation, they can stay alive without eating new food during the winter. Some animals that hibernate are bats, chipmunks, bears, snakes, and turtles.

Waterland

"Hurray!" cried Meghan. "Today is the day we're going to Waterland!" It was a hot July day, and Meghan's mom was taking her to cool off on the water slides. Meghan's new friend, Natasha, was going, too.

Just then, Meghan's mom came out of her bedroom. She did not look very happy. "What's the matter, Mom? Are you afraid to get wet?" Meghan teased. "I'll bet you'll melt, just like the Wicked Witch of the West!"

Mrs. Millett didn't laugh at the joke. Instead, she told the kids that she wasn't feeling well. She was too tired to drive to the water park.

Meghan and Natasha were disappointed. "My mom has chronic fatigue syndrome," Meghan explained. "Her illness makes her really tired. She's still a great mom."

"Thank you, dear," said Mrs. Millett. "I'm too tired to drive, but I have an idea. You can make your own waterland, and I'll rest in the lawn chair."

Meghan and Natasha set up three different sprinklers. They dragged the play slide over to the wading pool and aimed the sprinkler on the slide. Meghan and Natasha got soaking wet. Mrs. Millett sat in a lawn chair and rested. The kids played all day.

"Thank you for being so understanding," Meghan's mom said. "Now I feel better, but I'm really hot! There's only one cure for that." She stood under the sprinkler with all her clothes on. She was drenched from head to toe.

Meghan laughed and said, "Now you have chronic wet syndrome." Mrs. Millett rewarded her daughter with a big, wet hug. It turned out to be a wonderful day after all, in the backyard waterland.

Identifying Literature Genres

Directions: Circle the characteristics that you think are true about each passage.

Hibernation	**Waterland**
(Includes facts)	Includes facts
Made up or fantasized	(Made up or fantasized)
(Main purpose is to inform)	Main purpose is to inform
Main purpose is to entertain	(Main purpose is to entertain)
Organized into setting, characters, problem, goal, events, and resolution	(Organized into setting, characters, problem, goal, events, and resolution)
(Organized according to the purpose the authors wish to achieve (steps to achieve a goal; explain why something happens; attempt to make an argument, etc.))	Organized according to the purpose the authors wish to achieve (steps to achieve a goal; explain why something happens; attempt to make an argument, etc.)

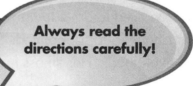

Always read the directions carefully!

Name _____ Date _____

Identifying Literature Genres

Directions: Read the passage, and answer the questions that follow

A Doomed Romance

You are my love, my love you are.
I worship you from afar;
I through the branches spy you.

You, Sir, are a climbing thug.
I do not like your fuzzy mug.
Away from me, please take you!

Oh, grant me peace, my love, my dove.
Climb to my home so far above
This place you call your warren.

I like my home in a sheltered hollow
Where fox and weasel may not follow.
Please go away, tree rodent!

I love your ears, so soft and tall.
I love your nose, so pink and small.
I must make you my own bride!

I will not climb, I cannot eat
the acorns that you call a treat.
Now shimmy up that oak; hide!

Now I hide up in my bower.
Lonesome still, I shake and cower.
Sadness overtakes me.

I must stay on the lovely ground
With carrots crisp and cabbage round.
I long for gardens, not trees

1. Which genre of literature is this passage?

(A) poetry

(B) biography

(C) nonfiction

(D) fable

2. What clues in the passage helped you decided what genre it is?

The first 2 sentences
of each paragraph
rhyme and the last
sentence of every 2
paragraphs rhyme

3. Who are the two speakers in this passage? Identify them, and write one adjective to describe the tone of each voice.

A Male squirrel
loves rabbit

B Female rabbit
doesn't like squirrel

4. What do you think the theme of this passage is? Write it in one phrase or sentence.

Love can't happen
if there is just one
lover.

Fiction

Directions: Read the passage. Choose the best answer for each question that follows.

Example

Misha stood on the stage. His hands shook so hard that he could barely hold his violin. A hush fell over the audience. He shut his eyes tightly and remembered that his music teacher had told him, "You can do it. Take a deep breath, and pretend that you're standing in your living room." Misha lifted his violin to his chin and played his solo perfectly from beginning to end.

From this passage, what do you know about Misha?

Ⓐ He has been playing the violin for many years.

Ⓑ He likes to play his violin in front of an audience.

Ⓒ He gets nervous when he is performing in front of others.

Ⓓ He and his music teacher are friends.

Answer: C

Floating the River

"Aren't we there yet?" Shiloh asked. At last, she and her family were on their way to their annual tubing trip. Floating down Glenn River on an inner tube was one of Shiloh's favorite things. This year, they would float five whole miles, all the way to Glenn Fork.

With each passing mile, Shiloh smiled more and more as she thought of the fun they would have. When they finally reached Glenn Fork and parked the car, she jumped out, all ready to go.

"Not so fast, Shiloh," said her mother. "Remember, we're just here to leave the car. We still have to drive up the river. After we float back here, we'll be able to drive the car upstream to the truck. Otherwise, we won't have any way to get home."

"Oh, yeah, false alarm," Shiloh said. She had forgotten the family's plan to leave one car at each end of the float.

The whole family piled into the truck and drove to Jenkins Ledge. Shiloh's father helped her unload her backpack and shiny tube from the truck. They walked down to the river's bank and put their toes in the water. Shiloh gasped as she felt how cold the water was. She took a deep breath and pushed herself out into the river. As Shiloh followed her family downstream, she thought to herself, "This will be the best tubing trip ever!"

Fiction

Directions: Use the passage on the previous page to answer the questions below.

1. This story is mostly about

(A) driving a truck.

(B) a family's adventure.

(C) a family's argument.

(D) a family's business.

2. The family will float between which two points?

(F) from Jenkins Ledge to Glenn Fork

(G) from Glenn Fork to Glenn River

(H) from Glenn River to Jenkins Ledge

(J) from Glenn Fork to Jenkins Ledge

3. How do you think Shiloh's parents feel about the tubing trip?

(A) bored

(B) disappointed

(C) frustrated

(D) excited

4. Why is the family driving both a car and a truck?

(F) so they don't get the truck wet and muddy

(G) so they can show that they have a lot of money

(H) so they can all have a ride to the river

(J) so they can have transportation back to where they started

5. Which character do you learn the most about in this passage?

(A) Shiloh's mother

(B) Shiloh

(C) Shiloh's father

(D) Shiloh's sister

6. When Shiloh says, "false alarm," she means

(F) she didn't tell the truth.

(G) that there is no danger.

(H) she made a mistake.

(J) there's been a warning.

> Read the questions first. Think about them as you read the passage.

Fiction

Directions: Read the passage. Choose the best answer for each question that follows.

Survivors

As far as Kiki was concerned, the island had always been her home, and she loved it. She had been just about a year old when the ship she and her family had been on was caught in a great storm. She didn't remember their home in England, where she had been born, or boarding the ship for Australia. Kiki certainly didn't remember how her family and a few dozen others had arrived on the island in lifeboats, or even how they had built houses and made new lives.

The Martin family and the others who had survived the shipwreck had worked hard to make the island livable. In the weeks following the wreck, chests of seeds, tools, and food washed up on the beach. These chests gave the survivors a chance to build a new life on the island. Now, ten years after the disaster, the island was a wonderful place to live. Everyone had a comfortable home, and there was plenty of food.

Kiki and the other children explored the island every day. It was on one of these outings that they saw the great ships. The children had climbed to the top of the highest peak on the island to study the sea birds that nested on the cliffs below. When they reached the top of the peak, Kiki spotted the four ships sailing toward the island.

By the time Kiki and her friends climbed down the mountain, the ships had reached the island. The captain and crew were surprised to find other English settlers there. They had known about the shipwreck, of course, but they had no idea there were survivors. The ships were heading to Australia, and the survivors were welcomed to join the crew on board.

That, however, was the problem. Almost none of the survivors wanted to leave the island, especially the children who had spent most of their lives there and the dozen who had been born there. For them, the island was their world, and they couldn't imagine leaving it.

Fiction

Directions: Use the passage on the previous page to answer the questions below.

1. What is the main idea of this story?

- (A) how people lived after a shipwreck
- (B) explorers discovering a deserted island
- (C) children studying sea birds
- (D) a family's journey to Australia

2. What helped the survivors begin their new lives on the island?

- (F) having the children explore the island
- (G) the captain and crew of the ships sailing to Australia
- (H) supplies that washed up on the beach
- (J) memories of England

3. If the children could vote on whether to leave the island or to stay, which of these would probably happen?

- (A) Most would vote to leave.
- (B) Most would vote to stay.
- (C) Most would not vote.
- (D) There would be a tie.

4. Which of the following sentences expresses an opinion?

- (F) Kiki didn't remember their home in England.
- (G) The children had climbed to the top of the highest peak.
- (H) The island was a wonderful place to live.
- (J) The captain and crew were surprised to find other English settlers there.

5. What do you know about the island from reading this passage?

- (A) The island has a desert climate.
- (B) There are cliffs on the island.
- (C) There are palm trees on the island.
- (D) Dangerous animals live on the island.

6. How do you suppose Kiki will feel if her family decides to leave the island?

- (F) disappointed
- (G) excited
- (H) proud
- (J) happy

If you don't know the answer to a question, skip it and come back to it later.

Fiction

Directions: Read the passage. Choose the best answer for each question that follows.

The Story of Arachne

Long ago in a faraway country, lived a young woman named *Arachne*. She was not rich or beautiful, but she had one great talent. Arachne could weave the most beautiful cloth anyone had ever seen. Everyone in Arachne's village had talked about her wonderful cloth, and soon she became famous. But as her fame grew, so did her pride.

"No one else can weave as well as I can," Arachne boasted. "Not even the goddess Minerva could make anything so lovely and fine."

Now Minerva wove cloth for all the gods. She was proud of her weaving, too, and thought that no human could ever match her skills. Soon, Arachne's words reached Minerva's ears, and the goddess became angry.

"So the human woman thinks she is better than I!" Minerva roared. "We will see about that!"

Minerva searched the countryside until she came upon Arachne's home. Minerva called to Arachne and challenged her to a contest. "Let us both weave a length of cloth. We will see whose is the most beautiful."

Arachne agreed. She set up two looms, and she and Minerva went to work. The goddess wove cloth of all the colors of the rainbow. It sparkled in the sun and floated on the breeze like a butterfly. But Arachne wove cloth that sparkled like gold and jewels. The villagers were dazzled by Arachne's cloth. When Minerva inspected it, she knew Arachne was the best weaver.

Minerva was enraged. She took out a jar of magic water and sprinkled it on Arachne. Instantly, poor Arachne began to change. She became smaller and smaller until she could almost not be seen. She grew more arms and became covered in fine brown hair. When it was all over, Arachne had become a tiny brown spider. Arachne would never boast again, but she would spend the rest of her life weaving fine webs.

Fiction

Directions: Use the passage on the previous page to answer the questions below.

1. **People in ancient times made up stories, or myths, to explain things in their world that they did not understand. This myth explains**

   (A) how to weave cloth.

   (B) why spiders weave webs.

   (C) how to turn a person into a spider.

   (D) why it is wrong to be boastful.

2. **Here is a sequence of events from the passage.**

Arachne becomes a famous weaver.

Arachne brags that her skills are better than the goddess Minerva's.

Minerva realizes that Arachne is the better weaver.

   Which of these events should go in the empty box?

   (F) Minerva sprinkles water on Arachne.

   (G) Minerva changes Arachne into a spider.

   (H) Minerva challenges Arachne to a weaving contest.

   (J) Arachne weaves webs.

3. **What might have happened if Arachne had not bragged about her talents?**

   (A) Minerva would have left her alone.

   (B) Arachne would not have become famous.

   (C) The villagers would not have appreciated Arachne's weaving.

   (D) Minerva would not be allowed to make cloth for the gods anymore.

4. **What caused Minerva to challenge Arachne to the contest?**

   (F) boredom and skill

   (G) contentment and humility

   (H) fear and confusion

   (J) pride and jealousy

5. **This passage tells us the most about the**

   (A) plot.

   (B) mood.

   (C) characters.

   (D) setting.

6. **This story might have been told to remind people not to**

   (F) brag about their talents.

   (G) weave cloth.

   (H) enter competitions.

   (J) kill spiders.

If you know which answer is correct, mark it and move on to the next question.

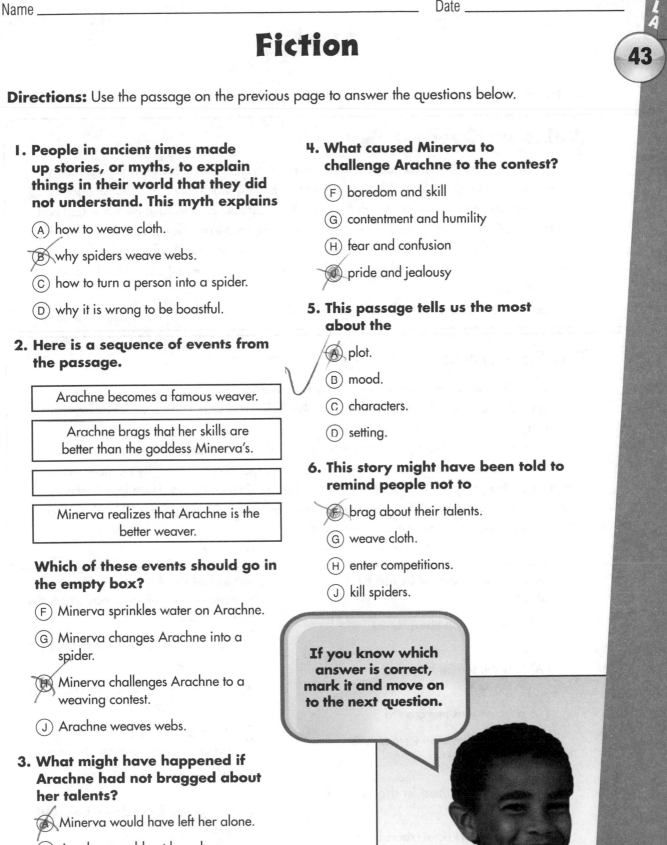

Fiction

Directions: Read the passages, and answer the questions that follow.

Walks All Over the Sky

Back when the sky was completely dark, there was a chief with two sons, a younger son, *One Who Walks All Over the Sky*, and an older son, *Walking About Early*. The younger son was sad to see the sky always so dark, so he made a mask out of wood and pitch (the sun) and lit it on fire. Each day, he travels across the sky. At night, he sleeps below the horizon and, when he snores, sparks fly from the mask and make the stars. The older brother became jealous. To impress their father, he smeared fat and charcoal on his face (the moon) and makes his own path across the sky.

—from the *Tsimshian of the Pacific Northwest*

The Porcupine

Once, Porcupine and Beaver argued about the seasons. Porcupine wanted five winter months. He held up one hand and showed his five fingers. He said, "Let the winter months be the same in number as the fingers on my hand."

Beaver said, "No," and held up his tail, which had many cracks or scratches on it. He said, "Let the winter months be the same in number as the scratches on my tail." They argued more, and Porcupine got angry and bit off his thumb. Then, holding up his hand with four fingers, he said, "There must be only four winter months." Beaver was afraid and gave in. For this reason, today porcupines have four claws on each foot.

—from the *Tahltan: Teit, Journal of American Folk-Lore*, xxxii, 226

1. What is explained in the first story?

(A) why the moon has different phases

(B) why the sun and moon appear in the sky

(C) how fire was first created

(D) how the Tsimshian were able to travel at night

2. What is explained in the second story?

(F) why beavers have cracks and scratches on their tails

(G) why there are four seasons

(H) why winter has four months

(J) why porcupines have four claws on each foot

3. Which of the following does not describe a similarity between the two stories?

(A) Both stories explain how something in nature came to be.

(B) In both stories, there is conflict between the main characters.

(C) The characters in both stories are animals with human characteristics.

(D) Neither story is true.

4. Which genre best describes these stories?

(F) nonfiction

(G) myth

(H) article

(J) science fiction

Nonfiction

Directions: Read the passage. Choose the best answer for each question that follows.

> **Example**
>
> Wasps build new nests every year. The potter wasp creates a mud "jar" nest for each of its eggs. The wasp then stings caterpillars to paralyze them and places them in the jar nests. The nests are sealed, and the caterpillars are used as food for the developing wasps.
>
> **How does the potter wasp paralyze caterpillars?**
>
> (A) by stinging them
>
> (B) by spitting on them
>
> (C) by biting them
>
> (D) by sealing them in jars
>
> Answer: (A)

Exploring a Coral Reef

A coral reef is a beautiful undersea wilderness filled with fascinating plants and animals. It is one of the most populated environments on Earth. Coral reefs are found where ocean water is warm, clean, and shallow.

For hundreds of years, people thought that coral was a type of flowering plant. Amazingly, coral reefs are actually formed by little tube-shaped animals called *coral polyps*. Coral polyps have hard outer skeletons that cover and protect their soft bodies. Most coral polyps stay within their protective skeletons during the day. At night, fingerlike tentacles emerge from the skeleton and pull tiny animals into the coral's mouth. When the coral polyps die, their skeletons remain in place. New polyps make their homes on the rocky foundations of the skeletons. In this way, the reef grows larger and larger.

A living thing takes up every bit of space on a coral reef. Beautiful tropical fish swim among sea turtles, colorful marine worms, and giant clams. Sharks patrol the water looking for food. Sea cucumbers share the rocky, sandy bottom of the reef with sea urchins. At dusk, octopuses come out of their caves and begin searching for food.

Many people come to coral reefs to snorkel or scuba dive. They swim in the water and explore the beauty of the reef. Unfortunately, some people damage the reefs by handling the coral. It may take hundreds of years for a reef to restore itself after a careless person damages it.

Nonfiction

Directions: Use the passage on the previous page to answer the questions below.

1. What is the main idea of this passage?

(A) Coral polyps are animals, not plants.

(B) People should handle coral.

(C) A coral reef is a delicate habitat populated by a wide array of animals.

(D) Coral reefs need warm, clean, and shallow ocean water to survive.

2. How do coral polyps eat?

(F) Tentacles emerge and capture tiny animals.

(G) Tropical fish bring them food.

(H) Tiny animals cling to the skeletons.

(J) They are hand-fed by people.

3. How does the author of this passage feel about coral reefs?

(A) The author would not want to visit a coral reef.

(B) The author thinks reefs are easily replaced.

(C) The author thinks reefs are hideous.

(D) The author thinks reefs are beautiful.

4. Which of these sentences expresses an opinion?

(F) Coral polyps have hard outer skeletons that cover and protect their soft bodies.

(G) Some people damage the reefs by handling the coral.

(H) A coral reef is a beautiful undersea wilderness.

(J) Coral reefs are found where ocean water is warm, clean, and shallow.

5. Where would a passage like this be most likely to appear?

(A) in a nature magazine

(B) in an almanac

(C) in a thesaurus

(D) in a biography

6. Which of these is not explained in the passage?

(F) how coral polyps eat

(G) that people used to think coral was a plant

(H) how pollution damages reefs

(J) other types of animals that live in and around reefs

Nonfiction

Directions: Read the passage. Choose the best answer for each question that follows.

Swimming Star

Every day, thousands of people cross the channel of water between France and England in planes, ferries, and even trains. An American athlete, Gertrude Caroline Ederle, however, used a different method. She was the first woman to swim across the English Channel.

Gertrude Ederle was born in New York City in 1906. She dedicated herself to the sport of swimming at an early age and enjoyed great success. Before long, she was on her way to becoming one of the most famous American swimmers of her time. When she was 16, Ederle broke seven records in one day at a swimming competition in New York. Two years later, in 1924, she represented the United States at the Olympic Games, winning a gold medal in the 400-meter freestyle relay.

After her Olympic victory, she looked for an even greater challenge. One of the most difficult swims is to cross the 21-mile-wide English Channel. The seas in the channel can be rough, and the water is cold. In the past, the feat had only been accomplished by male swimmers. Most people believed that the swim was too difficult for a woman, but Ederle wanted to prove them wrong. She didn't make it on her first attempt, but in 1926, she tried again. Leaving from the coast of France, Ederle had to swim even longer than planned because of heavy seas. She went an extra 14 miles and still managed to beat the world record by almost two hours. This accomplishment made her an instant heroine at the age of 20.

Look for important facts in the passage. They can help you answer the questions that follow.

Nonfiction

Directions: Use the passage on the previous page to answer the questions below.

1. **What is the main idea of the passage?**

   (A) Swimming is a fun sport.

   (B) Winning an Olympic medal will make you wealthy.

   (C) If you want to be very successful at something, you have to start at a young age.

   (D) Hard work and dedication can lead to great success.

2. **Which event happened first in the passage about Ederle's life?**

   (F) She swam across the English Channel.

   (G) She broke seven swimming records in a single day of competition.

   (H) She won an Olympic gold medal.

   (J) She looked for more challenges.

3. **Based on the information in the passage, what word probably describes Ederle's personality?**

   (A) imaginative

   (B) passive

   (C) lazy

   (D) determined

4. **Why did Ederle decide to swim across the English Channel?**

   (F) someone dared her to

   (G) to earn a lot of money

   (H) to prove that women could do it

   (J) to win a gold medal

5. **Which sentence would describe what the water was like on the day Ederle swam across the channel?**

   (A) The water was cold and choppy.

   (B) The water was calm and warm.

   (C) The water was shallow.

   (D) The water was frozen.

6. **According to the passage, why was Ederle considered a heroine?**

   (F) because she was a generous person

   (G) because she had done something that no other woman had ever done.

   (H) because she was a great swimmer

   (J) because she had rescued someone

Nonfiction

Directions: Read the passage. Choose the best answer for each question that follows.

Jackie Robinson, born in 1919, was the first African-American man to play modern American major league baseball. In high school and college, he played many sports. He earned letters in track and field, basketball, football, and baseball. Unfortunately, Robinson had to quit college for financial reasons. It seemed his days of playing sports were over.

In 1942, Robinson was drafted into the army. He faced a lot of prejudice in the army. As an officer, he was asked to join the army football team. When other team members objected to playing against a team with a black member, he turned to the army baseball team. There, he was rejected again because of his race.

After leaving the army in 1945, Robinson played shortstop for the Kansas City Monarchs, one of several teams in the Negro League. Professional baseball was still segregated at that time, but the Brooklyn Dodgers' president, Branch Rickey, recognized Robinson's athletic skills. Rickey was determined to make Robinson the first African-American player in major league baseball.

Robinson started playing with the Dodgers' farm team. Rickey advised him not to fight back when people were unkind to him. Baseball players and fans alike thought that he should not be allowed to play. But Robinson played so well that in 1947, he joined the Brooklyn Dodgers.

At first, his teammates didn't like playing with him. However, when other people screamed at him, they came to his defense. Because of his great performance at second base and his outstanding batting average, Robinson was selected Rookie of the Year. In 1949, he was named the Most Valuable Player in the National League. One of his greatest thrills was when he helped the Dodgers win the 1955 World Series.

Jackie Robinson paved the way for African-American men to play in the minor leagues. In 1962, he was inducted in baseball's Hall of Fame. Ten years later, at the age of 53, Robinson died in Stamford, Connecticut.

Name _____ Date _____

Nonfiction

Directions: Use the passage on the previous page to answer the questions below.

1. What would be a good title for the passage?

Ⓐ "Jackie Robinson: A Major League Success"

Ⓑ "Rickey and Robinson Make It to the Majors"

Ⓒ "How to Play Second Base"

Ⓓ "The Baseball Hall of Fame"

2. Why was Robinson selected as Rookie of the Year?

Ⓕ for his batting average and his skills at second base

Ⓖ for his excellent attitude

Ⓗ for his skills as a shortstop

Ⓙ because he helped win the World Series

3. How do you think Jackie Robinson felt toward Branch Rickey?

Ⓐ hostile

Ⓑ disgusted

Ⓒ appreciative

Ⓓ embarrassed

4. What effect did segregation have on professional baseball?

Ⓕ White players were given the best positions.

Ⓖ Anyone with enough talent was invited to play.

Ⓗ People who did not graduate from college could not play professional baseball.

Ⓙ African Americans weren't allowed to play in the major leagues.

5. How do you think Robinson felt about his accomplishments?

Ⓐ disappointed

Ⓑ proud

Ⓒ dissatisfied

Ⓓ shy

6. Why did Robinson join the army?

Ⓕ He needed a job.

Ⓖ He wanted to travel.

Ⓗ He was drafted.

Ⓙ He didn't know what else to do after he left college.

Nonfiction

Directions: The passages below are from a newspaper, an instruction manual, a textbook, or a biography. Read the passages, and identify the source of each.

1. The best way to understand the food web is to study a model of it. Refer to Figure 2.3 to see a model of a food web in a deciduous forest. Recall that in Chapter 1 we identified animals as either herbivores, carnivores, or omnivores. Which animals in Figure 2.3 could best be described as herbivores?

_____textbook_____

2. LONDON, England—Buckingham Palace announced today that Queen Elizabeth will make a short visit to the United States early next week to attend the annual Westhampton Flower Show in Westhampton, Connecticut. The Queen has made several trips to the flower show, often accompanied by other members of the royal family. Last year, the prize-winning rose at the show was named in honor of the Queen.

_____newspaper_____

3. Wolfgang Amadeus Mozart was born on January 27, 1756, in Austria. When he was just three years old, he learned to play the harpsichord. He was composing music by the time he was five years old. At the age of six, he was invited to perform for the Empress of Austria. Mozart astonished people with his musical ability. He was called a child genius.

_____biography_____

4. Step 1: Find pieces A, B, and C and Main Frame 1.
   Step 2: Insert Piece A into the square slot of Piece B.
   Step 3: Insert Piece C into the round slot of Piece B.
   Step 4: Snap the assembled ABC assembly into Main Frame 1.

_____instruction manuel_____

Directions: Based on the titles below, identify the form of nonfiction of each.

5. *Sports Weekly*

   (A) magazine
   (B) textbook
   (C) essay
   (D) reference book

6. *Dinner in Under an Hour*

   (F) newspaper
   (G) cookbook
   (H) science journal
   (J) computer manual

Nonfiction

Directions: Read the selections below, and then answer the questions that follow.

February 10

I did it! Well, I didn't win first place, but I came in second. I'm really proud of that.

At first, I was scared when I looked out and saw all those people in the audience. I was afraid I'd forget everything. But then I told myself, "You studied hard. You know all those words. Come on, you can do it!"

My first word was *indicate*: i-n-d-i-c-a-t-e. It was easy. Then, I knew I could do the rest of them, too. The only word that really stumped me was *cannibal*. I spelled it c-a-n-n-i-b-l-e—oops. Rebecca spelled it correctly, along with her last word: *hydraulics*.

Oh, well. I won a dictionary and had my picture taken for the newspaper. When I came home, my family had a party to celebrate! Tomorrow, I'm going to start studying for next year's contest.

Local Boy Finishes Second in Regional Spelling Bee

February 10—Ben Hanson, age 10, of Park Creek, finished second in the Regional Spelling Bee sponsored by the Literacy Society. He spelled eight words correctly, finally stumbling over the word *cannibal*. Hanson won a new dictionary for his efforts.

Rebecca Cohen, from Detroit, Michigan, won first prize for spelling the word *hydraulics*. She will receive a $100 savings bond and go on to the National Spelling Bee held in Washington, D.C., next month.

1. Identify the form of nonfiction of each of the two passages.

journal, newspaper article

2. Who wrote the first passage? Where did the second passage appear?

Ben Hanson (first para)

In a newspaper

3. Name three similarities between the passages.

Ben messed up on cannibal
Rebecca won 1st place.
Ben won a dictionary

4. Name three differences between the passages.

2nd Ben spelled 8 words-2nd
has Rebecca's last name
1st Ben will celebrate

Nonfiction

Directions: Read the passage, and answer the questions that follow.

The late 1800s and early 1900s are sometimes referred to as the *Progressive Era*. During this time, reformers known as *progressives* fought to improve living and working conditions for the poor.

By the late 1800s, many poor people lived in crowded housing in city slums. Progressives worked to change these living conditions. In some cities, they set up settlement houses where they provided medical care and worked with slum residents to improve conditions. As a result of the progressives' work, many states established housing regulations.

Working conditions were also a problem during this time. Factory employees worked long hours for low pay. They often operated unsafe machinery. Workers who complained were often fired and replaced with others who faced similar conditions. Progressives fought to change these conditions for workers. They worked to pass laws that required factories to establish safety precautions. The laws also allowed workers to collect money from factory owners for injuries received on the job. In some states, progressives were able to get laws passed that required minimum pay for workers.

1. **Why did progressives set up settlement houses in some cities?**

   (A) so workers could be closer to the factories where they worked

   (B) to provide medical care and improve living conditions for the poor

   (C) to provide a free place for poorly-paid workers to live

   (D) to establish housing regulations

2. **Which is not described in the passage as an improvement to working conditions brought about by progressives?**

   (F) minimum wage

   (G) weekends off

   (H) safety precautions

   (J) payments for injured workers

3. **Which of the following best summarizes the third paragraph?**

   (A) Progressives helped establish laws to improve working conditions at factories.

   (B) During the Progressive Era, working conditions in factories were dangerous.

   (C) Factory owners began providing money to help workers injured on the job.

   (D) Factory workers made little money for the long hours they had to work.

4. **Write a title that would be appropriate for this passage.**

   The Work of Progressives

   _____

   _____

Sample Test 2: Reading Comprehension

Directions: Read the passage. Choose the best answer for each question that follows.

Example

Cats were first kept as pets in 2500 B.C. by the Egyptians. These first house cats were probably a type of wildcat called a *Caffre* cat. The idea of keeping a cat as a pet spread to Europe. Caffre cats were brought to Europe and are the ancestors of many of the modern cat breeds.

Europeans probably thought that keeping cats as pets was

(A) ridiculous.

(B) a health hazard.

(C) a good idea.

(D) dangerous.

Answer: (C)

The penguin is a seabird that is native to the waters of the Southern Hemisphere. Penguins cannot fly, but they are excellent swimmers. They spend most of their time out at sea but come to land to raise their young. Mother penguins lay one or two eggs each season.

Puffins are another kind of seabird, but they are native to the cold waters of the Northern Hemisphere. Puffins can fly, but not very well. Like penguins, they swim well and spend most of their time at sea. Mother puffins lay only one egg each season, and they raise their young on land.

1. This passage mostly describes

(A) how seabirds raise their young.

(B) how penguins and puffins are alike and different.

(C) how penguins and puffins swim.

(D) where penguins and puffins live.

2. Which of the following statements is true?

(F) Penguins live in the Northern Hemisphere.

(G) Puffins live in the Northern Hemisphere.

(H) Puffins lay more eggs than penguins.

(J) Both birds spend most of their time on land.

3. Given what you know from reading the passage, what do you think penguins most likely eat?

(A) fish

(B) other birds

(C) puffins

(D) eggs

4. Which sentence tells one way that penguins and puffins are alike?

(F) The birds live in the Southern Hemisphere.

(G) The birds lay 17 eggs each season.

(H) The birds can fly for long distances.

(J) The birds are good swimmers.

GO

Sample Test 2: Reading Comprehension (55)

Directions: Read the passage. Choose the best answer for each question that follows.

The Flying Congressman

The first major battle of the Civil War was fought near the small town of Manassas Junction, Virginia. The Union army called the battle *Bull Run*, after the creek by that name. This quaint little town lay just 30 miles southwest of Washington, D.C., so a number of citizens from the nation's capital thought it might be fun to pack a picnic lunch, load up the family, and take a buggy ride out to watch the Confederates "get what was coming to them." They viewed the upcoming battle as nothing more than a sporting event. Even members of Congress were in attendance. No fewer than six senators and an undetermined number of congressmen showed up, as did pretty ladies in fancy gowns, all traveling in style in expensive buggies and carriages.

One particular congressman provided what turned out to be the only entertainment of the day for the spectators from the big city. What was predicted to be an easy victory for the Union forces turned into a rout. Federal troops retreated to the capital at a record pace, followed by the carriages of Washington's elite—minus their picnic baskets. These were discarded when the rout began, and the Confederate soldiers had a feast when the battle was over.

Although those in flight were preoccupied with their safety, they could not help noticing a tall, long-legged congressman who, on foot, was leading the pack in its frantic race back to the capital. He was seen jumping ditches and gullies, and was said to have cleared a six-foot fence with a foot to spare. Many of the terror stricken refugees howled with laughter, despite their fear.

History does not relate the name of the fleet and agile congressman. But there is a chance he might be the same legislator who, after reaching the safety of the capital, was confronted by President Lincoln. The president glared at the panting legislator and is supposed to have said dryly, "I congratulate you on winning the race!"

GO

56 Sample Test 2: Reading Comprehension

Directions: Use the passage on the previous page to answer the questions below.

5. This story mostly shows that

(A) many people died at the Battle of Bull Run.

(B) congressmen during the Civil War were quite athletic.

(C) some people in Washington, D.C., did not take the beginning of the Civil War seriously.

(D) the Confederates would win the war.

6. According to the story, who ended up eating the picnic lunches?

(F) the Washington elite.

(G) President Lincoln.

(H) the Union soldiers.

(J) the Confederate soldiers.

7. Reread the last sentence of the passage. How do you suppose the president felt about the people who went to watch the battle?

(A) He was angry with them.

(B) He was worried about them.

(C) He was proud of them.

(D) He distrusted them.

8. Why did the spectators run away from the battle?

(F) because the Union soldiers were winning the battle

(G) because they had lost their picnic baskets

(H) because they were in buggies

(J) because the Union soldiers were losing the battle

9. This story tells us the most about

(A) Manassas Junction, Virginia.

(B) why the Civil War took place.

(C) the people who went to watch the battle.

(D) President Lincoln's approach to the war.

10. Why was the battle named *Bull Run*?

(F) because that was the name of the nearest town

(G) because the people had to run away

(H) because that was the name of a nearby creek

(J) because the Confederates liked the name

Sample Test 2: Reading Comprehension 57

Directions: Read the passage. Choose the best answer for each question that follows.

Bonkers for Baseball

I remember a special Mother's Day back in 1939. My mom was a big baseball fan, so my father treated us to tickets for the Brainford Bisons game. We sat in box seats owned by my father's company. It was an exciting day.

Before the game began, we started talking to a woman sitting in a nearby box seat. We learned that she was the mother of the Beulah Blaze's pitcher. Her son, Brian Falls, had been pitching in the minor leagues for three years. This was the first time she had ever seen him pitch in a professional game.

For the special event, Brian Falls had treated his mother to a box seat. He had the box decorated in flowers. Mrs. Falls was so excited. She told us that she had always encouraged Brian to become a baseball player. Her dream for her son had come true.

My team wasn't doing very well in the early innings. With Brian Falls pitching, the Brainford Bisons' batters kept striking out. Then, Falls threw a fastball to the plate. The batter swung at it. He caught a piece of it and fouled it off. The foul ball flew into the crowd. It came straight toward us! My dad and I reached into the air to catch it, but the ball veered left and hit Mrs. Falls in the head. She was knocked unconscious. We couldn't believe it—out of all the people in the stands, the ball hit the pitcher's mother! Mrs. Falls was rushed to the hospital. For the rest of the game, we wondered what had happened to her. Later, we learned the rest of the story.

Brian Falls left the game to accompany his mom to the hospital. He was so upset that he told her he would quit the game. His mother, who was recovering nicely, convinced him to stay in baseball. It's a good thing, because three years later, he joined the major leagues.

Sample Test 2: Reading Comprehension

Directions: Use the passage on the previous page to answer the questions below.

11. What would be another good title for this story?

Ⓐ "Mother's Day at the Ballpark"

Ⓑ "Making It in the Majors"

Ⓒ "Brian Falls: His Career in Baseball"

Ⓓ "The Brainford Bisons Steal Home"

12. Here is a time line of what happens in the story. Which sentence belongs in the empty box?

The family goes to the baseball game for Mother's Day.

A foul ball is hit into the stands.

Brian Falls joins the major leagues.

Ⓕ Mrs. Falls convinces Brian not to quit baseball.

Ⓖ Mrs. Falls is taken to the hospital.

Ⓗ The family discovers that the woman they've been talking with is the mother of the Beulah Blaze's pitcher.

Ⓙ The ball is almost caught by the narrator.

13. Why do you suppose Brian Falls had his mother's box seat decorated with flowers?

Ⓐ because he wanted to impress his friends

Ⓑ because it was the first time she had seen him pitch professionally

Ⓒ because he was in the major leagues

Ⓓ because she told him not to quit

14. Why was Mrs. Falls taken to the hospital?

Ⓕ because she needed to tell Brian to stay in the game

Ⓖ because she was a nurse

Ⓗ because she was sick

Ⓙ because she was hit by a foul ball

15. Mrs. Falls probably taught Brian to

Ⓐ follow his dreams.

Ⓑ give up when things got too hard.

Ⓒ play baseball.

Ⓓ fight against his opponents.

16. From reading the passage, how do you suppose the narrator feels about baseball?

Ⓕ He thinks it is a silly game.

Ⓖ He despises it.

Ⓗ He is bored with it.

Ⓙ He enjoys it.

GO

Sample Test 2: Reading Comprehension

Directions: Read the passage. Choose the best answer for each question that follows.

A Delicious Dinner

Molly's family is Chinese-American. They serve a traditional Chinese meal once a week. Molly invited her friend Chloe to join them this week.

Molly's family was busy preparing for dinner when Chloe arrived. The house was filled with good smells. "You can help me set the table," Molly told her friend. They laid the place settings on the table. They gave each person a pair of chopsticks, a soup bowl, a soup spoon, and a rice bowl on a saucer.

"Where are the forks and knives?" Chloe asked.

"Oh, you won't need those," Molly explained. "We use chopsticks. But don't worry. I'll show you how to use them."

The two girls went into the kitchen. Molly's father was slicing and chopping vegetables. He tossed the vegetables into a large cooking pan coated with hot oil.

"That's a wok," Molly said.

Chloe watched the vegetables sizzle. Then, Molly's mother asked the girls to carry platters of food to the table. Chloe carried the steamed rice. It was one of the few dishes she recognized. There were meat-filled bundles called *won-tons*, steamed noodles, stir-fried beef, sweet-and-sour chicken, and pork spareribs. The food was nutritious and seasoned with herbs, spices, and sauces.

Chloe was a little nervous about eating with chopsticks. Molly gave her instructions on how to hold and pinch with the chopsticks.

Chloe managed to pick up a piece of chicken in her chopsticks. Suddenly, her fingers slipped and the chicken flew across the table. It landed in Molly's soup with a splash. Everyone smiled. "We keep these on hand for emergencies," Molly's father said kindly. He brought out a knife and fork and handed them to Chloe. Chloe was relieved and ate her dinner. It was delicious!

At the end of the meal, Chloe was given a fortune cookie. She broke it open and read the fortune inside. It said, "If you practice hard, you will learn many things." Chloe laughed and said, "If you let me take home a pair of chopsticks, my fortune may come true!"

LANGUAGE ARTS

60 Sample Test 2: Reading Comprehension

Directions: Use the passage on the previous page to answer the questions below.

17. This story is mostly about

(A) Chinese food.

(B) a family's traditions.

(C) a girl trying to use chopsticks.

(D) what it takes to have friends.

18. What food was the most familiar to Chloe?

(F) sweet-and-sour chicken

(G) rice

(H) won-tons

(J) steamed noodles

19. How do you think Molly's parents felt when Chloe dropped her food?

(A) They understood that Chloe wasn't used to using chopsticks.

(B) They felt Chloe had insulted their culture.

(C) They thought Chloe had bad manners.

(D) They wished Chloe hadn't come to dinner.

20. Why did Chloe's fortune make her laugh?

(F) because she was trying to act brave

(G) because she spilled her food

(H) because she thought it was a joke

(J) because she knew she needed to practice using chopsticks

21. In this story, we learn the most about

(A) Molly.

(B) Chloe.

(C) Molly's mother.

(D) Molly's father.

22. Molly's father said, "We keep these on hand for emergencies." What was he referring to?

(F) platters of food

(G) a wok

(H) a knife and fork

(J) chopsticks

STOP

Name _____ Date _____

Practice Test 1: Reading
Part 1: Vocabulary

Directions: Choose the word that means the same, or about the same, as the underlined word.

1. a <u>bundle</u> of goods

- (A) sweater
- (B) burden
- (C) rumble
- (D) package

2. <u>restore</u> the wood

- (F) repair
- (G) retread
- (H) relieve
- (J) reduce

3. The dishes <u>clattered</u> in the sink.

- (A) rattled
- (B) broke
- (C) jumped
- (D) washed

4. Max planted a <u>sapling</u> in the yard.

- (F) type of vegetable
- (G) flower
- (H) shrub
- (J) young tree

Directions: Choose the word that means the opposite of the underlined word.

5. <u>scamper</u> away

- (A) waltz
- (B) crawl
- (C) stroll
- (D) spring

6. <u>contemporary</u> art

- (F) modern
- (G) ancient
- (H) imaginative
- (J) folksy

7. the <u>collapse</u> of the government

- (A) creation
- (B) structure
- (C) downfall
- (D) laws

8. <u>reckless</u> behavior

- (F) foolish
- (G) carefree
- (H) juvenile
- (J) thoughtful

GO

Name _____ Date _____

Practice Test 1: Reading
Part 1: Vocabulary

Directions: Choose the word that best completes both sentences.

9. Jameeka plays in a _____.
   Tie a _____ around the tree.

   (A) group

   (B) ribbon

   (C) band

   (D) string

10. What is the _____ of your birth?
    His family has a _____ farm.

    (F) date

    (G) month

    (H) citrus

    (J) year

11. The ship sailed into the <u>bay</u>.
    In which sentence does the word *bay* mean the same thing as in the sentence above?

    (A) The <u>bay</u> horse was my favorite.

    (B) Coyotes <u>bay</u> at the moon.

    (C) Johan sat in the <u>bay</u> window.

    (D) Marnie found buried treasure at the bottom of the <u>bay</u>.

Directions: Choose the answer that best defines the underlined part of the words.

12. <u>tri</u>athlon   <u>tri</u>angle

    (F) two

    (G) three

    (H) four

    (J) five

13. teach<u>er</u>   wait<u>er</u>

    (A) the study of

    (B) small

    (C) art or skill of

    (D) one who

14. Which of these words probably comes from the Latin word *bini oculus,* meaning *two eyes at a time?*

    (F) bindery

    (G) bingo

    (H) binoculars

    (J) binomial

15. Which of these words probably comes from the Italian word *ombra,* meaning *shade?*

    (A) umbrella

    (B) omelet

    (C) omit

    (D) umpire

GO

Practice Test 1: Reading
Part 1: Vocabulary

Directions: Read the paragraph. Choose the word that best fits in each numbered blank

The armadillo is _____ (16) in several ways. First, the female gives birth to four babies, and they are always the same sex. Second, when an armadillo is _____ (17) and cannot escape to its _____ (18) or quickly dig itself into the ground, it rolls itself into a tight, protective ball. This is possible because of the joined _____ (19) plates of its shell. The armadillo also tucks in its head and feet. If, by chance, it _____ (20) to reach the safety of its burrow, the armadillo can hold on so tightly with its strong claws that it is virtually _____ (21) to pull it out.

16. F honored
    G unusual
    H motivated
    J typical

17. A assisted
    B free
    C cornered
    D released

18. F burrow
    G vehicle
    H porch
    J dormitory

19. A overlapping
    B detached
    C soft
    D disconnected

20. F endeavors
    G insists
    H actually
    J manages

21. A simple
    B impossible
    C likely
    D difficult

Name _____ Date _____

Practice Test 1: Reading
Part 2: Comprehension

Directions: Read the passage, and answer the questions that follow.

Autumn Dance

Every October, autumn bullies summer into letting go of the skies. The wind breathes a chill into the air. The sun gets tired and goes to bed earlier each night, and night sleeps in later each day. The trees dress in bright gowns for the last celebration of the season, and the leaves skip and dance down the sidewalk. This is autumn, standing firm with hands on her hips, until winter peers over the edge of the world.

1. This passage tells about

(A) winter turning into spring.

(B) fall turning into winter.

(C) spring turning into summer.

(D) summer turning into fall.

2. How does the sun change during autumn?

(F) It rises and sets earlier than in the summer.

(G) It rises and sets later than in the summer.

(H) It rises later but sets earlier than in the summer.

(J) It rises earlier but sets later than in the summer.

3. What is the author referring to when she describes the trees dressed in "bright gowns"?

(A) leaves that have changed color but have not yet fallen from the trees

(B) green leaves

(C) formal dresses

(D) the trees' empty branches

4. Personification means *giving human qualities to animals or objects*. Which sentence is not an example of personification?

(F) Every October, autumn bullies summer into letting go of the skies.

(G) A cold wind blows.

(H) The leaves skip and dance down the sidewalk.

(J) The sun gets tired and goes to bed.

GO

Practice Test 1: Reading
Part 2: Comprehension

Directions: Read the passage, and answer the questions that follow.

Tough Tumbleweed

I'm a travelling tumbleweed, rolling along the dusty trails of the wild, wild West. Well, actually I'm blowing across somebody's backyard in suburban Texas. These days, it's hard to find a large open space. Back in the good old days, my ancestors tumbled across miles and miles of deserts or plains. Today, it's hard to find a mile without a strip mall or housing complex. Life for tumbleweeds just isn't that exciting anymore.

My great-great-grandfather was one of the first immigrants to America. He sneaked into the country with a load of wheat from Russia. He and the other tumbleweeds used to be called *Russian thistle* before they came to America. Tumbleweeds can live on very little water, so my ancestors were able to spread across dry western lands that previously couldn't support plants. When a tumbleweed matures, it becomes dry and brittle. A strong wind comes along and—snap!—off it goes, tumbling across the landscape. As it rolls, it drops seeds in new places.

My family has had many adventures over the years. My great-great uncle tumbled with Crazy Horse, the legendary American Indian. My great-grandmother tumbled with the covered wagons. My father even tumbled on the set of a Hollywood western movie.

Modern times are not as kind to us tumbleweeds. We get caught in fences and ditches. Our worst enemy is the automobile. My cousin was trapped under a car and caught fire from the heat of the muffler. He became a tumbleweed torch! Some people hate tumbleweeds and try to burn us up. They can burn all they want, because tumbleweeds are not in danger of becoming extinct. We will be around for a long, long time. Our species wouldn't have lasted this long if we weren't stubborn. We've learned to adapt to civilization and to deal with humans who have taken over our land. Tumbleweeds aren't called tough for nothing!

Practice Test 1: Reading
Part 2: Comprehension

Directions: Use the passage on the previous page to answer the questions below.

5. What is the main idea of this story?

(A) how tumbleweeds have been used throughout history

(B) how modern times have affected tumbleweeds

(C) how people feel about tumbleweeds

(D) how tumbleweeds are used in Hollywood movies

6. Tumbleweeds came to America from

(F) Russia.

(G) Texas.

(H) Hollywood.

(J) the West.

7. How does the narrator of this story feel?

(A) He is happy with modern inventions.

(B) He longs for the days when there were more wide-open spaces.

(C) He appreciates the need for housing complexes.

(D) He wishes he could be in a Hollywood movie.

8. Which of these sentences is an opinion?

(F) Tumbleweeds used to be called *Russian thistle*.

(G) Tumbleweeds are not in danger of becoming extinct.

(H) Tumbleweeds are able to live on very little water.

(J) Life for tumbleweeds just isn't that exciting anymore.

9. The narrator in this story is

(A) a covered wagon.

(B) an American Indian.

(C) a tumbleweed.

(D) a Russian immigrant.

10. What would be a good word to describe tumbleweeds?

(F) hardy

(G) ragile

(H) irritable

(J) delicate

Practice Test 1: Reading
Part 2: Comprehension

Directions: Read the passage, and answer the questions on the following page.

There lived in Virginia in the early 1600s a beautiful girl named *Pocahontas*. Her name meant *playful one*. She was the daughter of Powhatan, the chief of some 30 Indian tribes in Virginia.

Pocahontas is remembered for saving the life of Captain John Smith. Smith was the leader of the Jamestown colony founded by the English in 1607. In that same year, he was captured by the Indians and sentenced to death by Chief Powhatan. According to Smith's own account, he was ordered to lay his head on large stones in anticipation of being clubbed to death by several braves. At this point, Pocahontas is said to have knelt beside the Englishman and placed her head on his. Powhatan was apparently touched by this gesture, and he ordered that Smith be set free.

It is not certain if the above story is true. What casts doubt on its validity is that Smith later claimed to have been saved in the same manner by an Indian girl in New Hampshire.

Regardless, Pocahontas was a real person who did much to improve relations between her people and the English settlers. After the Smith incident, it was mostly peaceful between the two peoples until Powhatan's death in 1618.

In 1613, Pocahontas was captured and held hostage by the English. During her year of captivity, she met and married John Rolfe, a Virginia tobacco planter. In 1616, she accompanied Rolfe to England, where she was presented at the royal court. Pocahontas died there of smallpox in 1617, shortly before her planned return to America. She was buried at Gravesend, England.

John Rolfe returned to Virginia where he died in 1622. Thomas, the son of Rolfe and Pocahontas, later became a distinguished Virginian. Today, a number of Virginia families claim to be descendants of Pocahontas and John Rolfe.

Name _____   Date _____

Practice Test 1: Reading
Part 2: Comprehension

Directions: Use the passage on the previous page to answer the questions below.

11. Which of the following would make a good title for this story?

(A) "Chief Powhatan and His Thirty Tribes"

(B) "The Capture of John Smith"

(C) "The Life of Pocahontas"

(D) "Life on a Virginia Tobacco Farm"

12. Here is a sequence of events that happened in the story.

Pocahontas improved relations between her tribe and the English.

The English capture Pocahontas..

Pocahontas traveled to England.

Which of these events should go in the empty box?

(F) Chief Powhatan died.

(G) Pocahontas married John Rolfe.

(H) Pocahontas saved John Smith.

(J) John Rolfe was killed.

13. Why do some people think John Smith's story about being saved by Pocahontas is not true?

(A) because John Rolfe also claimed he was rescued by Pocahontas

(B) because Pocahontas was not a real person

(C) because there were no witnesses

(D) because he said the same thing happened to him with another tribe

14. How did Pocahontas die?

(F) She died of smallpox.

(G) She was clubbed to death.

(H) She was killed during an Indian uprising.

(J) She drowned on her way to England.

15. In this story, you learn the most about

(A) Powhatan.

(B) John Rolfe.

(C) Pocahontas.

(D) John Smith.

16. The people who claim to be descendants of Pocahontas and John Rolfe are probably

(F) members of a historical society.

(G) proud of their heritage.

(H) ashamed by their family history.

(J) good storytellers.

Practice Test 1: Reading
Part 2: Comprehension

Directions: Read the passage, and answer the questions that follow.

Mammal, Fish, or Fowl?

When scientists in England received reports from Australia about the duckbill platypus in the late 1700s, they thought they were the victims of a hoax. Surely, they must have reasoned, some jokester had sewn body parts from several different animals together in an attempt to trick them.

Indeed, the duckbill platypus is a strange animal. It has a bill resembling a duck, a flat, paddle-shaped tail like a beaver, and it scuffles along the ground in the manner of an alligator. Both its front and hind feet are webbed and have claws. Unlike most mammals, it has neither lips nor exterior ears. Although it nurses its young, it does not give birth to live babies. Instead it lays eggs—like a chicken! Small wonder that scientists were confused and not certain whether they were dealing with fish, fowl, or some kind of new species. They eventually classified the platypus with mammals.

17. This story mostly describes

(A) why scientists decided that the platypus was a mammal.

(B) the unique features of the platypus.

(C) where the platypus can be found.

(D) a scientific hoax.

18. Which of the following statements is false?

(F) The platypus has a tail that resembles a beaver's tail.

(G) English scientists first learned about the platypus in the late 1700s.

(H) The platypus does not have lips.

(J) The platypus is a type of bird.

19. Which sentence is probably true?

(A) One scientist probably made the decision on how the platypus would be classified.

(B) Scientists were probably in complete agreement on how to classify the platypus.

(C) Scientists probably debated over how the platypus should be classified.

(D) Scientists probably let the people of England vote on how the platypus should be classified.

20. Which of these characteristics would have helped the scientists decide that the platypus was a mammal?

(F) The platypus nurses its young.

(G) The platypus lays eggs.

(H) The platypus does not have external ears.

(J) The platypus has a bill like a duck. **GO**

Practice Test 1: Reading
Part 2: Comprehension

Directions: Identify the genre that describes each item.

21. The children woke to a happy sight. While they slept, the world had turned white. Their mother peered into their room and said, "No school today. Go back to bed!"

(A) biography

(B) nonfiction

(C) fiction

(D) fable

22. "I can hop so far and so fast," boasted the frog. "There is no animal who is faster than me." He stretched his legs and hopped a few times for show. The turtle shrugged and yawned. "Hopping can be useful, I suppose," he agreed, "but there are other talents I'd rather have."

(F) fable

(G) biography

(H) poetry

(J) nonfiction

23. Frank Lloyd Wright was one of America's most memorable and talented architects. The buildings he designed had a very unique look. They fit into the landscape in a way that few other buildings of the time did.

(A) science fiction

(B) myth

(C) biography

(D) realistic fiction

24. Dark skies, clouds are gathering,
Children run inside.
Rumble above, whipping winds,
Close the windows tight.
Yellow lights, books in bed,
No place I'd rather be.

(F) mystery

(G) fable

(H) nonfiction

(J) poetry

25. I remember coming downstairs on winter mornings. The floors were cold under my bare feet, but the kitchen was always warm. Mama was up earlier than the rest of us every day of the year, and by the time we started trickling downstairs, the kitchen was filled with the smell of fresh bread and the sound of sizzling bacon.

(A) myth

(B) memoir

(C) poetry

(D) tall tale

Punctuation

Directions: Read each sentence. Choose the punctuation mark that is needed in the sentence. If no more punctuation is needed, choose "None."

Example

No I wasn't late for practice.

- (A) ;
- (B) ,
- (C) "
- (D) None

Answer: (B)

---

1. The team carried in the bats balls, and gloves.

- (A) ;
- (B) ,
- (C) :
- (D) None

2. "Great catch" yelled the pitcher.

- (F) ?
- (G) .
- (H) !
- (J) None

3. Did you see that foul ball

- (A) ?
- (B) .
- (C) ,
- (D) None

4. Matilda hit a homerun.

- (F) !
- (G) "
- (H) ,
- (J) None

5. That's three strikes," said the umpire.

- (A) ,
- (B) "
- (C) !
- (D) None

6. Yes the Fifth-Grade Firecrackers won the game.

- (F) ,
- (G) .
- (H) !
- (J) None

Read each sentence carefully. Pay special attention to the punctuation marks that are shown.

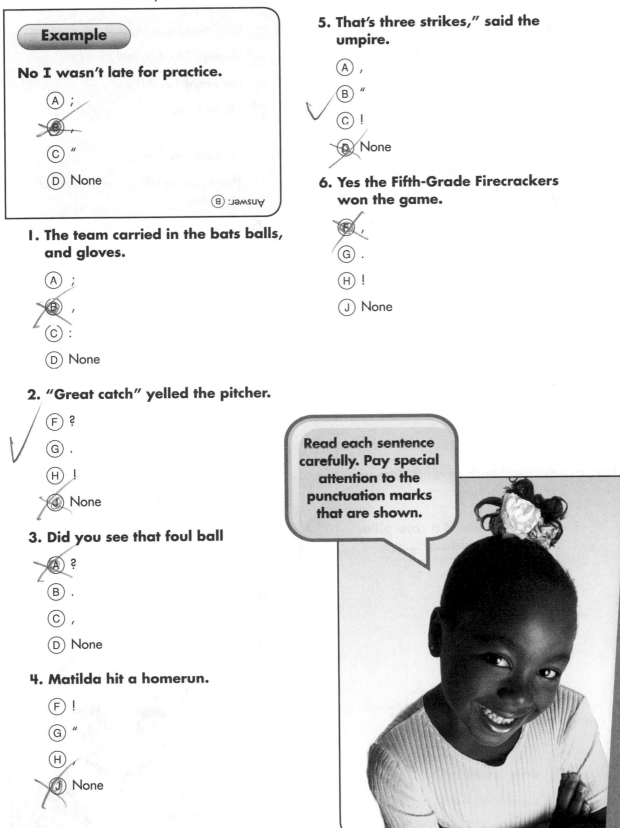

Name _____   Date _____

Punctuation

Directions: Read each item. Choose the answer that has a punctuation error. If there is no mistake, choose "No mistakes."

1. (A) Samuel Clemens had no money

   (B) He began writing articles

   (C) for a newspaper called the *Territorial Enterprises.*

   (D) No mistakes

2. (F) Samuel's newspaper articles

   (G) were eventually compiled

   (H) into his first book, Roughing It

   (J) No mistakes

3. (A) Samuel Clemens

   (B) first used the pen name:

   (C) Mark Twain while he worked as a writer in Virginia City, Nevada.

   (D) No mistakes

4. (F) 742 West Main Street

   (G) Virginia City, NV, 80235

   (H) December 12, 2012

   (J) No mistakes

5. (A) Dear Mr. Pendelton,

   (B) Thank you for telling our class about Mark Twain.

   (C) He was a real character?

   (D) No mistakes

Directions: Read each sentence. Choose the word or words that best fit in the blank and show the correct punctuation.

6. **Gabriel watched a caterpillar climb up the side of _____ aquarium.**

   (F) its

   (G) it's

   (H) its'

   (J) its's

7. **He placed bits of grass, _____ small twigs inside.**

   (A) some lettuce and

   (B) some lettuce, and

   (C) some lettuce, and,

   (D) some lettuce and,

Keep the directions in mind when choosing your answers.

Chapter 3: Mechanics

Capitalization and Punctuation

Directions: Read each item. Choose the answer that shows correct punctuation and capitalization.

Example

A "Where is your sunscreen," Emma asked Veronica.

B "Oh, I dont use that," veronica told her. "I want a great tan."

Ⓒ "That's not a good idea," Emma said, shaking her head.

D "We'll be outside from Noon until 3:00."

Answer: Ⓒ

1. A In the years following the civil war Chicago became the railroad and commercial center in America.

B With business thriving, no one was prepared for what happened on October 8, 1871.

C A fire broke out in the Lumber district.

D The fire was one of the worst in u.s. history.

2. F Crocodiles are on every continent except europe and antarctica.

G Alligators except for a species native to eastern China are limited to the United States.

H Alligators inhabit Swamps, Rivers, and Coastal Areas of many southern states.

J The best way to tell a crocodile from an alligator is by observing its snout.

3. **On December 7, 1941, Japanese planes attacked the U.S. naval base at <u>Pearl Harbor, Hawaii.</u>**

A Pearl Harbor Hawaii

B Pearl, Harbor, Hawaii

C pearl harbor, Hawaii

D Correct as it is

4. **Many acts of heroism <u>were recorded, in the hours</u> following the attack.**

F were recorded; in the hours

G were recorded in the hours

H were recorded; in the hours,

J Correct as it is

5. **An army <u>pilot, lieutenant George Bickell</u> was one man honored for his heroics.**

A pilot, lieutenant George Bickell,

B pilot, Lieutenant George Bickell

C pilot, Lieutenant George Bickell,

D Correct as it is

Capitalization and Punctuation

Directions: Read each sentence. Choose the word or words that best fit in the blank and show the correct punctuation.

1. School is in session from _____

(A) september through june!

(B) September, through June.

(C) September through June?

(D) September through June.

2. We took a tour of _____ office.

(F) Dr. Eli Hansen's

(G) Dr Eli Hansens'

(H) Dr. Eli Hansens

(J) dr. Eli Hansen's

3. The waiter _____ I get you anything else?"

(A) "Asked can

(B) asked, "Can

(C) asked. "Can

(D) asked "Can

4. Pilar takes _____ lessons after school.

(F) Piano lessons, Art lessons, and Dance

(G) piano lessons art lessons and dance

(H) piano lessons, art lessons, and dance

(J) piano, lessons, art, lessons, and dance,

5. The _____ of students at my school is 48 inches.

(A) Average Height

(B) average height

(C) average height,

(D) Average height

6. I was surprised by what I had _____ would ever believe me.

(F) found; No one

(G) found? No one

(H) found, no one

(J) found. No one

7. I am interested in buying stickers, _____ the best.

(A) and yours are

(B) and your's are

(C) and yours' are

(D) and yours, are

8. The people who live on _____ about the noise from the airport.

(F) Grant street complain

(G) Grant Street. Complain

(H) grant street complain

(J) Grant Street complain

> To narrow your choices, eliminate answers you know are incorrect.

Chapter 3: Mechanics

Name _____ Date _____

Spelling

Directions: Find the word that is spelled correctly and fits best in the blank.

Example

Elliot _____ a song for the contest.

(A) composed

(B) compossed

(C) compoosed

(D) compoased

Answer: (A)

1. Samantha had to renew her driver's _____.

(A) licensse

(B) lisense

(C) liesense

(D) license

2. Roger certified that the table was a _____ antique.

(F) genuwine

(G) genuine

(H) genuin

(J) genuinn

3. Please call a _____ to repair the sink.

(A) plumber

(B) plummer

(C) plumbner

(D) plumer

4. Crystal _____ on her mother's help.

(F) relys

(G) relies

(H) realize

(J) reelies

5. The waiter forgot to give us our _____.

(A) receipt

(B) receiept

(C) recete

(D) recite

6. The detective will _____ the crime.

(F) innvestigate

(G) envestigate

(H) investagate

(J) investigate

7. Shinook addressed the _____ of elders.

(A) counsill

(B) cowncil

(C) council

(D) counsell

Spelling

Directions: Mark the choice that has a spelling error. If there is no mistake, mark the space for "No mistakes."

1. (A) kindle
   (B) billyun
   (C) focus
   (D) No mistakes

2. (F) kwaint
   (G) loyal
   (H) pillar
   (J) No mistakes

3. (A) pursue
   (B) jealous
   (C) heroic
   (D) No mistakes

Directions: One of the underlined words is not spelled correctly for the way it is used in the phrase. Mark the circle for that phrase.

4. (F) worldwide <u>piece</u>
   (G) <u>idle</u> behavior
   (H) wounds will <u>heal</u>
   (J) light the <u>flare</u>

5. (A) $50 <u>fare</u>
   (B) <u>lesson</u> learned
   (C) <u>fowl</u> ball
   (D) apple <u>core</u>

6. (F) <u>write</u> a message
   (G) <u>herd</u> of buffalo
   (H) results will <u>vary</u>
   (J) tie a <u>not</u>

Directions: Find the underlined part of the sentence that is misspelled. If all the words are spelled correctly, mark "No mistakes."

7. I <u>beleive</u> the <u>experiment</u> will prove the <u>existence</u> of fat in this recipe. <u>No mistakes</u>
   (A)   (B)   (C)   (D)

8. If you are <u>board</u>, you may go <u>outside</u> and rake the <u>leaves</u>. <u>No mistakes</u>
   (F)   (G)   (H)   (J)

Spelling

Directions: Choose the phrase in which the underlined word is not spelled correctly.

1. (A) locked in a dungeon
   (B) casual conversation
   (C) betraid the trust
   (D) introduce your friends

2. (F) reckreation area
   (G) knight in shining armor
   (H) hoarse voice
   (J) medium height

3. (A) raise sheep
   (B) enough said
   (C) bouquet of balloons
   (D) aunts, uncles, and cusins

4. (F) get into trubble
   (G) loose tooth
   (H) stormy weather
   (J) their bikes

5. (A) free sample
   (B) mental image
   (C) a small morsul
   (D) fried potatoes

6. (F) airtight container
   (G) horse-driven carriage
   (H) hopeful fuchure
   (J) countless stars

7. (A) collapse under pressure
   (B) elderlie people
   (C) recite the poem
   (D) club members were initiated

8. (F) scholarly pursuits
   (G) sparkling diamonds
   (H) went down in defeat
   (J) difficult profesion

9. (A) cast your ballot
   (B) buy a trinkette
   (C) drive the vehicle
   (D) play the lyre

> **Be sure you know if you are supposed to find a word that is spelled correctly or incorrectly!**

Sample Test 3: Mechanics

Directions: Fill in the circle next to the punctuation mark that is needed in the sentence. Fill in the space for "None" if no additional punctuation marks are needed.

Example

"You can see the Grand Canyon out the left-hand windows" announced the pilot.

- (A) ?
- (B) ,
- (C) .
- (D) None

Answer: (B)

1. When we left the cafeteria this afternoon we headed for the library.

- (A) ;
- (B) ,
- (C) .
- (D) None

2. "Hey, Mitzi. Are you okay? asked Charles.

- (F) ;
- (G) ,
- (H) "
- (J) None

3. "I'm King of the Mountain" cried Madeline.

- (A) !
- (B) .
- (C) ?
- (D) None

Directions: Fill in the circle next to the choice that has a punctuation error. If there is no mistake, mark the space for "No mistakes."

4. (F) I cant finish
- (G) the project, because
- (H) I'm going on vacation.
- (J) No mistakes

5. (A) Yes, I'll go.
- (B) I always enjoy a day
- (C) at the park
- (D) No mistakes

6. (F) John still has to
- (G) clear the table wash the dishes and wipe down the counters
- (H) before he can watch television.
- (J) No mistakes

Name _____ Date _____

Sample Test 3: Mechanics

Directions: Read each sentence. Fill in the circle for the answer choice that best fits in the blank and has correct capitalization and punctuation.

7. I like to play _____ I like basketball even better.

Ⓐ baseball, but,

Ⓑ baseball but,

Ⓒ baseball. But

Ⓓ̶ baseball, but

8. The _____ were lined up for miles, and not one of them was moving.

Ⓕ cars's

Ⓖ̶ cars

Ⓗ cars'

Ⓙ car's

Directions: Read each group of sentences. Fill in the circle next to the sentence that is written correctly and shows the correct capitalization and punctuation.

9. Ⓐ Jake and Tristan went to the movies

Ⓑ They paid for their tickets popcorn and sodas.

Ⓒ They watched the previews?

Ⓓ̶ When the movie started, they stopped talking.

10. Ⓕ̶ Los Angeles, California, is a favorite vacation spot.

Ⓖ People come to see the Beaches, Amusement Parks, and Movie Studios.

Ⓗ Some people like to find celebrity homes in beverly hills.

Ⓙ The hollywood sign, is a famous landmark.

11. Ⓐ Native americans used stories to tell about nature and the world.

Ⓑ̶ The Cherokees have a legend about how fire came to Earth.

Ⓒ A bolt of lightning struck a Sycamore Tree on an island.

Ⓓ A water spider, carried a chunk of coal, across the water, to the mainland.

Directions: Look at the underlined part of each sentence. Fill in the circle for the answer choice that shows correct punctuation and capitalization. Fill in the circle for "Correct as it is" if the underlined part is correct.

12. The primary colors of pigments are <u>red blue and yellow</u>

Ⓕ red, blue and yellow?

Ⓖ red blue, and yellow.

Ⓗ̶ red, blue, and yellow.

Ⓙ Correct as it is

13. Many times, <u>Earths plates</u> move along an existing fault.

Ⓐ Earths' plates

Ⓑ Earths's plates

Ⓒ̶ Earth's plates

Ⓓ Correct as it is

GO

Name _____ Date _____

Sample Test 3: Mechanics

Directions: Fill in the circle for the answer that shows the correct punctuation and capitalization for the underlined word or words.

Firefighters work day and night. When there is a <u>fire each</u> (**14**) firefighter has a special duty. The duty may be to <u>connect hoses to Water Hydrants</u> (**15**), set up ladders, look for and rescue people, break windows, or cut holes in the roof or walls of the building to let smoke, gas, and heat escape. When <u>firefighters</u> (**16**) are not fighting fires, they clean and maintain their equipment. They attend classes and have practice drills so they can become better firefighters. They also exercise to stay in shape.

14. (F) a fire. Each

(G) a fire, each

(H) a fire; each

(D) Correct as it is

15. (A) connect hoses, to water hydrants

(B) connect hoses to water hydrants.

(C) connect hoses to water hydrants

(D) Correct as it is

16. (F) Firefighters

(G) firefighters'

(H) firefighter's

(J) Correct as it is

Directions: Read the passage, and use it to answer the questions that follow.

(**1**) The lower and middle slopes of a mountain are usually forest areas. (**2**) Coniferous forests have trees like <u>Pines and Spruces</u>. (**3**) These trees have leaves shaped like needles that stay green all year. (**4**) Deciduous forests have trees like oaks and maples. (**5**) <u>These tree's</u> have broad leaves that change colors and fall off in autumn. (**6**) The trees serve as home for many birds and rodents. (**7**) Forest predators stalk their prey among the trees. (**8**) The forest area comes to an end at a point called the *timberline*. (**9**) This is the point beyond which it is too cold for trees to grow.

17. In sentence 2, <u>Pines and Spruces</u> is best written

(A) pines and spruces?

(B) pines and spruces.

(C) Pines and Spruces;

(D) Correct as it is

18. In sentence 5, <u>These tree's</u> is best written

(F) These trees

(G) These trees's

(H) These trees'

(J) Correct as it is

GO

Sample Test 3: Mechanics

Directions: Read each item. Fill in the circle for the choice that has a spelling error. If there is not a mistake, fill in "No mistakes."

19. (A) grone
(B) leather
(C) reason
(D) No mistakes

20. (F) auction
(G) caught
(H) autumn
(J) No mistakes

21. (A) retreive
(B) sleigh
(C) receive
(D) No mistakes

Directions: One of the underlined words is not spelled correctly for the way it is used in the phrase. Mark the circle for that phrase.

22. (F) a <u>flair</u> for acting
(G) <u>minor</u> damage
(H) <u>plane</u> clothes
(J) a fishing <u>pier</u>

23. (A) <u>our</u> books
(B) <u>its</u> raining
(C) <u>they're</u> in charge
(D) <u>find</u> a few

24. (F) <u>die</u> the fabric
(G) a broken window <u>pane</u>
(H) <u>hail</u>, sleet, and snow
(J) move <u>forth</u>

Directions: Find the underlined part of the sentence that is misspelled. If all the words are spelled correctly, mark "No mistakes."

25. A <u>worrisome</u> <u>rumor</u> spread <u>threw</u> the school. <u>No mistakes</u>
(A)   (B)   (C)   (D)

26. The <u>village</u> <u>residants</u> were <u>wary</u> of the newcomer. <u>No mistakes</u>
(F)   (G)   (H)   (J)

27. He <u>adjusted</u> the <u>bandage</u> to cover the <u>blister</u>. <u>No mistakes</u>
(A)   (B)   (C)   (D)

STOP

LANGUAGE ARTS

82

Word Choice

Directions: Choose the word or phrase that best completes the sentence.

Example

They _____ only two days to go until the science fair.

- (A) hads
- (B) haves
- (C) had
- (D) half

Answer: C

1. Jeremy taught _____ to play the guitar.
   - (A) hisself
   - (B) itself
   - (C) themselves
   - (D) himself

2. The sleek steamer _____ through the quiet night.
   - (F) slided
   - (G) slipped
   - (H) slipping
   - (J) sliding

3. The dog _____ under the fence.
   - (A) crawled
   - (B) to crawl
   - (C) crawling
   - (D) crawlings

4. Tomorrow, I _____ my friend.
   - (F) to meet
   - (G) will meet
   - (H) meets
   - (J) met

5. Addison is _____ than I am.
   - (A) more hungrier
   - (B) hungriest
   - (C) most hungry
   - (D) hungrier

6. The twins can take care of _____.
   - (F) themselves
   - (G) herself
   - (H) himself
   - (J) yourselves

7. The roses _____ than the carnations.
   - (A) are more fragranter
   - (B) is more fragrant
   - (C) was more fragrant
   - (D) were more fragrant

8. He was the _____ member of the club.
   - (F) more louder
   - (G) louder
   - (H) loudest
   - (J) most loud

If you are not sure which answer is correct, try each one in the blank. Choose the one that sounds the best.

Word Choice

Directions: Choose the answer that is a complete and correctly written sentence.

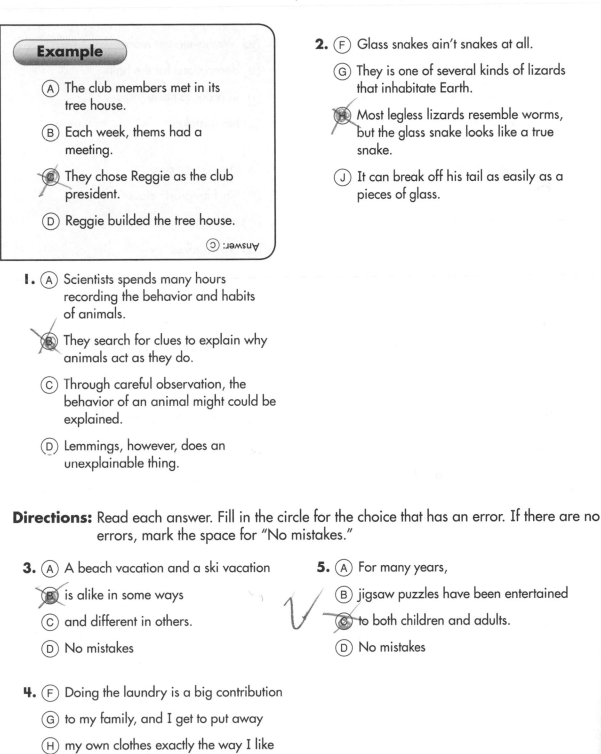

Example

(A) The club members met in its tree house.

(B) Each week, thems had a meeting.

(C) They chose Reggie as the club president.

(D) Reggie builded the tree house.

Answer: (C)

1. (A) Scientists spends many hours recording the behavior and habits of animals.

(B) They search for clues to explain why animals act as they do.

(C) Through careful observation, the behavior of an animal might could be explained.

(D) Lemmings, however, does an unexplainable thing.

2. (F) Glass snakes ain't snakes at all.

(G) They is one of several kinds of lizards that inhabitate Earth.

(H) Most legless lizards resemble worms, but the glass snake looks like a true snake.

(J) It can break off his tail as easily as a pieces of glass.

Directions: Read each answer. Fill in the circle for the choice that has an error. If there are no errors, mark the space for "No mistakes."

3. (A) A beach vacation and a ski vacation

(B) is alike in some ways

(C) and different in others.

(D) No mistakes

4. (F) Doing the laundry is a big contribution

(G) to my family, and I get to put away

(H) my own clothes exactly the way I like them.

(J) No mistakes

5. (A) For many years,

(B) jigsaw puzzles have been entertained

(C) to both children and adults.

(D) No mistakes

Name _____ Date _____

Word Choice

Directions: Choose the line that has a usage error. If there is no error, choose "No mistakes."

1. (A) George Washington
   (B) are called the father
   (C) of our country.
   (D) No mistakes

2. (F) Binoculars are helpful
   (G) because they let you
   (H) observe things closely.
   (J) No mistakes

3. (A) We missed the
   (B) baseball game however
   (C) there was a train crossing.
   (D) No mistakes

4. (F) He hasn't never made
   (G) a mistake on any of
   (H) his reading assignments.
   (J) No mistakes

5. (A) The junior high
   (B) play takes place on
   (C) Friday and Saturday night.
   (D) No mistakes

6. (F) We haveta get more
   (G) decorations for the hall
   (H) in order to finish.
   (J) No mistakes

7. (A) Mrs. Green give
   (B) her fifth-grade class
   (C) a surprise quiz.
   (D) No mistakes

8. (F) Carlos and Will are
   (G) best friends who play
   (H) on the same basketball team.
   (J) No mistakes

9. (A) Jada and Kerry decided
   (B) to fix the bike themself
   (C) and not ask for help.
   (D) No mistakes

10. (F) Did anyone
    (G) find the assignment
    (H) I finish yesterday.
    (J) No mistakes

Name _____   Date _____

Word Choice

Directions: Read the passage, and use it to find the correct answers.

Example

(1) We was reading an article called "Food for Thought." (2) It is about what we should and shouldn't eat as snacks. (3) Some of the ideas in the article are very good, such as choosing an apple instead of chips. (4) The article makes me think, but it also makes me hungry.

In sentence 1, <u>We was</u> is best written _____.

(A) We are

(B) We wasn't

(C) We is

(D) Correct as it is

Answer: (A)

Read the underlined phrases carefully.

Think of the best way to write those phrases before you look at the answer choices.

---

(1) In Great Britain 150 years ago, hospitals for the sick <u>have been</u> unpleasant places. (2) The surgeons would be found wearing blood-stained and grime-splattered clothing. (3) They often <u>refuse</u> to change clothing or equipment between surgeries. (4) Diseases traveled readily <u>under</u> patients in a filthy atmosphere where bedding and clothing went unwashed. (5) Hospital food was of meager benefit, sometimes tainted and barely nourishing. (6) <u>Them</u> who provided nursing care had little or no training and lacked motivation. (7) The wealthy in this period did not send their family members to the hospital, but had doctors and nurses come to their homes.

---

1. In sentence 1, <u>have been</u> is best written _____.

(A) were

(B) was

(C) are

(D) Correct as it is

2. In sentence 3, <u>refuse</u> is best written _____.

(F) refused

(G) refuses

(H) refusing

(J) Correct as it is

3. In sentence 4, <u>under</u> is best written _____.

(A) around

(B) through

(C) between

(D) Correct as it is

4. In sentence 6, <u>Them</u> is best written _____.

(F) Those

(G) They

(H) Themselves

(J) Correct as it is

Word Choice

Directions: Circle the correct word in each sentence.

1. Nikki _____ (led, (lead)) the class in singing the national anthem.

2. Show Brendan _____ ((where), wear) we keep the extra towels.

3. Jamal, the social studies report is _____ (do, dew, (due)) tomorrow!

4. Call me when _____ (it's, (its)) my turn to use the computer.

5. We can rest when_____ (their, (there), they're) is nothing left to put away.

6. The keys were_____ ((here), hear) on the table this morning.

7. Remember, _____ (your, (you're)) responsible for returning the videos.

8. Nathan _____ (red, (read)) a chapter of the book every day after dinner.

10. Aunt Jess _____ ((sent) cent, scent) the package to me on Monday.

Sentences

Directions: Find the underlined part of each sentence that is the simple subject of the sentence.

Example

The <u>cat</u> <u>jumped</u> from the <u>bed</u> to the <u>floor</u>.
Ⓐ   Ⓑ   Ⓒ   Ⓓ

Answer: Ⓐ

1. <u>My</u> <u>dad</u> <u>cooked</u> <u>spaghetti and meatballs</u> for dinner.
   Ⓐ   Ⓑ   Ⓒ   Ⓓ

2. <u>Last</u> <u>year</u>, <u>we</u> were in fourth <u>grade</u>.
   Ⓕ   Ⓖ   Ⓗ   Ⓙ

3. The <u>team</u> <u>celebrated</u> its <u>victory</u> at the <u>pizza</u> parlor.
   Ⓐ   Ⓑ   Ⓒ   Ⓓ

Directions: Find the underlined part of each sentence that is the simple predicate of the sentence.

4. <u>Ramona</u> <u>performed</u> a <u>dance</u> routine for the <u>talent</u> show.
   Ⓕ   Ⓖ   Ⓗ   Ⓙ

5. The <u>animals</u> at the zoo <u>usually</u> <u>eat</u> around sunset.
   Ⓐ   Ⓑ   Ⓒ   Ⓓ

6. <u>Often</u>, <u>Juan</u> <u>delivers</u> his packages <u>before</u> lunchtime.
   Ⓕ   Ⓖ   Ⓗ   Ⓙ

Read each sentence carefully. Decide who the sentence is about and what action is taking place.

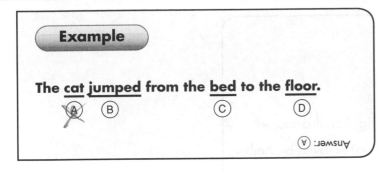

Sentences

88

Directions: Choose the answer that best combines the underlined sentences.

Example

Amber enjoys horseback riding.
Amber enjoys soccer.

(A) Amber enjoys horseback riding, but also soccer.

(B) Soccer and horseback riding are enjoyed by Amber.

(C) Amber enjoys horseback riding and soccer.

(D) Amber enjoys soccer but not horseback riding.

Answer: C

---

1. The computer is working.
I can't connect to the Internet.

(A) I can't connect to the Internet if the computer is working.

(B) I can't connect to the Internet with the computer.

(C) The computer is working, so I can't connect to the Internet.

(D) The computer is working, but I can't connect to the Internet.

2. We raked leaves yesterday.
The wind blew the leaves off the trees.

(F) Yesterday, we raked the leaves that the wind blew off the trees.

(G) The wind blew the leaves off the trees because we raked them up yesterday.

(H) The leaves, that we raked were blown.

(J) We raked the leaves yesterday and the wind blew the leaves off the trees.

3. The lodge is over 200 years old.
The lodge is still a comfortable place to stay.

(A) The lodge, which is over 200 years old, is still a comfortable place to stay.

(B) Still a comfortable place to stay, the lodge is over 200 years old.

(C) The lodge is over 200 years old, because it is still a comfortable place to stay.

(D) Because it is over 200 years old, the lodge is still a comfortable place to stay.

4. George left early.
Colette left early.
They are going to the band festival.

(F) George and Colette left early because to the band festival they are going.

(G) George and Colette left early to go to the band festival.

(H) George left early and Colette because they are going to the band festival.

(J) Leaving early, George and Colette are going to the band festival.

Sentences

Directions: Choose the best way to express the idea. Fill in the circle for the correct answer.

Example

(A) Though once calm in the morning, the seas were choppy by afternoon.

(B) The seas became choppy in the afternoon, and it was calm in the morning.

(C) The seas were calm in the morning, but by the afternoon they had become choppy.

(D) The seas were calm in the morning, because they were choppy in the afternoon.

Answer: C

---

(1) Last Saturday, the Wilson family drove to Chicago to watch a Cubs baseball game. (2) The bustling streets around the ballpark were filled with activity. (3) The children spotted a booth outside the stadium that was selling Cubs' baseball caps. (4) They begged their dad to buy each of them a hat. (5) He insisted that they wait until they got inside the park. (6) When they got to the front of the line, the children saw a woman handing out free Cubs' hats. (7) It was Free-Hat Day! (8) Mr. Wilson smiled, and the children cheered.

1. How is sentence 1 best written?

(A) On a drive to Chicago last Saturday, the Wilson family was watching a Cubs baseball game.

(B) To watch a Cubs baseball game, the Wilson family drove to Chicago last Saturday.

(C) Last Saturday, the Wilson family was driving to Chicago and watching a Cubs baseball game.

(D) Correct as it is

If you are not sure which answer is correct, say each one to yourself. The correct answer will usually sound the best.

2. What is the best way to combine sentences 4 and 5 without changing their meaning?

(F) They begged their dad to buy each of them a hat, but he insisted that they wait until they got inside the park.

(G) They begged their dad to buy each of them a hat, because he insisted that they wait until they got inside the park.

(H) They begged their dad to buy each of them a hat; therefore, he insisted that they wait until they got inside the park.

(J) Since their dad insisted that they wait until they got inside the park, they begged him to buy each of them a hat.

Name _____   Date _____

Sentences

Directions: For each paragraph below, underline the declarative sentences. Then, in each blank, write **IN** if the paragraph also contains an interrogative sentence, **EX** if it contains an exclamatory sentence, **IM** if it contains an imperative sentence, or **none** if it contains only declarative sentences.

A **declarative** sentence makes a statement: *Karim walked home from school with Jaime.*

An **interrogative** sentence asks a question: *Will you feed the fish today?*

An **exclamatory** sentence shows excitement or emotion: *Watch out for that car!*

An **imperative** sentence expresses a command or request: *Come to the principal's office now.*

1. __IN__ You are on a deserted island: no town, no people—just you and those crazy, noisy seagulls. What are you going to do?

2. __IM__ Toward the castle she fled. She begged the gatekeeper for entrance. He did not hear her cries. Past the stone walls she scurried, the hounds in pursuit.

3. __none__ Maggie bit her lip. No use crying about it. She pulled her math homework out of the sink and just stared at her little sister.

4. __IN__ The music is playing those lovely tunes, but you're not listening. You can't. You have too many important things to plan. What should you buy for Teddy? Who should you invite to the party?

5. __EX__ Columbus stood on the deck of the ship. Land was on the horizon. Land! Not the edge of the world, not dragons to devour the ship, but the land that would make his fortune . . . his and Spain's.

6. __EX__ I think Mama forgot me. Otherwise, she would come and find me. Oh, no! Mama said not to go see the toys because I'd get lost. Mama is going to be mad at me!

7. __IM__ Do not stop reading until you reach the end of this story. What you are about to read is so amazing that you simply must hear about it now. So settle back and get ready for the most incredible tale you've ever heard.

Name _____   Date _____

Sentences

Directions: Rewrite each run-on sentence to make it correct. Write **C** if the sentence is correct as it is.

1. **Let's ask David to come with us. He knows about a great bike trail.**

   C

2. **I can ride faster than you can let's race to the stop sign.**

   I can ride faster than you can. Lets race to the stop sign.

3. **I'm thirsty does anyone have some bottled water?**

   I'm thirsty, does anyone have some bottled water?

4. **We need to be careful on the bike trail in-line skaters can appear out of nowhere.**

   We need to be careful on the bike trail. In-line skaters can appear out of nowhere.

5. **Do you know how to recognize a happy bicyclist? He has bugs in his teeth.**

   C

Directions: Rewrite each sentence fragment below to make it a sentence.

6. **found a hidden staircase in the old house**

   I found a hidden staircase in the old house.

7. **a mysterious note tacked up on the wall**

   A mysterious note was tacked upon the wall.

8. **lay behind the creaking door**

   She lay behind the creaking door.

9. **up the ladder and into the attic**

   I climbed up the ladder and into the attic.

Name _____ Date _____

Paragraphs

Directions: Find the best topic sentence for the paragraph. Fill in the circle next to the sentence.

Example

_____ Snails produce a liquid on the bottom of their feet. They "surf" on the rippling waves of this sticky liquid. Sea stars have slender tube feet with tiny suction cups that help them grip. Dolphins whip their tails up and down to thrust their bodies through the water.

Ⓐ Animals eat a variety of foods found in nature.

Ⓑ There are many different animals in the United States.

Ⓒ Animals move about in many unusual ways.

Ⓓ Animals have different kinds of feet.

Answer: C

---

1. _____ A honeybee collects pollen and nectar from a flower. When the bee goes to the next flower, some of the pollen from the first flower falls onto the second. The second flower uses this pollen to make seeds.

Ⓐ It is estimated that honeybees pollinate billions of dollars worth of crops each year.

Ⓑ The most important role of the honeybee is to pollinate plants.

Ⓒ If you are stung by a bee, remove the stinger carefully.

Ⓓ Bees are considered pests.

2. _____ Toads and tree frogs croak in the evenings. Sometimes, the chirping of the crickets is so loud that you can't hear the little frogs. But the booming of the big bullfrogs can always be heard. I don't know how Lane Roy sleeps.

Ⓕ Crickets are louder than frogs.

Ⓖ Swamps are homes to many different creatures.

Ⓗ Frogs make a variety of sounds.

Ⓙ The swamp beside the house is filled with sound.

Directions: Find the answer choice that best develops the topic sentence.

3. Anne Frank was born into a prosperous German family.

Ⓐ Her father, Otto, was a businessman. But the Franks were Jews, and when Adolf Hitler took power, Otto moved his family to Amsterdam.

Ⓑ For two years, Anne and seven other people lived in a secret annex. They had to remain still and quiet during the day.

Ⓒ When Otto was released from the concentration camp, he returned to Amsterdam. He was the only person in his family who had survived.

Ⓓ Anne found comfort writing in her diary. She wrote about the cramped space she lived in, about the quarrels and difficulties of life in their hiding place, and about her fears and joys.

Name _____ Date _____

Paragraphs

Directions: Read the paragraph. Fill in the circle next to the sentence that does not belong in the paragraph.

(1) In 1567, Francis Drake, John Hawkins, and other English seamen were on a voyage. **(2)** They hoped to make a profit by selling smuggled goods to some of the Spanish colonies. **(3)** On their way back from their voyage, they stopped at a Mexican port. **(4)** By far, Drake is best known as the first Englishman to sail around the world.

1. Ⓐ sentence 1
   Ⓑ sentence 2
   Ⓒ sentence 3
   Ⓓ sentence 4

> Read each paragraph carefully to determine which sentence does not fit with the main topic.

(1) In his book *Over the Top of the World*, Will Steger relates the travels of his research party across the Arctic Ocean from Siberia to Canada in 1994. **(2)** With a team of 6 people and 33 dogs, Steger set out by dogsled to complete this daring mission. **(3)** At other times, they boarded their canoes to cross chilly stretches of water. **(4)** Along the way, the party would exchange dogsleds for canoe sleds because of the breaking ice packs.

2. Ⓕ sentence 1
   Ⓖ sentence 2
   Ⓗ sentence 3
   Ⓙ sentence 4

(1) The "Great Zimbabwe" is one of many stone-walled fortresses built on the Zimbabwean plateau. **(2)** The Shona spoke a common Bantu language, and all were herdsmen and farmers. **(3)** Researchers believe that the Shona people built this structure over a course of 400 years. **(4)** More than 18,000 people may have lived in the "Great Zimbabwe."

3. Ⓐ sentence 1
   Ⓑ sentence 2
   Ⓒ sentence 3
   Ⓓ sentence 4

Name _____   Date _____

Paragraphs

Directions: Read the paragraph. Use it to answer the questions.

Example

Some people in South Africa keep meerkats as pets. They are convenient to have around the house when mice and rats are a problem.

Which is the best last sentence?

- (A) The meerkat eats plants.
- (B) Meerkats can stand as straight as boards.
- (C) Meerkats are not cats.
- (D) Meerkats seem capable of performing some of the same duties as working cats.

Answer: D

---

(1) There are many differences between frogs and toads. (2) Frogs have narrow bodies and ridges down their backs. (3) They have large, round ear membranes and small teeth in their upper jaws. (4) Their long hind legs enable them to take long leaps. (5) A toad's short legs limit it to only short jumps. (6) Frogs have smooth, moist, soft skin. (7) Most frogs are water-dwellers.

1. If another paragraph about toads were added, what would make a good first sentence for that paragraph?

- (A) Their ear membranes are smaller than frogs'.
- (B) In contrast, toads have chubby bodies and ridges on their heads.
- (C) Toads and frogs are similar to each other in many ways.
- (D) However, they lay their eggs in strings rather than clumps.

2. Which sentence should be left out of this paragraph?

- (F) sentence 3
- (G) sentence 4
- (H) sentence 5
- (J) sentence 6

3. Choose the best last sentence for this paragraph.

- (A) They lay clumps of eggs in their watery habitat.
- (B) Toads have no teeth.
- (C) Frogs make a loud croaking sound.
- (D) Most toads make their homes on land.

Think about the topic of the paragraph.
Make sure that all the sentences you choose match the same topic.

Paragraphs

Directions: Read each paragraph. Use the paragraphs to answer the questions.

Example

I am writing a report in school about the state of Illinois. I think some of the stories about our family moving there would make it more interesting. Can you tell me about the time Grandma lived on the farm?

Who would be an appropriate person to send this letter to?

(A) a business owner

(B) a state congressman

(C) a travel agent

(D) a relative

Answer: D

My family is planning a trip to Chicago, Illinois. We will arrive on July 1, and we plan to stay for five nights. Can you please help us find a hotel? Also, any information you can share about things to do in Chicago would be appreciated.

1. Who would be an appropriate person to send this letter to?

(A) the owner of a restaurant

(B) the mayor of Chicago

(C) a hotel manager

(D) a travel agent

2. What needed information is missing from this letter?

(F) the number of nights the family will be staying

(G) the number of hotel rooms needed

(H) where the family is coming from

(J) the type of food the family likes to eat

I would like to make dinner reservations at your restaurant for July 3. We would like to be seated by 7:00. Please let me know if you can accommodate us.

3. Who would be an appropriate person to send this letter to?

(A) a relative

(B) a business owner

(C) a restaurant manager

(D) a friend

4. What needed information is missing from this letter?

(F) the number of people who want to eat at the restaurant

(G) the type of food the people like to eat

(H) how much money the people plan to spend

(J) the name of the hotel where the people are staying

Study Skills

Directions: Use the table of contents and index to answer the questions that follow.

The Gold Rush
Table of Contents

Chapter	Page
1 The Overland Trail...........1	
2 Sea Routes....................27	
3 In the Diggings.............42	
4 Children in the Mines 68	
5 After the Gold Rush 85	

Index

children
  jobs in the mines, 68–73
  schools, 76–77
  traveling to California, 4–8, 31–32
daily life
  in the diggings, 44–46
  in the mines, 68–73
desert
  crossing the desert, 7–10
gold
  discovery, 1–3, 44–46
  gold fever, 1–6, 52–53
routes to California
  Cape Horn, 27–32
  Overland Trail, 3–12
  Panama, 33–36
San Francisco
  after the gold rush, 85–86, 90–92
  before the gold rush, 1–3, 42–44
  Winnemuca, Sara, 87

1. Look at the table of contents. Which two chapters might tell about how people came to California?

  (A) Chapters 1 and 2

  (B) Chapters 2 and 3

  (C) Chapters 3 and 4

  (D) Chapters 4 and 6

2. Compare the index to the table of contents. What information do you think the book would provide about Sara Winnemuca?

  (F) how she came to California

  (G) what her life was like in the gold mines

  (H) what her life was like as a child

  (J) what her life was like after the Gold Rush

3. Look at the table of contents. Which of these might you find in Chapter 1?

  (A) traveling on a ship

  (B) traveling in a covered wagon

  (C) panning for gold

  (D) schools for the children of gold miners

Study Skills

Directions: Use the table of contents and index on the previous page to answer the questions that follow.

1. Which route to California is not listed in the index?

(A) Panama

(B) Cape Horn

(C) Overland Trail

(D) San Francisco ✗

2. How is the index organized?

(F) in time order

(G) in alphabetical order ✗

(H) randomly

(J) in order of importance

3. Information about crossing the desert can be found on pages _____.

(A) 44–46

(B) 27–32

(C) 7–10 ✗

(D) 68–73

4. Where in the book are you likely to find the table of contents?

(F) in the beginning ✗

(G) in the middle

(H) in the end

(J) after the index

5. According to the index, page 43 probably contains information about

(A) San Francisco after the gold rush.

(B) San Francisco before the gold rush. ✗

(C) jobs in the mines.

(D) gold fever.

6. How long is Chapter 2?

(F) 17 pages

(G) 25 pages

(H) 13 pages

(J) 15 pages ✗

> Think through your answers carefully. Ask yourself if your answer makes sense.

Study Skills

Directions: Read each item. Fill in the circle next to the best answer.

1. Bianca is writing a report on the Liberty Bell. Which of these would she not want to include in her report?

Ⓐ a physical description of the Liberty Bell

Ⓑ events in which the Liberty Bell has been rung

Ⓒ where the Liberty Bell is hung

Ⓓ a description of Pennsylvania

2. In writing her report, Bianca used a book titled *Let Liberty Ring*. Where in the book should she look to get a general overview of the book's contents?

Ⓕ the title page

Ⓖ the introduction

Ⓗ the glossary

Ⓙ the index

3. Where could Bianca look to find the book's publication information?

Ⓐ the glossary

Ⓑ the table of contents

Ⓒ the copyright page

Ⓓ the index

Directions: Mark the space beside the word that would come first in an alphabetical list.

4. Ⓕ phase
Ⓖ pharmacy
Ⓗ pheasant
Ⓙ phantom

5. Ⓐ amber
Ⓑ amble
Ⓒ ambassador
Ⓓ ambulance

6. Ⓕ legend
Ⓖ lemonade
Ⓗ legacy
Ⓙ lend

7. Ⓐ Great Britain
Ⓑ growl
Ⓒ granola
Ⓓ grapefruit

Study Skills

Directions: Choose the best source of information, and mark your answer.

1. **What was Amelia Earhart's childhood like?**

   (A) an almanac

   (B) a thesaurus

   (C) a book about how to fly a plane

   (D) a biography of Earhart

2. **You want to find the correct way to pronounce *incorrigible*. Where could you look?**

   (F) in a thesaurus

   (G) in an encyclopedia

   (H) in a dictionary

   (J) in an almanac

3. **How much water does the town of Springbrook use a week?**

   (A) an encyclopedia

   (B) the town's Web site

   (C) a road atlas

   (D) a book about water sanitation

4. **Which of these would tell you another word for *beautiful*?**

   (F) an encyclopedia

   (G) a book of quotations

   (H) a thesaurus

   (J) an almanac

5. **Which of these would help you understand the water cycle?**

   (A) a map

   (B) a dictionary

   (C) a history book

   (D) an encyclopedia article

6. **Which of these would help you plan a driving route from Los Angeles to San Francisco?**

   (F) an almanac

   (G) a road atlas

   (H) an encyclopedia

   (J) the owner's manual for an automobile

7. **Which of these would tell you how fast a cheetah can run?**

   (A) an encyclopedia

   (R) a dictionary

   (C) a history book

   (D) a map of a zoo

8. **What is the capital of California?**

   (F) an almanac

   (G) a history book

   (H) a dictionary

   (J) a road atlas

Name _____ Date _____

Study Skills

Directions: Study the map below. Use it to answer the questions that follow.

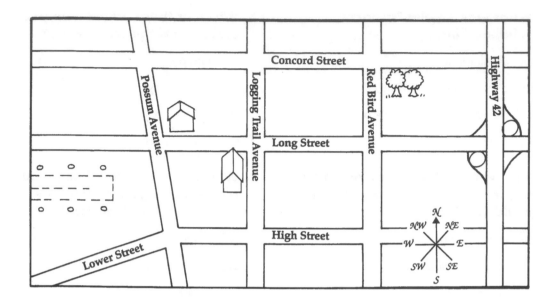

1. Where is the airport located?

(A) north of Lower Street and east of High Street

(B) south of Long Street and west of Possum Avenue

(C) east of Highway 42 and west of Red Bird Avenue

(D) south of Concord Street and north of Long Street

2. If you were to walk from the house at the corner of Long Street and Possum Avenue to the park, which directions would you follow?

(F) travel south on Logging Trail Avenue and west on High Street

(G) travel north on Possum Avenue and west on Long Street

(H) travel east on Long Street and north on Red Bird Avenue

(J) travel north on Possum Avenue and west on Concord Street

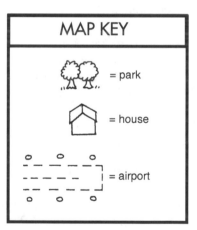

MAP KEY

= park

= house

= airport

Name _____ Date _____

Sample Test 4: Usage

Directions: Fill in the circle of the choice that has an error. If there are no errors, choose "No mistakes."

1. (A) A more better place
   (B) to see bats
   (C) is the Carlsbad Caverns in New Mexico.
   (D) No mistakes

2. (F) Mom and Aunt Emily
   (G) aren't in no aerobics class
   (H) this Saturday.
   (J) No mistakes

3. (A) After they finished the book,
   (B) Colby and Marcos
   (C) wrote the report.
   (D) No mistakes

Directions: Find the underlined part of each sentence that is the simple subject of the sentence.

4. The <u>old red</u> <u>barn</u> <u>needed</u> to be <u>painted</u>.
   (F)   (G)   (H)   (J)

5. The <u>setting</u> of the <u>play</u> <u>was</u> a <u>castle</u>.
   (A)   (B)   (C)   (D)

Directions: Find the underlined part of each sentence that is the simple predicate of the sentence.

6. The <u>lions</u> at the <u>park</u> <u>roared</u> <u>loudly</u>.
   (F)   (G)   (H)   (J)

7. <u>Sumiko</u> <u>wants</u> <u>herbs</u> in her <u>garden</u>.
   (A)   (B)   (C)   (D)

Directions: Choose the answer that best combines the underlined sentences.

8. <u>Isaac will create a collage tomorrow.</u>
   <u>Isaac will use photographs for his collage.</u>
   (F) Isaac will create a collage tomorrow, but he will use photographs.
   (G) Isaac will use photographs tomorrow, and he will create a collage.
   (H) Isaac will create a collage tomorrow and he will use photographs.
   (J) Isaac will create a collage tomorrow using photographs.

GO

Name _____ Date _____

Sample Test 4: Usage

Directions: Read the paragraph below. Find the best topic sentence for it.

_____ Since they were so rare, the sight of early motor cars was exciting to the American public.

9. Ⓐ Today's cars are much more varied, comfortable, and fun to drive.

Ⓑ Taking a car trip was quite a challenge in the early days.

Ⓒ Not everyone welcomed the first automobiles.

Ⓓ Gasoline-powered automobiles were available only to a few wealthy individuals before the early 1900s.

Directions: Rewrite each run-on sentence to make it correct. Write **C** if the sentence is correct as it is.

10. I love the playground it has great swings.

I love the playground because it has great swings

11. When I swing too high, I get sick do you?

When I swing too high, I get sick. Do you?

12. I like the slide the best. I've always liked slides.

_C_

Directions: Rewrite each sentence fragment below to make it a complete sentence.

13. several small boxes stacked in the backyard

Several small boxes were stacked in the backyard.

14. an old key covered with rust

I saw an old key covered with rust.

15. hugged the yellow dog wagging its tail

She hugged the dog wagging its tail.

GO ▶

Sample Test 4: Usage

Directions: Read the passage, and answer the questions that follow.

---

(1) Imagine going to a college where you can major in video games! (2) Well, all the students at DigiPen School is <u>doing</u> exactly that. (3) A man named *Claude Comair* founded the college in Vancouver, British Columbia. (4) It has a goal that is to teach students to create computer animation and to also program video games. (5) While this may sound like fun, the school's curriculum is serious business. (6) The teachers are professional programmers and engineers. (7) The classes are taught year-round for two years of intense study. (8) Students typically from 8 A.M. to 9 P.M. Monday through Friday and for much of the day on Saturday.

---

16. How is sentence 4 best written?

(F) Its goal is to teach students to create computer animation and program video games.

(G) For its goal, it aims to teach students to create computer animation and program video games.

(H) Creating computer animation and programming video games is the goal the school sets for all of its students.

(J) Teaching creating computer animation and programming video games is its goal.

17. Which sentence is incomplete?

(A) sentence 2

(B) sentence 4

(C) sentence 6

(D) sentence 8

18. In sentence 2, <u>is doing</u> is best written _____.

(F) are doing

(G) was doing

(H) would be doing

(J) Correct as it is

19. Which sentence could be added after sentence 6?

(A) Each game requires several programmers, artists, musicians, and designers to make it marketable.

(B) The classes include advanced mathematics and physics, computer languages, and art.

(C) The video game industry earns billions of dollars each year.

(D) The graduates of DigiPen will tell you that they make a living doing what they love best—playing video games.

Name _____ Date _____

Sample Test 4: Usage

Directions: Use the sample dictionary entries and the pronunciation guide to answer the questions that follow.

camp /'kamp/ *n.* 1. a place, usually away from cities, where tents or simple buildings are put up to provide shelter for people working or vacationing there 2. a place, usually in the country, for recreation or instruction during the summer months [goes to summer camp each July] 3. a group of people who work to promote a certain idea or thought or who work together in support of another person *v.* 4. to live temporarily in a camp or outdoors

cam·paign /kam-'pan/ *n.* 1. a series of military operations that make up a distinct period during a war 2. a series of activities designed to bring about a desired outcome [an election campaign] *v.* to conduct a campaign

cam·pus /'kam-pen/ *n.* 1. the grounds and buildings of a school

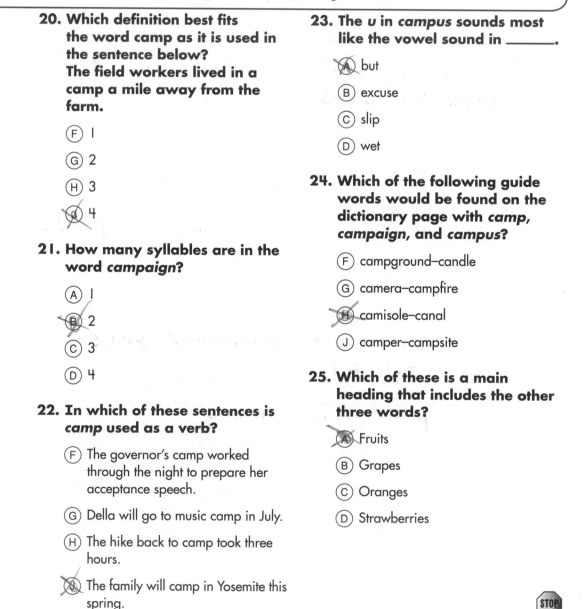

20. Which definition best fits the word camp as it is used in the sentence below?
The field workers lived in a camp a mile away from the farm.

(F) 1

(G) 2

(H) 3

(J) 4 ⨯

21. How many syllables are in the word campaign?

(A) 1

(B) 2

(C) 3

(D) 4

22. In which of these sentences is camp used as a verb?

(F) The governor's camp worked through the night to prepare her acceptance speech.

(G) Della will go to music camp in July.

(H) The hike back to camp took three hours.

(J) The family will camp in Yosemite this spring. ⨯

23. The u in campus sounds most like the vowel sound in _____.

(A) but ⨯

(B) excuse

(C) slip

(D) wet

24. Which of the following guide words would be found on the dictionary page with camp, campaign, and campus?

(F) campground–candle

(G) camera–campfire

(H) camisole–canal ⨯

(J) camper–campsite

25. Which of these is a main heading that includes the other three words?

(A) Fruits ⨯

(B) Grapes

(C) Oranges

(D) Strawberries

STOP

Writing a Personal Narrative

Directions: Read the paragraph that tells about one student's experience. Then, think about your good experiences as you answer each question below.

> My violin competition was one of the best experiences I've ever had. I met people from all over the city. I learned to feel comfortable in front of an audience. I felt good about playing for so many people. When everyone clapped, I felt very proud.

1. **Think about all your good experiences. List the top three.**

   3rd Math Competition

   1st Piano Recital

   Summer Camp

2. **For each item you listed in question 1, briefly tell why this experience was so good.**

   • 3rd Math Competition, did stuff differently, brave

   • 1st Piano Recital, 1st time, get trophy, rememberable

   • Summer Camp, 1st time, met people

3. **Pick one of the items you listed in question 1. Outline the three most important things about that experience that you would want to include in an essay.**

   I. did stuff differently, brave, experienced

   II. 1st time, trophy, rememberable

   III. 1st time, met people, did different stuff

Name _____ Date _____

Writing with Organization

Directions: Write three short paragraphs about things you think need to be improved in your community. Structure your composition as follows:

Paragraph 1: Choose at least three things that you think could use improvement.

Paragraph 2: Give reasons why you think these things should be improved.

Paragraph 3: Conclude by explaining what you personally would do to make these improvements.

    I think the park, public bathrooms, and some restaraunts.

    The parks should be improved because there is a bunch of poop there and people can step on those. Also, they should add some new equipment or polish it up every 4 months. ← Public bathrooms should be improved because unsanitary conditions can cause you to be sick. Finally restaraunts should be improved because if the kitchen is dirty, the consumers might get sick.

    I will help by not making too much trash and cleaning up my messes.

Writing a Narrative Procedure

Directions: Read the paragraph below about how to plant a seed. Then, think of something you know how to do well. Write a narrative procedure that explains how to do it. Use paragraphs and words such as *first, next, then, finally,* and *last.* Use details to explain how you learned to do this activity and why you enjoy it.

I recently learned how to plant a seed and make it grow. First, I found a spot where the plant would get enough sunlight. Next, I dug a hole and put the seed into the soil. I covered the seed with soil, and then I watered it. I checked the soil each day to make sure that it stayed moist, and after a week, I could see the first shoots of the seedling poking through the ground.

I learned how to make a peanut butter and jelly sandwich. First, get 2 slices of bread. Next, spread peanut butter on one slice and jelly on the other. Finally, put those 2 together. Voilā! A peanut butter and jelly sandwich. Enjoy!

Who is your audience? As you write, keep them in mind!

Name _____   Date _____

Writing Using Figurative Language

Directions: Complete each of the following sentences with a simile.

1. **As we walked down the street, the leaves under our feet crunched like** _cookies_ .

2. **After our game, drinking a glass of water was as refreshing as** _jumping into_ . _a pool_

3. **The flowers on Amelia's dress were as bright and cheerful as** _a bunny_ .

4. **Music suddenly filled the room like** _water_ .

> Figurative language is used to make writing and descriptions more interesting. **Similes** use the words *like* or *as* to compare things that may seem unlike each other. *The tree was as tall as a skyscraper.* **Metaphors** also compare two unlike things. *Callie's voice was music to my ears.*

Directions: Picture a beautiful scene, like a beach, a mountaintop, or a cool stream. Write a short paragraph describing what you see. Use at least two metaphors in your paragraph.

A cool wind brushed my face as I look
at the stream. The waterfall was a lion. The
fish, were orange streaks in the water. I
dipped my feet in the icy water. I felt the
stress melt away and get replaced by relief.

o it roared at me,

Writing a Persuasive Essay

Directions: Read the persuasive paragraph below. Then, answer the questions that follow.

> I believe that a portion of Beatty Park should be turned into a dog park. Dogs are the most popular pets for people in Lydenville. Since Sinclair Dog Park closed two years ago, dog owners have not had a place for their pets to socialize. Beatty Park is the largest park in town. It is also within walking distance for most people. Making a new dog park would make the residents (and dogs) of Lydenville very happy.

1. What is the author's purpose in writing?

Making a dog park.

2. What reasons does the author give for his or her argument?

Dogs could not socialize. Beatty Park is the largest part in town and it is within walking distance. Finally, it would make the residents and dogs of Lydenville happy.

3. Think of something you feel strongly about. Write a paragraph to explain your position, and include examples to support your reasons. Be sure to use as many details as possible to persuade readers.

_____
_____
_____
_____
_____
_____
_____
_____

Writing with Organization

Directions: Write a paragraph about a change that you feel should happen at your school. Make sure your paragraph has a main idea and details that support the main idea. Use the chart below to create a rough draft of your paragraph. Then, write the final paragraph on the lines below.

Main Idea:	More time for homework
Detail 1:	Quality work
Detail 2:	Less Trouble
Detail 3:	Practice using Computer
Detail 4:	Don't have to stress too much.
Conclusion:	Students should have more time for homework

Students should have more time for their homework. That way, they can turn in better work, otherwise known as "quality work." It will cause less trouble and time in class. More students will be able to complete their work. Also, the students can practice using the computer by turning things in by Google Classroom. Finally, the students won't stress too much because of the limited time to finish the work. In conculsion, students should have more time to finish homework.

Sample Test 5: Writing

Directions: Write about a time when you had to try something new. It could be a new school, a new sport, a new type of food—any experience that you hadn't had before. Include descriptions of places and people, interesting details, and feelings you had during your experience.

My First Piano Recital

I had my first piano recital at a place called   . I was nervous. As soon as my name was called, I stepped up and started playing. It went like a breeze. After my turn was over, I felt relieved. That is, until I remembered the duet. I anxiously waited for my turn. When it was my turn, I played the duet with my teacher. It sounded beautiful. After that, we went home.

STOP

Name _____ Date _____

Practice Test 2: Language
Part 1: Language Mechanics

Directions: Fill in the circle next to the punctuation mark that is needed in the sentence. Fill in the space for "None" if no additional punctuation marks are needed.

1. Who ate the last meatball?" asked Bella.

- (A) .
- (B) ,
- (C) "
- (D) None

2. Mike, Jaden and I took a baby-sitting course last summer.

- (F) ,
- (G) ;
- (H) !
- (J) None

3. Who's going sledding with me today?

- (A) "
- (B) ,
- (C) .
- (D) None

4. On Saturday morning all the neighborhood kids meet to play soccer.

- (F) :
- (G) .
- (H) ,
- (J) None

Directions: Fill in the circle next to the choice that has a punctuation error. If there is no mistake, mark "No mistakes."

5.
- (A) Most people
- (B) love pizza but
- (C) Albert hates it.
- (D) No mistakes

6.
- (F) What do you think
- (G) is in the bag. I think
- (H) it's a new pair of shoes.
- (J) No mistakes

7.
- (A) Maria plants flowers and
- (B) raises vegetables
- (C) in her garden.
- (D) No mistakes

Directions: Fill in the circle next to the choice that has a punctuation error. If there is no mistake, mark "No mistakes."

8. On Valentine's Day, _____ class had a party.

- (F) Miss Jacksons
- (G) Miss Jacksons'
- (H) Miss Jackson's
- (J) Miss Jacksons's

9. _____ you may carry the water.

- (A) Yes
- (B) Yes,
- (C) Yes?
- (D) Yes.

Practice Test 2: Language

Practice Test 2: Language
Part 1: Language Mechanics

Directions: Fill in the circle next to the sentence that is correctly written and shows the correct capitalization and punctuation.

10. (F) Mrs. Ling may I check out this book?

(G) Moms candles come in handy when the power goes out.

(H) In the morning, dad read us a story.

(J) Troy and Kenneth sit in the grass and watch the clouds.

11. (A) Ballet dancers create graceful patterns using formal precise movements.

(B) Last spring, four baby robins hatched.

(C) Charles Lindbergh was the first person to fly nonstop across the atlantic ocean by himself.

(D) Suzette and Jacques speak french at home.

12. (F) A bears home is a den.

(G) A. A. Milne was born on january 18 1882.

(H) At our house, green jelly beans are always eaten first.

(J) Since we don't drive, our mom's are glad to drop us off.

13. (A) Kate helped Blanca and Sierra hang up art projects.

(B) Joels favorite subject is Aviation.

(C) Maybe I shouldnt have had a second helping of that lasagna.

(D) Ava who left her keys in the car was scolded for her carelessness.

Directions: Choose the word or words that best fit in the blank and show the correct punctuation and capitalization.

14. **The hospital is on _____ near the park.**

(F) Grant Ave.

(G) Grant Ave,

(H) Grant, Ave.

(J) grant ave.,

15. **Many camels live in the _____.**

(A) African And Arabian Deserts

(B) African And Arabian deserts

(C) African and Arabian deserts

(D) african and arabian deserts

16. **Every summer, I go with my _____ to Camp Muckamucka.**

(F) friends Ben and Javier

(G) friends, Ben and Javier

(H) friends Ben and Javier,

(J) friends, ben and javier,

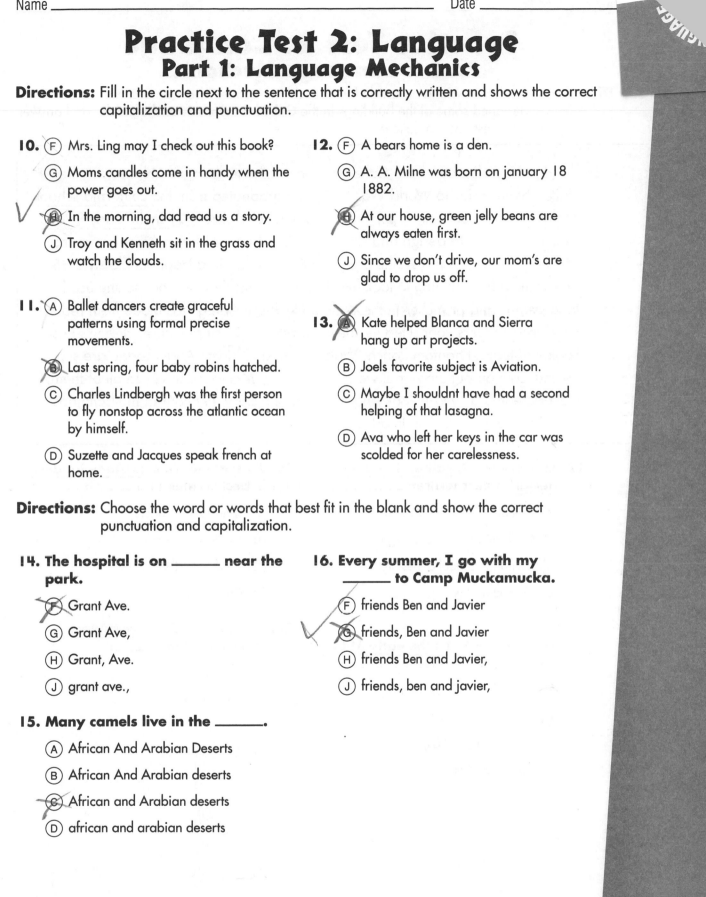

GO

Practice Test 2: Language
Part 1: Language Mechanics

Directions: Braden is writing an article for his local newspaper about an architect who designed some of the buildings in the Grand Canyon. Read the article, and answer the questions that follow.

(1) Mary Elizabeth Jane Colter was one of the few female architects in the United States prior to World War I. (2) She graduated from the <u>california school of design</u> and taught art to support her mother and sister. (3) <u>In the early 1900s Colter</u> was hired to design and decorate a building for Native American crafts at the Grand Canyon. (4) She designed the building in a Hopi pueblo style. (5) She wanted her building to look like it had been made long ago, so she used long beams and branches in the ceiling. (6) The building was made from red <u>sandstone ladders</u> connected its uneven rooftops. (7) Hopi House, <u>Hermit's Rest</u>, Lookout Studio, Phantom Ranch, Watchtower, and Bright Angel Lodge are six Grand Canyon buildings that were designed by Mary Colter. (8) In all of them, Colter created a lived-in look and a feeling of history. (9) Four of the buildings are National Historic Landmarks.

17. In sentence 2, <u>california school of design</u> is best written _____.

- (A) California School Of Design
- (B) California School of Design
- (C) California school of design
- (D) Correct as it is

18. In sentence 3, <u>In the early 1900s Colter</u> is best written _____.

- (F) In the early 1900s, Colter
- (G) In the early 1900's Colter,
- (H) In the early, 1900s, Colter
- (J) Correct as it is

19. In sentence 6, <u>sandstone ladders</u> is best written _____.

- (A) sandstone! Ladders
- (B) sandstone, ladder
- (C) sandstone. Ladders
- (D) Correct as it is

20. In sentence 7, <u>Hermit's Rest</u> is best written _____.

- (F) Hermits Rest
- (G) Hermits Rest
- (H) Hermits's Rest
- (J) Correct as it is

GO

Practice Test 2: Language
Part 1: Language Mechanics

Directions: Mark the circle for the word that is spelled correctly and fits best in the blank.

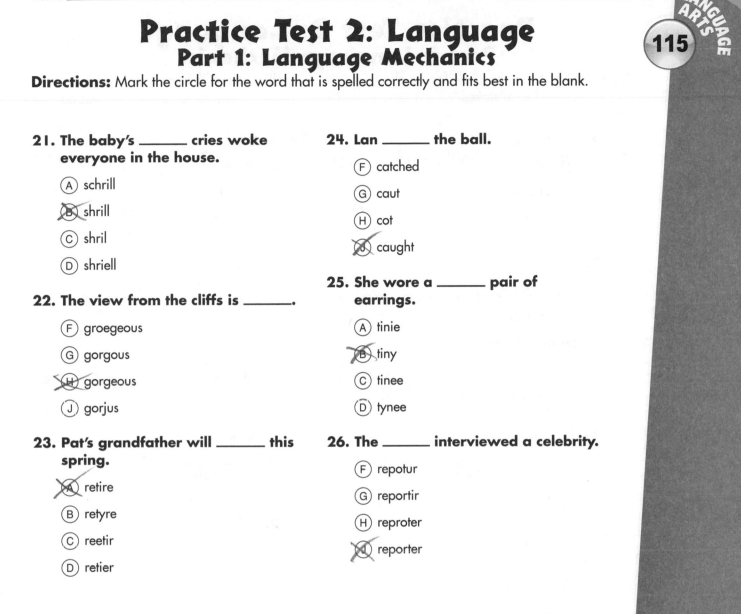

21. The baby's _____ cries woke everyone in the house.

- (A) schrill
- (B) shrill
- (C) shril
- (D) shriell

22. The view from the cliffs is _____.

- (F) groegeous
- (G) gorgous
- (H) gorgeous
- (J) gorjus

23. Pat's grandfather will _____ this spring.

- (A) retire
- (B) retyre
- (C) reetir
- (D) retier

24. Lan _____ the ball.

- (F) catched
- (G) caut
- (H) cot
- (J) caught

25. She wore a _____ pair of earrings.

- (A) tinie
- (B) tiny
- (C) tinee
- (D) tynee

26. The _____ interviewed a celebrity.

- (F) repotur
- (G) reportir
- (H) reproter
- (J) reporter

Directions: Choose the phrase in which the underlined word is not spelled correctly.

27.
- (A) <u>filtered</u> water
- (B) deep <u>raveene</u>
- (C) <u>herbal</u> tea
- (D) <u>lofty</u> goals

28.
- (F) <u>desparate</u> measures
- (G) <u>fictional</u> story
- (H) expert <u>opinion</u>
- (J) <u>impressive</u> performance

29.
- (A) <u>previously</u> unknown
- (B) <u>musical</u> talent
- (C) bright <u>future</u>
- (D) a well-deserved <u>promoshun</u>

30.
- (F) <u>declare</u> your goals
- (G) make a <u>promise</u>
- (H) <u>profess</u> the truth
- (J) swear an <u>othe</u>

GO

Name _____ Date _____

Practice Test 2: Language
Part 1: Language Mechanics

Directions: Fill in the circle for the choice that has a spelling error. If there is no mistake, mark "No mistakes."

31. Ⓐ emerge
    Ⓑ batery
    Ⓒ disease
    Ⓓ No mistakes

33. Ⓐ tost
    Ⓑ shrink
    Ⓒ sparkle
    Ⓓ No mistakes

32. Ⓕ prosper
    Ⓖ literature
    Ⓗ release
    Ⓙ No mistakes

Directions: Read each phrase. Fill in the circle for the word that is not spelled correctly for the way it is used in the phrase.

34. Ⓕ <u>chews</u> activities wisely
    Ⓖ <u>too</u> many projects
    Ⓗ <u>straight</u> hair
    Ⓙ <u>weed</u> the garden

36. Ⓕ <u>made</u> by hand
    Ⓖ the mountain's <u>peak</u>
    Ⓗ mist and <u>rain</u>
    Ⓙ <u>creeky</u> stairs

35. Ⓐ <u>tow</u> the boat
    Ⓑ turn <u>right</u>
    Ⓒ <u>reel</u> diamond ring
    Ⓓ sweet <u>potatoes</u>

Directions: Find the underlined word that is misspelled. If all the words are spelled correctly, fill in the circle for "No mistakes."

37. It seems that <u>every</u> year, there are more <u>flotes</u> than the year <u>before</u>. <u>No mistakes</u>
    　　　　　　　Ⓐ　　　　　　　　　　　　　　Ⓑ　　　　　　　　　　Ⓒ　　　　Ⓓ

38. Niko paints <u>nature</u> <u>scenes</u> <u>especially</u> well. <u>No mistakes</u>
    　　　　　　　Ⓕ　　　Ⓖ　　　Ⓗ　　　　　　　Ⓙ

39. Camels have <u>bony</u> <u>ridges</u> above each eye to <u>sheild</u> them from the sun. <u>No mistakes</u>
    　　　　　　　Ⓐ　　　Ⓑ　　　　　　　　　　　Ⓒ　　　　　　　　　　　　Ⓓ

STOP

Practice Test 2: Language
Part 2: Usage

Directions: Choose the word or phrase that best completes the sentence.

1. Falling stars _____ the sky above.

   Ⓐ was streaked

   Ⓑ streaking

   Ⓒ were streaked

   Ⓓ streak

Directions: Choose the answer that is a complete and correctly written sentence.

2. Ⓕ I can't never keep my room clean for very long.

   Ⓖ My grandma has his own way of doing things.

   Ⓗ Jamie and Olly built a fort in their backyard.

   Ⓙ Brianna and Maya went snorkels in the ocean

Directions: Fill in the circle for the choice that has a usage error. If there is no mistake, mark "No mistakes."

3. Ⓐ The fifth-grade class

   Ⓑ are studying

   Ⓒ Aesop's fables.

   Ⓓ No mistakes

4. Ⓕ All winter long,

   Ⓖ the sleeping tulips waited

   Ⓗ for the warm spring sun.

   Ⓙ No mistakes

Directions: Mark the underlined word that is the simple subject of the sentence.

5. <u>My</u> <u>parents</u> <u>speak</u> <u>German</u> and sing German songs.
   Ⓐ   Ⓑ   Ⓒ   Ⓓ

Directions: Mark the underlined word that is the simple predicate of the sentence.

6. Every <u>Saturday</u> <u>morning</u>, the club <u>members</u> <u>meet</u> at the tree house.
   Ⓕ   Ⓖ   Ⓗ   Ⓙ

GO

Name _____ Date _____

Practice Test 2: Language
Part 2: Usage

Directions: Choose the answer that best combines the underlined sentences.

7. Taylor wanted corn on the cob for dinner.
Taylor wanted potato salad for dinner.

   (A) Taylor wanted corn on the cob but not potato salad for dinner.

   (B) Taylor wanted corn on the cob for dinner, and she wanted potato salad to go with it.

   (C) Taylor wanted corn on the cob and potato salad for dinner.

   (D) Taylor wanted corn on the cob but potato salad for dinner.

8. Uncle Sid always plants tulip bulbs around the garden.
He plants the tulip bulbs in October.

   (F) Uncle Sid plants tulip bulbs in October around the garden.

   (G) Uncle Sid always plants tulip bulbs around the garden in October.

   (H) In October, Uncle Sid around the garden plants the tulip bulbs.

   (J) Uncle Sid always plants tulip bulbs around the garden, and he plants the tulip bulbs in October.

9. Nikhil lives around the corner.
Nikhil came over to help me clean the garage.

   (A) He lives around the corner, Nikhil, who came over to help me clean the garage.

   (B) Nikhil came over to help me clean the garage, and he lives around the corner.

   (C) Nikhil, who lives around the corner, who came over to help me clean the garage.

   (D) Nikhil, who lives around the corner, came over to help me clean the garage.

Directions: For each item below, choose the best way of expressing the idea.

10. (F) When I baby-sit, I will play games with the children and read them books.

   (G) To baby-sit, I will play games and read books to children.

   (H) The children will play games and read books when I am there to baby-sit.

   (J) I will play games when I baby-sit and read books.

11. (A) Our vacation was made from a scrapbook of photographs and postcards.

   (B) A scrapbook of photographs and postcards were used for our vacation.

   (C) I used photographs and postcards to make a scrapbook of our vacation.

   (D) Photographs and postcards is what I used to make a scrapbook of our vacation.

GO

Practice Test 2: Language
Part 2: Usage

Directions: Read the paragraph below. Choose the best topic sentence for it.

_____ Wampum was used to decorate personal items such as clothing, and it was common practice to weave thousands of these beads into wampum belts. The Iroquois exchanged wampum belts as promises to maintain peace and to confirm friendships.

12. (F) If a chief was given a wampum belt, it meant he was being invited to come for a visit.

(G) The Iroquois arranged the beads in designs that had special meaning for keeping records.

(H) The Keepers of the Wampum were respected people.

(J) Wampum is the name Native Americans gave to white or purple beads made from shells.

Directions: Find the answer choice that best develops the topic sentence.

13. To scientists who study plants, corn is a mystery.

(A) It can be eaten in many ways. Some people grind it into flour. Others roast it and eat it whole.

(B) They know that people in the Americas planted corn as long ago as 4,000 years. However, they have not found a wild plant that is the ancestor of corn.

(C) Ancient people like the Anasazi planted it. They used a sharp stick to make a hole in the soil and then dropped kernels of corn into the hole.

(D) Look at home or in the grocery store for things that contain corn. Read the label on packages of food. You'll probably discover that many more things contain corn than you might have guessed.

Directions: Read the paragraph below. Find the sentence that does not belong in the paragraph.

(1) The Pony Express operated from April 3, 1860, to November 20, 1861. (2) Though it lost money for its owner, it successfully established a 2,000-mile mail route between St. Joseph, Missouri, and Sacramento, California. (3) San Francisco was an important city in California during the 1860s. (4) The mail route was an important way to keep communications open between the North and the West at the beginning of the Civil War.

14. (F) sentence 1

(G) sentence 2

(H) sentence 3

(J) sentence 4

Name _____ Date _____

Practice Test 2: Language
Part 1: Language Usage

Directions: Read the passage below, and answer the questions that follow.

(1) Many years ago, a young Navajo boy was told that he must not speak his Navajo language in school. (2) Later in his life, he became a United States Marine. (3) As a Marine, he served in World War II. (4) That's when using his Navajo language gained new respect from the outside world. (5) He was one of a special group of Navajo code talkers, a communications unit that was sent to islands in the Pacific.

(6) In battle, the code talkers were often among the first to land on beaches. (7) They used their Navajo language to send secret messages by radio to headquarters. (8) For example, in code talk, the Navajo word *tsidi*, which means *bird*, stood for *aircraft*. (9) The code talkers information about the location.

(10) Code talkers could speak both Navajo and English fluently. (11) The code talkers had a dangerous job carrying heavy radios and cables, and the enemy was always on the lookout for them. (12) Some code talkers <u>was awarded</u> medals, such as the Bronze Star, for their bravery and service. (13) The enemy was never able to break the secret code during the war.

15. How would sentences 2 and 3 best be combined without changing their meaning?

Ⓐ Later in his life, he became a United States Marine and served in World War II.

Ⓑ Later in his life, he became a United States Marine, but not in World War II.

Ⓒ He became a United States Marine during World War II.

Ⓓ In World War II, he became a United States Marine and served the United States.

16. Which sentence is not a complete thought?

Ⓕ sentence 1

Ⓖ sentence 4

Ⓗ sentence 9

Ⓙ sentence 13

17. How is sentence 6 best written?

Ⓐ In battle, and among the first to land on the beaches, were the code talkers.

Ⓑ Code talkers, who often were among the first to land on the beaches, were in battle.

Ⓒ Landing on beaches first, the code talkers were often in battle.

Ⓓ Correct as it is

18. In sentence 12, <u>was awarded</u> is best written

Ⓕ were awarded.

Ⓖ is awarded.

Ⓗ been awarded.

Ⓙ have awarded.

STOP

Practice Test 2: Language
Part 3: Usage

Directions: Use the map below to answer the questions that follow.

1. According to the map, most of Iowa's land is used for _____.

   (A) grazing
   (B) crops
   (C) forests
   (D) unproductive uses

2. What is the main use for the land around the city of Duluth?

   (F) forests
   (G) grazing
   (H) unproductive uses
   (J) crops

3. According to the map, what type of land is not found in South Dakota?

   (A) cropland
   (B) grazing
   (C) forest land
   (D) unproductive uses

4. What is the main use for the land around the city of Valentine?

   (F) forest land
   (G) grazing
   (H) cropland
   (J) unproductive uses

GO

Practice Test 2: Language
Part 2: Usage

Directions: Use this card from an electronic library card catalog to answer the questions that follow.

> 930.67
> Cr   **Craft, Brenda**
> Lewis and Clark/Brenda Craft; illustrations
> and maps by Drew Allot. Introduction by Marla Singh.
> New York: EdBook Publishing Company, 2002.
> 125 pages; illustrations and maps; 2 cm
> (The Explorers series, volume 8)
>
> 1. U.S. History   2. Biography   3. Native Americans

5. What is the title of this book?

(A) U.S. History

(B) Lewis and Clark

(C) Explorers Series

(D) Lewis

6. How did Drew Allott contribute to this book?

(F) He was the illustrator.

(G) He was the author.

(H) He wrote the introduction.

(J) He was the publisher.

7. How did Brenda Craft contribute to this book?

(A) She was the publisher.

(B) She was the illustrator.

(C) She was the author.

(D) She wrote a review for it.

8. In what year was this book published?

(F) 1999

(G) 2000

(H) 2001

(J) 2002

Directions: Read each question below. Mark the circle for your answer.

9. Look at these guide words from a dictionary page. Which word would be found on this page?

| reason | reduce |

(A) realize

(B) reign

(C) refer

(D) receive

10. Which of these is a main heading that includes the other three words?

(F) Baseball

(G) Track and Field

(H) Summer Olympic Events

(J) Gymnastics

11. Which of these might be found in a book chapter entitled "Community Service Careers"?

(A) architect

(B) firefighter

(C) engineer

(D) stockbroker

STOP

Practice Test 2: Language
Part 3: Writing

Directions: Write about your favorite way to spend a day. Give details about why the activities are your favorites. Use words that express your feelings.

My favorite ways to spend the day is to read and play games on the computer.

Reading takes up many hours of a day. It is very enjoyable. All you need is a book, a comfy chair, and some light. It is an guarenteed hour that you will never miss.

Playing games on the computer is also an enjoyable way to pass the time. There is a lot of games, so you won't be bored. The games are also fun.

Those are my favorite ways to spend a day.

Number Sense

Directions: Read and work each problem. Choose the correct answer, and mark it.

Example

Which two numbers are both factors of 63?

- (A) 6, 10
- (B) 6, 12
- (C) 7, 8
- (D) 7, 9

Answer: (D)

---

1. 25 =

- (A) 10^3
- (B) 12^2
- (C) 5^5
- (D) 5^2

2. Which point on this number line shows 654?

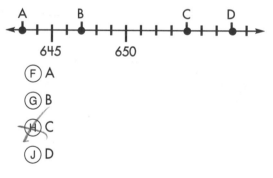

645   650

- (F) A
- (G) B
- (H) C
- (J) D

3. Which of these will have a remainder when it is divided by 8?

- (A) 40
- (B) 45
- (C) 24
- (D) 56

4. Which of these has a 6 in both the millions and the ten thousands place?

- (F) 6,690,021
- (G) 6,562,428
- (H) 6,286,383
- (J) 5,665,419

5. Maria is fourteenth in line to buy a movie ticket. Exactly how many people are in front of her in line?

- (A) 13
- (B) 15
- (C) 14
- (D) 12

Use scratch paper to work the problems.

If you need to, draw a picture—it can help you find the answer!

Name _____ Date _____

Number Sense

Directions: Use the chart to answer the questions that follow.

6
5
4
3
2
1
Sea level 0
−1
−2
−3
−4
−5
−6
−7
−8
−9
−10
−11
−12

1. Write an integer to represent approximately where the following are located.

−2	porpoise
4	bird
−9	eel
1	flag on sailboat
−7	sea horse
−4	octopus
6	clouds
−6	jellyfish

2. In each pair, circle the item that represents the greater integer.

sea horse, (porpoise)

eel, (flag)

(buoy,) octopus

(clouds,) eel

(sail of boat,) bottom of ocean

(bird,) sea horse

3. Put the following items in order from least to greatest by the integers they represent: jellyfish, buoy, eel, porpoise, bird, octopus, clouds.

clouds, bird, buoy, porpoise, octopus, jellyfish, eel

4. Which of these rules is correct?

F. Half of any even number is odd.

G. Half of any even number is even.

H. All odd numbers can be divided by 3.

J. All even numbers can be divided by 2.

5. Which of these has a 4 in the hundreds place?

A. 4,523

B. 8,634

C. 3,844

D. 7,498

Number Sense

Directions: Read each problem. Choose the correct answer, and mark it.

1. Which of these numbers cannot be evenly divided into 28?

(A) 1

(B) 4

(C) 6 ~~(crossed out)~~

(D) 7

2. A librarian was putting books on shelves. There were 58 books and 6 shelves. The librarian wanted to put the same number of books on each shelf, but she had some extras. How many books did not fit on the 6 shelves?

(F) 4 ~~(crossed out)~~

(G) 6

(H) 8

(J) 9

3. What is the meaning of 640?

(A) 6 tens and 4 ones

(B) 6 tens and 0 ones

(C) 4 hundreds and 6 ones

(D) 6 hundreds and 4 tens ~~(crossed out)~~

4. Which of these is not another way to write 4,860?

(F) 400 + 800 + 6 + 0 ~~(crossed out)~~

(G) four thousand, eight hundred, sixty

(H) 4,000 + 800 + 60

(J)

thousands	hundreds	tens	ones
4	8	6	0

5. How many of these numbers are common multiples of 3 and 9?

18   27   58   63   144

(A) 2

(B) 3

(C) 4 ~~(crossed out)~~

(D) 5

6. What is the smallest number that can be divided evenly by 6 and 15?

(F) 24

(G) 30 ~~(crossed out)~~

(H) 45

(J) 60

> Read the problems carefully. If you misread a number, it could cause you to mark the wrong answer!

Number Sense

Directions: Read each problem. Choose the correct answer, and mark it.

1. Which two numbers are both factors of 64?

(A) 3 and 16

(B) 4 and 24

(C) 8 and 32

(D) 8 and 48

2. How much would the value of 42,369 be increased by replacing the 3 with a 5?

(F) 200

(G) 300

(H) 400

(J) 500

3. What does the 6 in 678,009 mean?

(A) 6,000

(B) 600

(C) 600,000

(D) 60,000

4. Which of these has a 2 in the ten thousands place and a 7 in the tens place?

(F) 528,197

(G) 8,298,672

(H) 129,374

(J) 2,076

5. 795,643 =

(A) seven hundred million, ninety-five thousand, six hundred forty-three

(B) seven hundred ninety-five thousand, six hundred forty-three

(C) seven hundred ninety-five million, six thousand forty-three

(D) seven hundred ninety-five, six hundred forty-three

6. Which statement about place value is true?

(F) 10 thousands are equal to 1,000,000.

(G) 10 hundreds are equal to 10,000.

(H) 10 tens are equal to 1,000.

(J) 10 tens are equal to 100.

7. Which number is 2,000 less than 765,422?

(A) 565,422

(B) 763,422

(C) 745,422

(D) 765,222

8. The 7 in 68,743 means _____.

(F) 7,000

(G) 700

(C) 70

(D) 7

Number Sense

Directions: Read each problem. Choose the correct answer, and mark it.

1. **Which of the following statements is not true?**

   (A) 73 is not a prime number.

   (B) 59 is a prime number.

   (C) 6, 9, 18, and 27 are factors of 54.

   (D) There are 6 factors of 63.

2. **Which number is between 38,000 and 39,000 and has a 4 in the hundreds place?**

   (F) 39,456

   (G) 38,422

   (H) 38,541

   (J) 37,498

3. **Extend the number pattern.**
   2.5, 2.8, 3.1, 3.4, _____

   (A) 3.2

   (B) 3.9

   (C) 3.5

   (D) 3.7

4. **Which number is less than 5.7?**

   (F) 5.9

   (G) 6.7

   (H) 5.2

   (J) 5.78

5. **What is the smallest number that can be divided evenly by 4 and 7?**

   (A) 16

   (B) 21

   (C) 28

   (D) 36

6. **Which number sentence is not true?**

   (F) $\frac{3}{12} = \frac{1}{4}$

   (G) 5.26 < 5.1

   (H) 12.75 = $12\frac{3}{4}$

   (J) 25% > 18%

7. **At her party, Emily wants to serve each of her friends a turkey hot dog and bun. There are 8 hot dogs in a package but only 6 buns in a bag. What is the least amount of hot dogs Emily must buy so that she has an equal number of hot dogs and buns?**

   (A) 48

   (B) 16

   (C) 8

   (D) 24

8. **An employee in a warehouse has 84 games to pack into boxes. Each box can hold 18 games. How many boxes will the employee need for all the games?**

   (F) 6

   (G) 4

   (H) 5

   (J) 8

Number Concepts

Directions: Read each problem. Choose the correct answer, and mark it.

Example

Which number is expressed as
(9 × 1,000) + (4 × 100)
+ (2 × 10) + (3 × 1)?

(A) 9,420

(B) 9,400

(C) 90,423

(D) 9,423

Answer: (D)

---

1. What is another name for the Roman numeral XII?

(A) 5

(B) 7

(C) 12

(D) 20

2. What is the rule shown by the number sequence in the box?

$$3, 5, 7, 9, 11$$

(F) $n \div 2$

(G) $n \times 2$

(H) $n - 2$

(J) $n + 2$

3. Which of these is 6,809,465?

(A) six billion, eight hundred million, nine thousand, four hundred sixty-five

(B) six million, eight hundred nine, four hundred sixty-five

(C) sixty-eight thousand, nine thousand, four hundred sixty-five

(D) six million, eight hundred nine thousand, four hundred sixty-five

4. Which is the numeral for four million, six hundred ninety-three thousand, three hundred twenty-one?

(F) 400,693,321

(G) 4,693,321

(H) 469,321

(J) 4,963,231

5. Which of these statements is true about the numbers in the box?

$$4, 9, 16, 25, 36$$

(A) They are all even numbers.

(B) They are all odd numbers.

(C) They are all perfect squares.

(D) They are all prime numbers.

Look for key words, numbers, and patterns to help you find the answers.

Name _____ Date _____

Number Concepts

Directions: Read each problem. Choose the correct answer, and mark it.

1. These squares show groups of numbers that are related by the same rule. What number is missing from the third square?

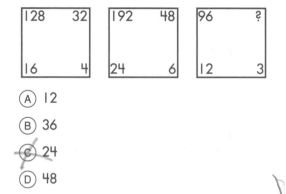

128	32
16	4

192	48
24	6

96	?
12	3

Ⓐ 12

Ⓑ 36

Ⓒ 24

Ⓓ 48

2. Which of the following expressions does not equal 144?

Ⓕ $8^2 + 80$

Ⓖ 12^2

Ⓗ $424 \div 4$

Ⓙ $288 - 144$

3. Which number can be expressed as (28 + 54) + (16 × 7) − 12?

Ⓐ 128   82   112

Ⓑ 182

Ⓒ 176

Ⓓ 162

4. Suppose you have the digits 1, 5, and 9. Without repeating a digit, how many three-digit numbers could you make with 9 as the ones digit?

Ⓕ 2

Ⓖ 3

Ⓗ 4

Ⓙ 5

5. What is another name for the Roman numeral XVI?

Ⓐ 9

Ⓑ 11

Ⓒ 14

Ⓓ 16

6. What is the rule shown by the number sequence in the box?

128, 64, 32, 16, 8, 4, 2

Ⓕ $n \div 2$

Ⓖ $n \times 2$

Ⓗ $n - 2$

Ⓙ $n + 2$

Look carefully at the position of the digits within each numeral. The position tells you what value the number has.

Name _____ Date _____

Number Concepts

MATH
131

Directions: Read each problem. Choose the correct answer, and mark it.

1. Which number makes this number sentence true?
$\frac{1}{2} + \square = \frac{3}{4}$
- (A) $\frac{1}{8}$
- (B) $\frac{1}{2}$
- (C) $\frac{1}{4}$
- (D) $\frac{2}{3}$

2. Which number makes this number sentence true?
$(3 \times 5) + (64 \div 8) =$
- (F) 12
- (G) 16
- (H) 22
- (J) 23

3. Which number makes this number sentence true?
$3.14 \times \square = 15.7$
- (A) 6
- (B) 9
- (C) 5
- (D) 4

4. Which number makes this number sentence true?
15% of $\square = 12$
- (F) 80
- (G) 100
- (H) 180
- (J) 92

5. Which number makes this number sentence true?
$2,455 - \square = 2,097$
- (A) 348
- (B) 358
- (C) 318
- (D) 352

6. Which number makes this number sentence true?
$\square \div 20 = 30$
- (F) 1,600
- (G) 550
- (H) 800
- (J) 600

7. Which number makes this number sentence true?
$\frac{3}{5}$ of 900 = $\square$
- (A) 540
- (B) 1,500
- (C) 3,150
- (D) 5,400

8. Which number makes this number sentence true?
23% of $\square = 126.5$
- (F) 5.5
- (G) 550
- (H) 2,909.5
- (J) 5,500

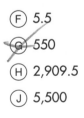

Chapter 6: Concepts

Ready to Test • Fifth Grade

Number Concepts

Directions: Read each problem. Choose the correct answer, and mark it.

1. 324 □ 4 = 81
   Which operation sign belongs in the box?

   (A) +

   (B) −

   (C) ×

   (D) ÷

2. 25 □ 95 = 2,375
   Which operation sign belongs in the box?

   (F) +

   (G) −

   (H) ×

   (J) ÷

3. $2\frac{2}{3}$ □ $1\frac{3}{4}$ = $4\frac{5}{12}$
   Which operation sign belongs in the box?

   (A) +

   (B) −

   (C) ×

   (D) ÷

4. 68.4 □ 22.4 = 90.8
   Which operation sign belongs in the box?

   (F) +

   (G) −

   (H) ×

   (J) ÷

5. $\frac{4}{36} = \frac{□}{9}$
   What does the □ equal?

   (A) 6

   (B) 3

   (C) 1

   (D) 4

6. $□^2 = 225$
   What does the □ equal?

   (F) 12

   (G) 5

   (H) 25

   (J) 15

7. 49 × □ = 147
   What does the □ equal?

   (A) 3

   (B) 4

   (C) 7

   (D) 9

8. 101.1 + □ = 108.8
   What does the □ equal?

   (F) 7.1

   (G) 8.7

   (H) 8.8

   (J) 7.7

Fractions

Directions: Write <, >, or = in the box to make the statement true.

1. $\frac{1}{2}$ ☐ $\frac{1}{4}$ >

2. $\frac{1}{12}$ ☐ $\frac{1}{2}$ <

3. $\frac{1}{7}$ ☐ $\frac{1}{8}$ >

4. $\frac{2}{8}$ ☐ $\frac{1}{4}$ =

5. $\frac{1}{10}$ ☐ $\frac{1}{11}$ >

6. $\frac{3}{4}$ ☐ $\frac{9}{12}$ =

7. $\frac{1}{6}$ ☐ $\frac{1}{12}$ >

8. $\frac{3}{6}$ ☐ $\frac{1}{2}$ =

9. $\frac{1}{4}$ ☐ $\frac{1}{6}$ >

10. $\frac{1}{3}$ ☐ $\frac{1}{5}$ >

11. $\frac{1}{3}$ ☐ $\frac{3}{9}$ =

12. $\frac{1}{9}$ ☐ $\frac{1}{4}$ <

13. $\frac{2}{7}$ ☐ $\frac{3}{4}$ <

14. $\frac{5}{6}$ ☐ $\frac{2}{3}$ >

15. $\frac{1}{9}$ ☐ $\frac{1}{3}$ <

16. $\frac{6}{16}$ ☐ $\frac{3}{8}$ =

17. $\frac{5}{5}$ ☐ $\frac{3}{6}$ >

18. $\frac{9}{10}$ ☐ $\frac{4}{5}$ >

Fractions

Directions: Read each problem. Fill in the circle for the correct answer.

1. Place these fractions in order from smallest to largest.

$\frac{1}{5}, \frac{1}{12}, \frac{1}{4}, \frac{1}{8}, \frac{1}{2}$

(A) $\frac{1}{12}, \frac{1}{2}, \frac{1}{4}, \frac{1}{5}, \frac{1}{8}$

(B) $\frac{1}{2}, \frac{1}{12}, \frac{1}{4}, \frac{1}{5}, \frac{1}{8}$

(C) $\frac{1}{2}, \frac{1}{4}, \frac{1}{5}, \frac{1}{8}, \frac{1}{12}$

(D) $\frac{1}{12}, \frac{1}{8}, \frac{1}{5}, \frac{1}{4}, \frac{1}{2}$ ✗

2. Place these fractions in order from largest to smallest.

$\frac{1}{11}, \frac{1}{3}, \frac{1}{9}, \frac{1}{7}, \frac{1}{6}$

(F) $\frac{1}{11}, \frac{1}{9}, \frac{1}{7}, \frac{1}{6}, \frac{1}{3}$

(G) $\frac{1}{3}, \frac{1}{6}, \frac{1}{7}, \frac{1}{9}, \frac{1}{11}$ ✗

(H) $\frac{1}{11}, \frac{1}{9}, \frac{1}{6}, \frac{1}{7}, \frac{1}{3}$

(J) $\frac{1}{3}, \frac{1}{7}, \frac{1}{6}, \frac{1}{9}, \frac{1}{11}$

3. Place these fractions in order from smallest to largest.

$\frac{1}{6}, \frac{1}{26}, \frac{1}{16}, \frac{1}{36}, \frac{1}{64}$

(A) $\frac{1}{64}, \frac{1}{36}, \frac{1}{26}, \frac{1}{16}, \frac{1}{6}$ ✗

(B) $\frac{1}{16}, \frac{1}{26}, \frac{1}{36}, \frac{1}{64}, \frac{1}{6}$

(C) $\frac{1}{6}, \frac{1}{16}, \frac{1}{26}, \frac{1}{36}, \frac{1}{64}$

(D) $\frac{1}{64}, \frac{1}{6}, \frac{1}{16}, \frac{1}{26}, \frac{1}{36}$

4. Place these fractions in order from largest to smallest.

$\frac{1}{24}, \frac{1}{32}, \frac{1}{16}, \frac{1}{12}, \frac{1}{4}$

(F) $\frac{1}{12}, \frac{1}{16}, \frac{1}{24}, \frac{1}{32}, \frac{1}{4}$

(G) $\frac{1}{32}, \frac{1}{24}, \frac{1}{16}, \frac{1}{12}, \frac{1}{4}$

(H) $\frac{1}{4}, \frac{1}{32}, \frac{1}{24}, \frac{1}{16}, \frac{1}{12}$

(J) $\frac{1}{4}, \frac{1}{12}, \frac{1}{16}, \frac{1}{24}, \frac{1}{32}$ ✗

5. Place these fractions in order from smallest to largest.

$\frac{3}{4}, \frac{3}{8}, \frac{5}{16}, \frac{7}{7}, \frac{9}{36}$

(A) $\frac{3}{4}, \frac{7}{7}, \frac{3}{8}, \frac{5}{16}, \frac{9}{36}$

(B) $\frac{9}{36}, \frac{5}{16}, \frac{3}{8}, \frac{3}{4}, \frac{7}{7}$ ✗

(C) $\frac{3}{4}, \frac{3}{8}, \frac{5}{16}, \frac{7}{7}, \frac{9}{36}$

(D) $\frac{9}{36}, \frac{5}{16}, \frac{3}{8}, \frac{7}{7}, \frac{3}{4}$

6. Place these fractions in order from largest to smallest.

$\frac{3}{18}, \frac{5}{9}, \frac{6}{27}, \frac{44}{45}, \frac{9}{81}$

(F) $\frac{9}{81}, \frac{44}{45}, \frac{6}{27}, \frac{3}{18}, \frac{5}{9}$

(G) $\frac{44}{45}, \frac{9}{81}, \frac{6}{27}, \frac{3}{18}, \frac{5}{9}$

(H) $\frac{44}{45}, \frac{5}{9}, \frac{6}{27}, \frac{3}{18}, \frac{9}{81}$ ✗

(J) $\frac{3}{18}, \frac{5}{9}, \frac{6}{27}, \frac{44}{45}, \frac{9}{81}$

It's important to eat a good breakfast before your test!

Name _____   Date _____

Fractions

Directions: Look closely at each group of statements. Fill in the circle next to the statement that is not true.

1. (A) $\frac{3}{4} < \frac{13}{16}$

   (B) $1\frac{3}{8} = 1\frac{9}{24}$

   (C) $5 = \frac{5}{5}$ ~~crossed out~~

   (D) $\frac{9}{16} < \frac{5}{8}$

2. (F) $\frac{23}{46} = \frac{16}{32}$

   (G) $\frac{8}{32} < \frac{3}{16}$ ~~crossed out~~

   (H) $\frac{7}{27} > \frac{2}{9}$

   (J) $\frac{4}{5} < \frac{23}{25}$

3. (A) $\frac{60}{100} > \frac{3}{5}$ ~~crossed out~~

   (B) $\frac{6}{7} = \frac{54}{63}$

   (C) $\frac{12}{12} = \frac{13}{13}$

   (D) $3\frac{3}{8} > \frac{25}{8}$

4. (F) $\frac{15}{5} = 3$

   (G) $2\frac{6}{7} < \frac{23}{7}$

   (H) $\frac{14}{3} = 3\frac{2}{3}$ ~~crossed out~~

   (J) $\frac{13}{12} > \frac{12}{13}$

5. (A) $6\frac{1}{8} = \frac{49}{8}$

   (B) $\frac{3}{9} > \frac{6}{27}$

   (C) $8\frac{1}{9} > \frac{100}{25}$

   (D) $\frac{3}{3} < \frac{45}{47}$ ~~circled~~

6. (F) $\frac{5}{25} < \frac{1}{5}$ ~~crossed out~~

   (G) $12\frac{1}{4} > \frac{48}{4}$

   (H) $3\frac{1}{2} = \frac{14}{4}$

   (J) $\frac{3}{19} < \frac{19}{38}$

7. (A) $\frac{8}{88} < \frac{88}{8}$

   (B) $\frac{10}{100} = 10$ ~~crossed out~~

   (C) $\frac{7}{7} > \frac{7}{77}$

   (D) $\frac{1}{13} < \frac{3}{11}$

8. (F) $\frac{17}{34} > \frac{1}{4}$

   (G) $4 = \frac{60}{15}$

   (H) $3\frac{3}{8} > 3\frac{1}{4}$

   (J) $\frac{19}{4} = 4\frac{1}{9}$ ~~crossed out~~

9. (A) $\frac{21}{22} > \frac{1}{2}$ ~~circled~~

   (B) $3\frac{1}{3} = \frac{10}{3}$

   (C) $\frac{4}{9} < \frac{9}{4}$

   (D) $\frac{1}{8} > \frac{8}{16}$

10. (F) $\frac{10}{12} = \frac{5}{6}$

   (G) $\frac{3}{7} < \frac{9}{21}$

   (H) $\frac{3}{2} > \frac{18}{24}$ ~~circled~~

   (J) $\frac{8}{48} = \frac{2}{12}$

Fractions and Decimals

Name _____ Date _____

Directions: Read and work each problem. Choose the correct answer, and mark it.

Example

Which figure below is $\frac{4}{9}$ shaded?

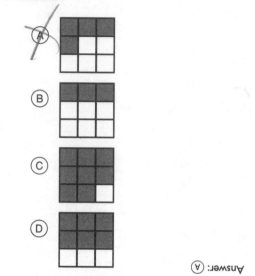

Answer: (A)

If you work on scratch paper, be sure that you transfer your answer correctly and fill in the right answer space.

1. Which fraction is shown by the x on this number line?

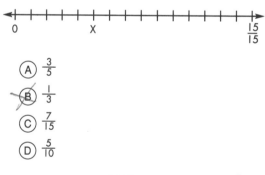

(A) $\frac{3}{5}$

(B) $\frac{1}{3}$

(C) $\frac{7}{15}$

(D) $\frac{5}{10}$

2. The length of $\overline{YZ}$ is what fraction of the length of $\overline{VX}$?

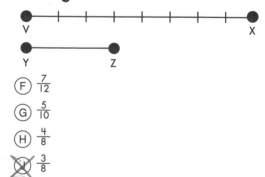

(F) $\frac{7}{12}$

(G) $\frac{5}{10}$

(H) $\frac{4}{8}$

(J) $\frac{3}{8}$

3. Which of these is another way to write $\frac{3}{10}$?

(A) 0.03

(B) 0.3

(C) 3.0

(D) 0.003

4. How do you write thirty-eight hundredths as a decimal?

(F) 03.8

(G) 0.038

(H) 0.38

(J) 3.8

Fractions and Decimals

Directions: Read and work each problem. Choose the correct answer, and mark it.

1. $\frac{3}{\square} = \frac{9}{21}$
   $\square = ?$

   Ⓐ 8

   Ⓑ 4

   Ⓒ 6

   Ⓓ 7

2. **Which number tells how much of this group of shapes is shaded?**

   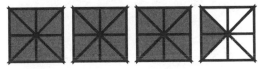

   Ⓕ $\frac{3}{4}$

   Ⓖ $3\frac{1}{2}$

   Ⓗ $3\frac{1}{4}$

   Ⓙ $3\frac{3}{4}$

3. **Which of these is another way to write 0.25?**

   Ⓐ $\frac{1}{4}$

   Ⓑ $\frac{25}{50}$

   Ⓒ $\frac{4}{25}$

   Ⓓ $\frac{3}{8}$

4. **Which of these has a value greater than $\frac{3}{4}$?**

   Ⓕ 0.25

   Ⓖ 0.68

   Ⓗ 0.86

   Ⓙ 0.75

5. **What is the least common denominator of $\frac{1}{2}$, $\frac{1}{4}$, and $\frac{1}{5}$?**

   Ⓐ 15

   Ⓑ 20

   Ⓒ 30

   Ⓓ 40

6. **Which decimal shows how much of the shape on the left is shaded?**

   Ⓕ 0.23

   Ⓖ 0.27

   Ⓗ 0.49

   Ⓙ 0.72

> Remember, with fractions, the smaller the denominator (the number on the bottom), the larger the value.

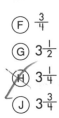

Fractions and Decimals

Directions: Read and work each problem. Choose the correct answer, and mark it.

1. Which of the following is not equivalent to $\frac{1}{2}$?

Ⓐ 50%

Ⓑ 0.5

Ⓒ 25%

Ⓓ $\frac{5}{10}$

2. Which of the following is not equivalent to $\frac{3}{4}$?

Ⓕ $\frac{9}{12}$

Ⓖ 75%

Ⓗ 0.75

Ⓙ 0.34

3. Which of the following fractions is equivalent to 25%?

Ⓐ $\frac{1}{8}$

Ⓑ $\frac{1}{4}$

Ⓒ $\frac{1}{2}$

Ⓓ $\frac{3}{4}$

4. $\frac{9}{4}$ can also be written as _____.

Ⓕ $9\frac{1}{4}$

Ⓖ $4\frac{1}{9}$

Ⓗ $2\frac{1}{4}$

Ⓙ $\frac{4}{9}$

5. 110% can also be written as _____.

Ⓐ $\frac{1}{10}$

Ⓑ $\frac{11}{10}$

Ⓒ 0.110

Ⓓ 11

6. 0.32 can also be written as _____.

Ⓕ 3.2%

Ⓖ $\frac{3}{2}$

Ⓗ $\frac{8}{25}$

Ⓙ 32

Change your answer only when you are sure of the correction. Your first answer is often correct!

Fractions and Decimals

Directions: Rewrite each fraction as a decimal rounded to the nearest hundredth.

1. $5\frac{3}{4}$ = _5.75_

4. $\frac{3}{8}$ = _.38_

2. $\frac{12}{5}$ = _2.4_

5. $\frac{23}{7}$ = _3.21_ ✓

3. $3\frac{1}{3}$ = _3.33_

6. $9\frac{1}{9}$ = _9.11_

Directions: Rewrite each decimal as a fraction in simplest form.

7. 9.25 = _$9\frac{1}{4}$_

10. 5.7 = _$5\frac{7}{10}$_ Simplest
← Fraction
?

8. 0.6 = _$\frac{6}{10}$_ ✓

11. 100.75 = _$100\frac{1}{4}$_ ✓

9. 4.12 = _$4\frac{12}{100}$_ ✓

12. 22.15 = _$22\frac{15}{100}$_ ✓

Properties

Directions: Read and work each problem. Choose the correct answer, and mark it.

Example

What is 654,909 rounded to the nearest thousand?

(A) 654,000

(B) 650,000

(C) 654,900

(D) 655,000

Answer: D

---

1. There are 324 students in the fifth grade. Each student pledged to read 50 books during the year. Which number sentence shows how to find the number of books the fifth graders pledged to read?

(A) $324 \div 50 = \square$

(B) $324 \times 50 = \square$

(C) $324 + 50 = \square$

(D) $324 - 50 = \square$

2. Which number sentence below is incorrect?

(F) $4 \times 12 = 48$

(G) $0 \div 12 = 12$

(H) $4 + 12 = 16$

(J) $48 - 12 = 36$

3. What number makes all the number sentences below true?

$3 \times \square = 15$
$\square \times 6 = 30$
$9 \times \square = 45$

(A) 3

(B) 6

(C) 4

(D) 5

4. The sum of 631 and 892 is closest to _____.

(F) 1,600

(G) 1,500

(H) 1,300

(J) 1,400

5. Another name for 20 × 10,000 is _____.

(A) $2 \times 200,000$

(B) $20,000 \times 100$

(C) $200 \times 1,000$

(D) $2,000 \times 1,000$

> **Some problems can be solved through estimation.**
>
> When estimating, it is especially important to look for key words and numbers to help you solve the problem.

Properties

Directions: Use the distributive property to rewrite the following expressions. Then, use the correct order of operations to solve both sides and check your answers.

The **distributive property** is used when there is a combination of multiplication over addition and subtraction.

$5(3 + 6) = 5 \times 3 + 5 \times 6$ $16 - 6 = (8 \times 2) - (3 \times 2)$
$5 \times 9 = 15 + 30$ $10 = (8 - 3)2$
$45 = 45$ $10 = 10$

1. $2(6 + 3) =$ $2 \times 6 + 2 \times 3$
$2 \times 9 = 12 + 6$
$18 = 18$

2. $12 + 9 =$
21

3. $4(9-1) =$
32

4. $18 - 6 =$
12

5. $(15 - 3)2 =$
24

6. $(7 + 5)8 =$ $8 \times 7 + 5 \times 8$
$8 \times 12 = 90 + 6$
$96 = 96$

7. $25 - 15 =$ $(5 \times 5) - (3 \times 5)$
$10 = (5 - 3)5$
$10 = 10$

8. $3(5 + 6) =$ $3 \times 5 + 3 \times 6$
$3 \times 11 = 15 + 18$
$33 = 33$

9. $8 + 12 =$ $(4 \times 8) + (6 \times 2)$
20

10. $3(8+3) =$
33

MATH
142

Properties

Directions: Read and work each problem. Choose the correct answer, and mark it.

Example

A factory has 314 workers. The owner gave a total bonus of $612,300. Which number sentence shows how to find the amount of bonus money each worker received? Let b = amount of bonus money.

Ⓐ $b + 314 = \$612,300$

Ⓑ $b \times 314 = \$612,300$

Ⓒ $b - 314 = \$612,300$

Ⓓ $b \div 314 = \$612,300$

Answer: Ⓑ

---

1. What number does a equal to make all the number sentences shown true?
$6 \times a = 12$
$a \times 10 = 20$
$9 \times a = 18$

Ⓐ 3

Ⓑ 4

Ⓒ 2

Ⓓ 5

2. Which statement is true about the value of z in the equation $6,896 \div 1,000 = z$?

Ⓕ z is less than 5.

Ⓖ z is between 5 and 6.

Ⓗ z is equal to 6.

Ⓙ z is between 6 and 7.

3. What is the value of m in the equation $81 \div 9 = (9 \div 3) \times (9 \div m)$?

Ⓐ 81

Ⓑ 27

Ⓒ 9

Ⓓ 3

4. Which of the following equations does not belong to the same family or group as the equation $c \times 9 = 36$?

Ⓕ $36 \div c = 9$

Ⓖ $36 \div c = 6$

Ⓗ $36 \div 9 = c$

Ⓙ $9 \times c = 36$

5. Suppose you wanted to double a number n and then add 10 to it. Which expression would you use?

Ⓐ $(n \times 2) + 10$

Ⓑ $n + 2 + 10$

Ⓒ $n \times 2 \times 10$

Ⓓ $(2 \times 10) + n$

6. What value of r makes these number sentences true?
$r + 21 = 30$
$63 \div 7 = r$

Ⓕ 19

Ⓖ 8

Ⓗ 11

Ⓙ 9

Name _____   Date _____

Properties

Directions: Use the patterns below to answer the questions that follow.

1. Look for a pattern in the following shapes. Fill in the table.

Pattern A:

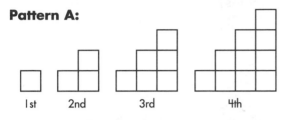

1st   2nd   3rd   4th

Shape	Number of Tiles
1st	1
2nd	3
3rd	6
4th	10
5th	15
6th	21
7th	27
8th	35

2. Explain how the pattern grows.

It goes like +1, +2, +3, +4, +5, +6, +7, +8.

3. If the pattern continues, how many tiles will be in the 10th shape?

(54) tiles

4. Kaleb is planning a party. He has to plan where to seat people. He can seat one guest on each open end of a table. He must group the tables in rectangles. Look for a pattern, and fill in the table below.

Pattern B:

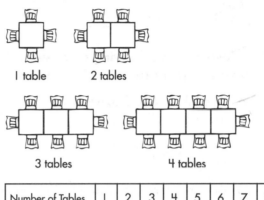

1 table   2 tables

3 tables   4 tables

Number of Tables	1	2	3	4	5	6	7	8
Number of Guests	4	6	8	10	12	14	16	18

5. Explain how the pattern grows.

Add 2 by 2

6. If the pattern continues, how many guests will be able to sit at 10 tables?

22 guests

Properties

Directions: Use the chart to answer the questions that follow.

	C1	C2	C3	C4	C5
R1	20	40	60	80	100
R2	18	36	54	72	90
R3	15	30	45	60	75
R4	11	22	33	44	55
R5	6	12	18	24	30

1. **Which of the following rules would give this pattern: 1, 2, 3, 5, 8, 13?**

   (A) Add the previous two numbers to get the next number.

   (B) Subtract by decreasing consecutive integers.

   (C) Add by increasing consecutive integers.

   (D) Add 2 and subtract 1.

2. **Which column has the rule of: Subtract by increasing consecutive integers?**

   (F) C1

   (G) C2

   (H) C3

   (J) C4

3. **Which column has the rule of: Subtract by integers increasing by threes?**

   (A) C1

   (B) C2

   (C) C3

   (D) C4

4. **Which column has the rule of: Subtract by integers increasing by fives?**

   (F) C1

   (G) C2

   (H) C3

   (J) C5

5. **Which column has the rule of: Subtract by integers increasing by twos?**

   (A) C1

   (B) C2

   (C) C3

   (D) C4

6. **What is the rule for the rows?**

   (F) The numbers increase across by a factor of two.

   (G) The numbers increase across by the first number in the row.

   (H) The numbers increase across by a factor of three.

   (J) The numbers increase across by the sum of the first two numbers.

Properties

Directions: Read each problem. Choose the correct answer, and mark it.

1. 18 + 5 □ 5 × 5

  (A) >
  (B) <
  (C) +
  (D) ≥

2. Which statement is true about the answer to the equation in the box?

8,986 ÷ 100 = □

  (F) is between 87 and 88
  (G) is between 88 and 89
  (H) is between 89 and 90
  (J) is between 90 and 91

3. Which of these is the best estimate of 66 × 98?

  (A) 60 × 90
  (B) 70 × 90
  (C) 60 × 100
  (D) 70 × 100

4. What symbol should replace the box in the number sentence below?
  64 □ 8 = 32 ÷ 4

  (F) ×
  (G) ÷
  (H) −
  (J) +

5. The amounts below show how much a student earned during a six-week time period.

$41.87	$36.23
$25.90	$42.36
$34.21	$27.83

What operations are necessary to find out the student's average weekly earnings?

  (A) subtraction and addition
  (B) addition and multiplication
  (C) addition and division
  (D) multiplication and division

6. Which of the following number facts does not belong to the same family or group as the number sentence in the box?

6 × 8 = 48

  (F) 48 ÷ 6 = 8
  (G) 8 × 6 = 48
  (H) 48 ÷ 8 = 6
  (J) 48 ÷ 12 = 4

The answer in an addition problem is always larger than the numbers being added.

Name _____   Date _____

Sample Test 6: Concepts

Directions: Read and work each problem. Choose the correct answer, and mark it.

Example

What is the value of *n* in the number sentence 6 × *n* = 30?

Ⓐ 4

Ⓑ 5

Ⓒ 6

Ⓓ 7

Answer: Ⓑ

---

1. What is the value of 6 in 89.634?

Ⓐ 6 tens

Ⓑ 6 hundreds

Ⓒ 6 tenths

Ⓓ 6 hundredths

2. Which of these is the same as the number in the place value chart?

thousands	hundreds	tens	ones
4	3	8	0

Ⓕ 4,830

Ⓖ four thousand, thirty-eight

Ⓗ 4,000 + 380 + 80

Ⓙ 4,380

3. What number makes these number sentences true?
9 + = 15
42 ÷ 7 =

Ⓐ 6

Ⓑ 4

Ⓒ 12

Ⓓ 9

4. Suppose you wanted to triple the value of 7 and then subtract 15 from it? Which number sentence would you use?

Ⓕ $15 - 7^3$

Ⓖ $(7 \times 7 \times 7) - 15$

Ⓗ $(7 \times 3) - 15$

Ⓙ $7 + 7 + 7 + 15$

5. What decimal goes in the box on the number line below?

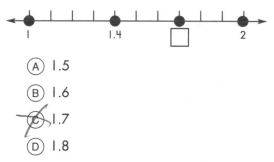

Ⓐ 1.5

Ⓑ 1.6

Ⓒ 1.7

Ⓓ 1.8

6. Which of these is a prime number?

Ⓕ 19

Ⓖ 21

Ⓗ 32

Ⓙ 48

7. What are all of the factors of the product of 5 × 4?

Ⓐ 2, 4, 5, 10

Ⓑ 1, 2, 4, 5, 10, 20

Ⓒ 1, 4, 5, 9

Ⓓ 1, 2, 3, 4, 5, 6, 10, 20

GO ▷

Sample Test 6: Concepts

Directions: Read and work each problem. Choose the correct answer, and mark it.

8. Which of these is between 673,904 and 678,042?

(F) 675,864

(G) 673,901

(H) 672,075

(J) 678,069

9. Which of these is another name for $\frac{7}{11}$?

(A) $\frac{21}{35}$

(B) $\frac{35}{66}$

(C) $\frac{28}{44}$

(D) $\frac{11}{15}$

10. If the pattern of the shaded blocks was continued, how many would be shaded in the last figure?

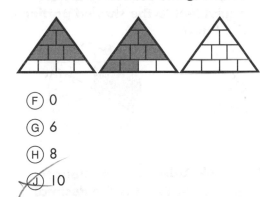

(F) 0

(G) 6

(H) 8

(J) 10

11. What number is 1,000 more than 4,568?

(A) 3,568

(B) 5,648

(C) 5,568

(D) 4,668

12. Which of these numbers is 10 less than the Roman numeral XXV?

(F) 10

(G) 17

(H) 15

(J) 25

13. Which of these is another name for 36 × 1,000?

(A) 360 × 100

(B) 360 × 1,000

(C) 36 × 100

(D) 360 × 10,000

14. In which numeral is there a 3 in both the hundreds and the hundred thousands place?

(F) 3,409,397

(G) 1,306,322

(H) 2,343,178

(J) 2,430,390

15. Which of these rules is not correct?

(A) $a \times b = b \div a$

(B) $a + b = b + a$

(C) if $a - b = c$, then $c + b = a$

(D) $(a \times b) + c = (b \times a) + c$

16. Which number shows the value of the shaded portion of this figure?

(F) 0.8

(G) 0.6

(H) 0.5

(J) 2.1

Name _____   Date _____

Sample Test 6: Concepts

Directions: Read and work each problem. Choose the correct answer, and mark it.

17. Tenisha made a number chart on which she shaded all the multiples of 5. Which pattern shows the shading on her number chart?

Ⓐ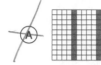

Ⓑ

Ⓒ

Ⓓ

18. What is the pattern for the number of triangles above?

Shape	1st	2nd	3rd	4th
Number of triangles	2	4	6	

Ⓕ The number of triangles increases by three each time.

Ⓖ The number of triangles increases by two each time.

Ⓗ The number of triangles increases by one each time.

Ⓙ The number of triangles increases by four each time.

19. How many triangles will be in the 15th shape?

Ⓐ 15

Ⓑ 20

Ⓒ 30

Ⓓ 35

20. What value does b have to be to make both equations true?
$$b - 7 = 15$$
$$2 \times 11 = b$$

Ⓕ 85

Ⓖ 12

Ⓗ 21

Ⓙ 22

21. Which of the following is not equivalent to the shaded portion of the figure?

Ⓐ $\frac{1}{3}$

Ⓑ $\frac{4}{8}$

Ⓒ $\frac{12}{36}$

Ⓓ $\frac{37}{111}$

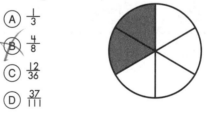

22. It took Aiden $\frac{3}{6}$ of an hour to get home. What is the decimal equivalent of $\frac{3}{6}$?

Ⓕ 0.5

Ⓖ 0.36

Ⓗ 2.0

Ⓙ None of these

Sample Test 6: Concepts

Directions: Read and work each problem. Choose the correct answer, and mark it.

23. Each column in the number pattern below equals 21. What numbers are missing?

Ⓐ 6 and 8

Ⓑ 7 and 5

Ⓒ 1 and 7

Ⓓ 4 and 3

3	5	2	1	6
2	7	8	9	1
9	8	4	6	7
	1	7		7

24. What number makes this number sentence true?
25% of □ = 75

Ⓕ 75

Ⓖ 200

Ⓗ 100

Ⓙ 300

25. Suppose you wanted to divide a number n by 10 and then subtract 26 from it. Which expression would you use?

Ⓐ $n - 26 \div 10$

Ⓑ $(n \div 10) + 26$

Ⓒ $(n \div 10) - 26$

Ⓓ $26 - (10 \div n)$

26. What is the value of s in the equation
$48 \div 4 = (18 \div 6) \times (12 \div s)$?

Ⓕ 6

Ⓖ 2

Ⓗ 3

Ⓙ 8

27. Which of these is not another way to write 22,586?

Ⓐ 2,000 + 500 + 86

Ⓑ 20 ten thousands, 2 thousands, 5 hundreds, 8 tens, 6 ones

Ⓒ 20,000 + 2,000 + 500 + 80 + 6

Ⓓ twenty-two thousand, five hundred eighty-six

28. Which of the following shows 35 as a Roman numeral?

Ⓕ XXV

Ⓖ XXXV

Ⓗ IIIV

XXXIV

29. $□^2 = 144$
What does the □ equal?

Ⓐ 16

Ⓑ 14

Ⓒ 12

Ⓓ 11

30. How much would the value of 16,128 be increased by replacing the 2 with a 7?

Ⓕ 5

Ⓖ 50

Ⓗ 500

Ⓙ 5,000

STOP

MATH 150

Addition and Subtraction of Whole Numbers

Directions: Solve each problem. Fill in the circle for the correct answer. Choose "None of these" if the correct answer is not given.

Example

2,554
−   9

Ⓐ 2,553

Ⓑ 2,555

Ⓒ 2,543

~~Ⓓ~~ None of these

Answer: Ⓓ

1. 30 + 15 + 27 =

Ⓐ 62

Ⓑ 78

~~Ⓒ~~ 72

Ⓓ None of these

2. 56 + 47 + 4 =

~~Ⓕ~~ 107

Ⓖ 93

Ⓗ 110

Ⓙ None of these

**3.   375
     246
    +381**

Ⓐ 902

~~Ⓑ~~ 1,002

Ⓒ 1,200

Ⓓ None of these

**4.   4,553
     8,120
     1,453
    +2,697**

Ⓕ 16,123

Ⓖ 14,144

Ⓗ 16,023

~~Ⓙ~~ None of these

5. 68 − 9 =

~~Ⓐ~~ 59

Ⓑ 61

Ⓒ 58

Ⓓ None of these

6. 74 − 6 =

Ⓕ 65

Ⓖ 69

Ⓗ 80

~~Ⓙ~~ None of these

**7.   9,003
    −7,685**

Ⓐ 1,428

Ⓑ 1,328

~~Ⓒ~~ 1,318

Ⓓ None of these

**8.   18,312
    − 9,264**

~~Ⓕ~~ 9,048

Ⓖ 9,124

Ⓗ 9,158

Ⓙ None of these

Addition and Subtraction
of Whole Numbers

Directions: Solve each problem. Fill in the circle for the correct answer. Choose "None of these" if the correct answer is not given.

1. 6,165
   −2,420

   Ⓐ 3,745
   Ⓑ 3,545
   Ⓒ 3,754
   Ⓓ None of these

2. 2,019
   − 86

   Ⓕ 1,923
   Ⓖ 1,930
   Ⓗ 1,733
   Ⓙ None of these

3. 86 + 14 + 9 =

   Ⓐ 111
   Ⓑ 119
   Ⓒ 109
   Ⓓ None of these

4. 8,212
   +3,111

   Ⓕ 12,323
   Ⓖ 11,323
   Ⓗ 11,333
   Ⓙ None of these

5. 5,014
   9,198
   2,228
   +3,468

   Ⓐ 19,912
   Ⓑ 20,918
   Ⓒ 19,908
   Ⓓ None of these

6. 189 − 92 =

   Ⓕ 99
   Ⓖ 87
   Ⓗ 88
   Ⓙ None of these

7. 325
   589
   120
   + 18

   Ⓐ 1,154
   Ⓑ 1,052
   Ⓒ 1,050
   Ⓓ None of these

8. 2,040 − 586 =

   Ⓕ 1,464
   Ⓖ 1,254
   Ⓗ 1,456
   Ⓙ None of these

Multiplication and Division of Whole Numbers

Directions: Solve each problem. Fill in the circle for the correct answer.

1. Find 777 ÷ 7.
- (A) 10
- (B) 11
- (C) 100
- (D) 111 ✗

2. Find 185 ÷ 5.
- (F) 37 ✗
- (G) 36
- (H) 180
- (J) 190

3. Find 304 × 57.
- (A) 361
- (B) 247
- (C) 17,328 ✗
- (D) 19,380

4. Find 46 × 82.
- (F) 3,772 ✗
- (G) 3,672
- (H) 3,662
- (J) 128

5. Find 444 ÷ 6.
- (A) 78
- (B) 63
- (C) 74 ✗
- (D) 64

6. Find 12 × 12.
- (F) 240
- (G) 144 ✗
- (H) 140
- (J) 24

7. Find 145 × 32.
- (A) 4,640 ✗
- (B) 725
- (C) 177
- (D) 4,760

8. Find 464 ÷ 4.
- (F) 460
- (G) 468
- (H) 116 ✗
- (J) 232

Check it out! You can check your answers in a division problem by multiplying your answer by the divisor.

$6 ÷ 3 = 2$

$2 × 3$ is 6, so your answer is correct.

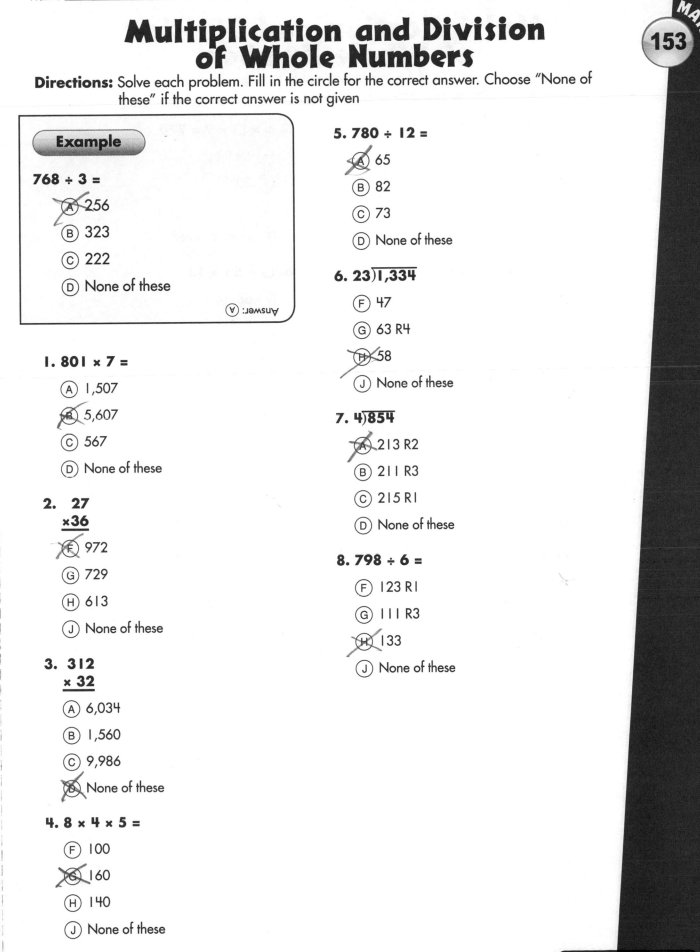

Multiplication and Division of Whole Numbers

Directions: Solve each problem. Fill in the circle for the correct answer. Choose "None of these" if the correct answer is not given

Example

768 ÷ 3 =

Ⓐ 256
Ⓑ 323
Ⓒ 222
Ⓓ None of these

Answer: A

1. 801 × 7 =
Ⓐ 1,507
Ⓑ 5,607
Ⓒ 567
Ⓓ None of these

2. 27
×36
Ⓕ 972
Ⓖ 729
Ⓗ 613
Ⓙ None of these

3. 312
× 32
Ⓐ 6,034
Ⓑ 1,560
Ⓒ 9,986
Ⓓ None of these

4. 8 × 4 × 5 =
Ⓕ 100
Ⓖ 160
Ⓗ 140
Ⓙ None of these

5. 780 ÷ 12 =
Ⓐ 65
Ⓑ 82
Ⓒ 73
Ⓓ None of these

6. 23)1,334
Ⓕ 47
Ⓖ 63 R4
Ⓗ 58
Ⓙ None of these

7. 4)854
Ⓐ 213 R2
Ⓑ 211 R3
Ⓒ 215 R1
Ⓓ None of these

8. 798 ÷ 6 =
Ⓕ 123 R1
Ⓖ 111 R3
Ⓗ 133
Ⓙ None of these

Name _____ Date _OK 4/14/16_

Multiplication and Division of Whole Numbers

Directions: Fill in the circle for the number that makes the equation true. Choose "None of these" if the correct answer is not given.

1. 2,088 ÷ □ = 58

(A) 30

(B) 36

(C) 2,030

(D) None of these

2. □ × 256 = 3,072

(F) 12

(G) 13

(H) 14

(J) None of these

3. □ ÷ 810 = 15

(A) 53

(B) 55

(C) 57

(D) None of these

4. 300 ÷ □ = 12

(F) 25

(G) 30

(H) 35

(J) None of these

5. 6 × □ × 9 = 270

(A) 54

(B) 30

(C) 45

(D) None of these

6. □ ÷ 55 = 13

(F) 68

(G) 715

(H) 4 R3

(J) None of these

7. □ × 54 × 40 = 2,160

(A) 40

(B) 54

(C) 1

(D) None of these

8. 1,980 ÷ □ = 20

(F) 97

(G) 98

(H) 99

(J) None of these

Adding Fractions

Directions: Solve each problem. Reduce the answer to its lowest terms. Fill in the circle for the correct answer. Choose "None of these" if the correct answer is not given.

Example

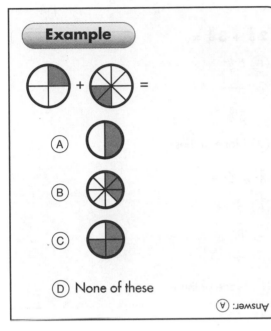

Answer: (A)

1. $\frac{6}{18} + \frac{2}{18} =$

  (A) $\frac{8}{36}$

  (B) $\frac{12}{18}$

  (C) $\frac{4}{9}$

  (D) None of these

2. $\frac{3}{13} + \frac{7}{13} =$

  (F) $\frac{4}{13}$

  (G) $\frac{10}{13}$

  (H) $\frac{10}{26}$

  (J) None of these

3. $\frac{3}{4} + \frac{1}{5} =$

  (A) $\frac{1}{5}$

  (B) $\frac{4}{9}$

  (C) $\frac{19}{20}$

  (D) None of these

4. $\frac{2}{8} + \frac{3}{4} =$

  (F) $\frac{5}{12}$

  (G) $\frac{5}{8}$

  (H) $\frac{3}{16}$

  (J) None of these

5. $1\frac{5}{9} + 4\frac{3}{9} =$

  (A) $5\frac{8}{9}$

  (B) $5\frac{2}{9}$

  (C) $2\frac{4}{9}$

  (D) None of these

6. $2\frac{4}{7} + 2\frac{3}{7} =$

  (F) 6

  (G) $4\frac{6}{7}$

  (H) 5

  (J) None of these

Don't forget—after you add the fractions, reduce the answer to its lowest term.

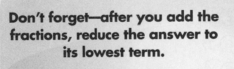

MATH
156

Adding Fractions

Directions: Solve each problem. Reduce the answer to its lowest terms. Fill in the circle for the correct answer. Choose "None of these" if the correct answer is not given.

1. $\frac{4}{14} + \frac{1}{7} =$

   (A) $\frac{2}{7}$

   (B) $\frac{3}{14}$

   (C) $\frac{3}{7}$

   (D) None of these

2. $3\frac{2}{8} + 4\frac{6}{8} =$

   (F) 8

   (G) $7\frac{7}{8}$

   (H) $8\frac{1}{4}$

   (J) None of these

3. $\frac{4}{8} + \frac{1}{3} =$

   (A) $\frac{5}{8}$

   (B) $\frac{6}{5}$

   (C) $\frac{5}{24}$

   (D) None of these

4. $\frac{1}{3} + \frac{3}{12} =$

   (F) $\frac{4}{12}$

   (G) $\frac{7}{12}$

   (H) $\frac{2}{3}$

   (J) None of these

5. $5\frac{6}{14} + \frac{4}{14} =$

   (A) $5\frac{10}{7}$

   (B) $5\frac{11}{14}$

   (C) $5\frac{5}{7}$

   (D) None of these

6. $2\frac{2}{9} + 3\frac{4}{9} =$

   (F) $5\frac{1}{3}$

   (G) $5\frac{1}{9}$

   (H) $5\frac{8}{9}$

   (J) None of these

7. $\frac{3}{9} + \frac{2}{6} =$

   (A) $\frac{5}{9}$

   (B) $\frac{5}{18}$

   (C) $\frac{2}{3}$

   (D) None of these

8. $\frac{4}{9} + \frac{2}{4} =$

   (F) $\frac{6}{9}$

   (G) $\frac{17}{18}$

   (H) $\frac{4}{36}$

   (J) None of these

9. $\frac{5}{6} + \frac{1}{12} + \frac{1}{3} =$

   (A) $\frac{7}{3}$

   (B) $1\frac{1}{4}$

   (C) $\frac{11}{12}$

   (D) None of these

10. $20\frac{2}{5} + 5\frac{5}{6} =$

   (F) $26\frac{7}{30}$

   (G) $25\frac{7}{12}$

   (H) $36\frac{3}{10}$

   (J) None of these

Adding Fractions

Directions: Solve each problem. Reduce the answer to its lowest terms.

1. $5\frac{3}{8} + 6\frac{3}{16} =$ _____

7. $\frac{17}{100} + \frac{3}{20} =$ _____

2. $7\frac{8}{9} + 3\frac{1}{4} =$ _____

8. $\frac{54}{8} + \frac{1}{2} =$ _____

3. $12\frac{1}{2} + 1\frac{1}{8} =$ _____

9. $82\frac{1}{4} + \frac{8}{32} =$ _____

4. $1\frac{4}{5} + \frac{3}{2} =$ _____

10. $4\frac{7}{49} + 7\frac{9}{63} =$ _____

5. $6\frac{2}{25} + 5\frac{3}{5} =$ _____

11. $\frac{23}{15} + \frac{14}{5} =$ _____

6. $18\frac{1}{6} + 3\frac{1}{72} =$ _____

12. $6\frac{3}{29} + 4\frac{1}{2} =$ _____

Subtracting Fractions

Directions: Solve each problem. Reduce the answer to its lowest terms. Fill in the circle for the correct answer. Choose "None of these" if the correct answer is not given.

Example

$\frac{5}{6} - \frac{2}{6} =$

(A) $\frac{2}{6}$

(B) $\frac{1}{2}$

(C) $\frac{4}{6}$

(D) None of these

Answer: (B)

1. $\frac{8}{15} - \frac{2}{15} =$

(A) $\frac{2}{5}$

(B) $\frac{6}{15}$

(C) $\frac{3}{5}$

(D) None of these

2. $\frac{6}{7}$
   $- \frac{3}{7}$

(F) $\frac{4}{7}$

(G) 3

(H) $\frac{9}{7}$

(J) None of these

3. $\frac{4}{5} - \frac{1}{6} =$

(A) $\frac{1}{10}$

(B) $\frac{29}{30}$

(C) $\frac{19}{30}$

(D) None of these

4. $\frac{3}{5}$
   $- \frac{4}{15}$

(F) $\frac{1}{3}$

(G) $\frac{13}{15}$

(H) $\frac{8}{15}$

(J) None of these

5. $6\frac{3}{8} - 5\frac{5}{8} =$

(A) $\frac{3}{8}$

(B) $\frac{3}{4}$

(C) $1\frac{1}{4}$

(D) None of these

6. $11\frac{12}{15}$
   $- 5\frac{8}{15}$

(F) $6\frac{1}{3}$

(G) $5\frac{4}{15}$

(H) $6\frac{3}{15}$

(J) None of these

When reducing fractions, be sure to divide the numerator and the denominator by the same number.

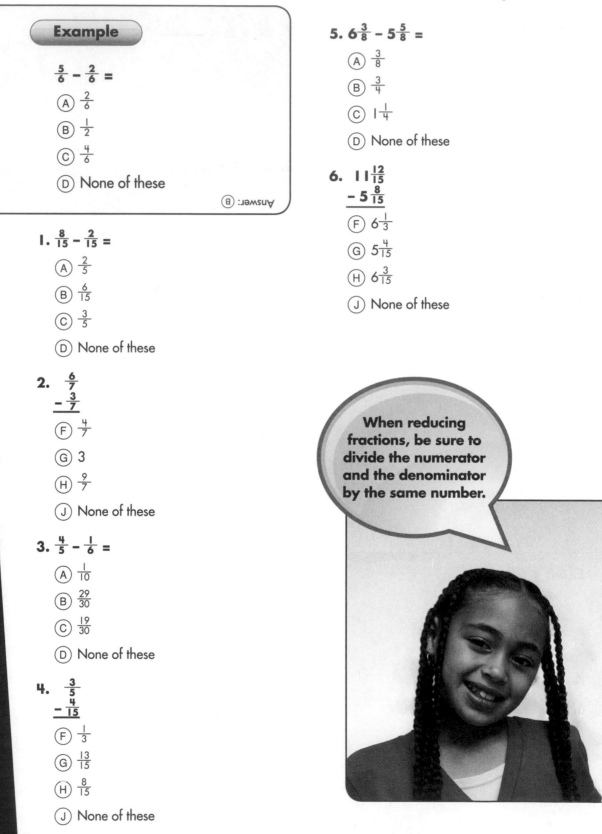

Subtracting Fractions

Directions: Solve each problem. Reduce the answer to its lowest terms. Fill in the circle for the correct answer. Choose "None of these" if the correct answer is not given.

1. $9\frac{5}{10} - 3\frac{5}{10} =$

   (A) $6\frac{1}{5}$

   (B) $5\frac{9}{10}$

   (C) 6

   (D) None of these

2. $2\frac{3}{12}$
   $-\ \frac{1}{12}$

   (F) $2\frac{1}{3}$

   (G) $2\frac{1}{6}$

   (H) $2\frac{1}{12}$

   (J) None of these

3. $\frac{5}{9} - \frac{2}{9} =$

   (A) $\frac{1}{9}$

   (B) $\frac{2}{3}$

   (C) $\frac{2}{9}$

   (D) None of these

4. $\frac{3}{7}$
   $-\ \frac{2}{14}$

   (F) $\frac{2}{7}$

   (G) $\frac{1}{7}$

   (H) $\frac{2}{14}$

   (J) None of these

5. $1\frac{6}{12} - 1\frac{3}{12} =$

   (A) $1\frac{1}{4}$

   (B) $\frac{1}{4}$

   (C) $\frac{3}{4}$

   (D) None of these

6. $\frac{2}{3} - \frac{3}{9} =$

   (F) $\frac{4}{9}$

   (G) $\frac{2}{3}$

   (H) $\frac{1}{4}$

   (J) None of these

7. $\frac{8}{10} - \frac{2}{10} =$

   (A) $\frac{4}{10}$

   (B) $\frac{3}{5}$

   (C) $\frac{6}{5}$

   (D) None of these

8. $\frac{5}{6}$
   $-\ \frac{2}{12}$

   (F) $\frac{7}{12}$

   (G) $\frac{1}{3}$

   (H) $\frac{2}{3}$

   (J) None of these

MATH
160

Subtracting Fractions

Directions: Solve each problem. Reduce the answer to its lowest terms.

1. $12\frac{6}{9} - 5\frac{5}{9} =$ _____

2. $56\frac{12}{15} - 13\frac{3}{4} =$ _____

3. $\frac{45}{12} - \frac{13}{24} =$ _____

4. $\frac{7}{8} - \frac{15}{32} =$ _____

5. $6\frac{8}{63} - 4\frac{8}{9} =$ _____

6. $\frac{48}{49} - \frac{6}{7} =$ _____

7. $32\frac{6}{55} - \frac{3}{11} =$ _____

8. $27\frac{9}{10} - \frac{1}{2} =$ _____

9. $112 - \frac{5}{12} =$ _____

10. $5\frac{3}{7} - \frac{72}{35} =$ _____

11. $16 - 14\frac{3}{16} =$ _____

12. $29\frac{1}{3} - 12\frac{17}{18} =$ _____

Adding and Subtracting Decimals and Percents

Directions: Solve each problem. Fill in the circle for the correct answer. Choose "None of these" if the correct answer is not given.

Example

50.25 + 45.36 =

Ⓐ 9,561

Ⓑ 95.61

Ⓒ 956.1

Ⓓ None of these

Answer: (B)

---

1. 48.3 + 6.7 =

Ⓐ 115.3

Ⓑ 54.1

Ⓒ 55

Ⓓ None of these

2. 0.583
**   +0.79**

Ⓕ 0.662

Ⓖ 1.373

Ⓗ 1.381

Ⓙ None of these

3. 38.03
**   −15.6**

Ⓐ 2.43

Ⓑ 36.47

Ⓒ 23

Ⓓ None of these

4. $49.39 − $12.87 =

Ⓕ $36.51

Ⓖ $37.54

Ⓗ $35.53

Ⓙ None of these

---

5. 27.03% + 39.65% =

Ⓐ 63.27%

Ⓑ 56.69%

Ⓒ 66.68%

Ⓓ None of these

6. 50.25%
**   +29.75%**

Ⓕ 77%

Ⓖ 87%

Ⓗ 80%

Ⓙ None of these

Get in line!
When adding and subtracting decimals, always make sure that the decimal points are lined up before you begin to solve the problem.

Adding and Subtracting Decimals and Percents

Directions: Solve each problem. Fill in the circle for the correct answer. Choose "None of these" if the correct answer is not given.

1. $145.67 + $63.25 =
- (A) $108.82
- (B) $208.92
- (C) $298.92
- (D) None of these

2. 32.8% – 16.24% =
- (F) 16.56%
- (G) 16.6%
- (H) 16.64%
- (J) None of these

3. 765.95 + 0.214 =
- (A) 768.09
- (B) 766.164
- (C) 979.95
- (D) None of these

4. 52.98 – 1.7 =
- (F) 51.28
- (G) 51.81
- (H) 35.98
- (J) None of these

5. $658.32 – $19.99 =
- (A) $458.42
- (B) $656.33
- (C) $656.32
- (D) None of these

6. 45.2% + 63.47% =
- (F) 108.67%
- (G) 108.7%
- (H) 100%
- (J) None of these

7. 0.245 + 2.35 =
- (A) 4.8
- (B) 2.3745
- (C) 2.595
- (D) None of these

8. $25.99 – $3.08 =
- (F) $29.07
- (G) $22.19
- (H) $22.91
- (J) None of these

9. 0.45 + 9.23 =
- (A) 8.78
- (B) 9.68
- (C) 9.86
- (D) None of these

10. 26.54% – 17.98% =
- (F) 44.52%
- (G) 5.85%
- (H) 8.55%
- (J) None of these

Multiplying and Dividing Decimals and Percents

Directions: Solve each problem. Fill in the circle for the correct answer. Choose "None of these" if the correct answer is not given

---

Example

13% of 4 =

- (A) 52%
- (B) 50%
- (C) 59%
- (D) None of these

Answer: (D)

---

1. 6.87 × 4 =

- (A) 27.48
- (B) 2.748
- (C) 274.8
- (D) None of these

2. 2.03
   ×0.02

- (F) 0.406
- (G) 0.0406
- (H) 2.006
- (J) None of these

3. 3)7.2

- (A) 2.4
- (B) 2 R12
- (C) 2.89
- (D) None of these

4. 12% of 6 =

- (F) 0.84
- (G) 0.96
- (H) 0.72
- (J) None of these

5. 34% of 2 =

- (A) 0.36
- (B) 0.70
- (C) 0.66
- (D) None of these

6. 37% ÷ 5 =

- (F) 8.6%
- (G) 7.4%
- (H) 6.5%
- (J) None of these

Check it out! You can check your answers in a division problem by multiplying your answer by the divisor.

$$6 \div 3 = 2$$

2 × 3 is 6, so your answer is correct.

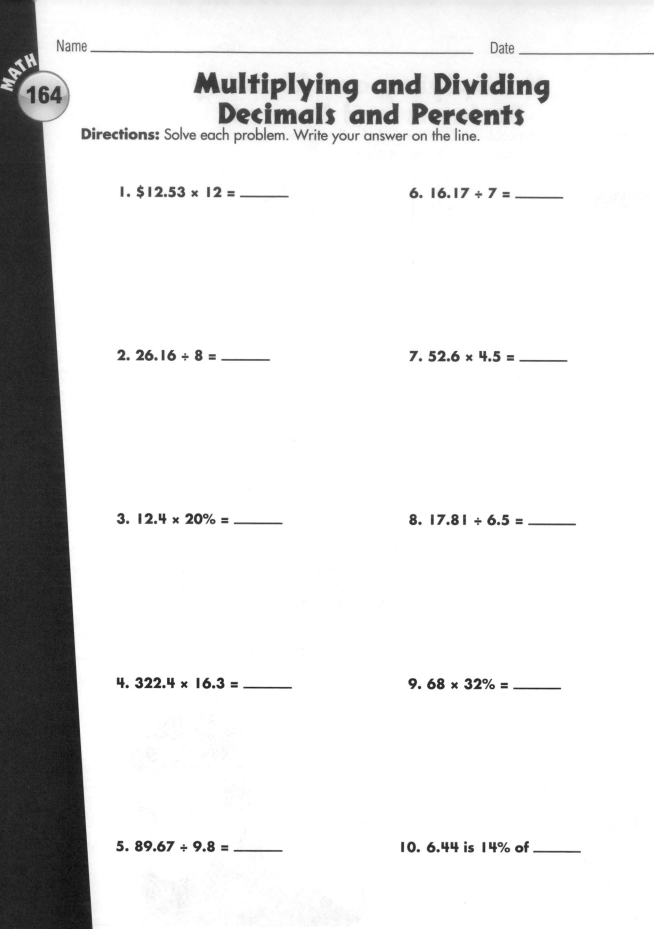

MATH
164

Multiplying and Dividing
Decimals and Percents

Directions: Solve each problem. Write your answer on the line.

1. $12.53 × 12 = _____

2. 26.16 ÷ 8 = _____

3. 12.4 × 20% = _____

4. 322.4 × 16.3 = _____

5. 89.67 ÷ 9.8 = _____

6. 16.17 ÷ 7 = _____

7. 52.6 × 4.5 = _____

8. 17.81 ÷ 6.5 = _____

9. 68 × 32% = _____

10. 6.44 is 14% of _____

Multiplying and Dividing Decimals and Percents

165

Directions: Solve each problem. Fill in the circle for the correct answer.

1. If 87% of the students passed the test, how many passed if there were 100 students?

- Ⓐ 13
- Ⓑ 87
- Ⓒ 100
- Ⓓ 43

2. There were a total of 100 people at the beginning of the concert. Thirty people left early. Which decimal shows how many left early?

- Ⓕ 1.00
- Ⓖ 0.70
- Ⓗ 0.30
- Ⓙ 0.00

3. 50 birds are sitting on a wire. Then 40 birds fly away. What percentage of the original 50 birds remain on the wire?

- Ⓐ 10%
- Ⓑ 20%
- Ⓒ 40%
- Ⓓ Not enough information

4. A gardener planted 200 carrot seeds. A few weeks later, 166 of the seeds have sprouted. What percentage of the seeds that were planted have sprouted?

- Ⓕ 166%
- Ⓖ 34%
- Ⓗ 68%
- Ⓙ 83%

5. A bookstore's shelves can hold a total of 100,000 books. Currently, there are 73,000 books on the shelves. Which decimal shows how full the bookstore's shelves are?

- Ⓐ 0.73
- Ⓑ 7.3
- Ⓒ 73.0
- Ⓓ 730

6. When a bucket is 100% full of soil, the total weight of the soil is 45 pounds. When the bucket is 32% full of soil, approximately how much does the soil in it weigh?

- Ⓕ 14.4 pounds
- Ⓖ 13 pounds
- Ⓗ 12 pounds
- Ⓙ 1.4 pounds

Sample Test 7: Computation

Directions: Solve each problem. Fill in the circle for the correct answer. Choose "None of these" if the correct answer is not given.

Example

109 + 356 + 498 + 253 =

- (A) 1,206
- (B) 1,358
- (C) 1,216
- (D) None of these

Answer: C

1.
```
  1,222
  2,907
  5,745
+ 4,306
```
- (A) 14,270
- (B) 14,320
- (C) 14,180
- (D) None of these

2. $7\frac{1}{5} - 5\frac{1}{4} =$
- (F) $1\frac{2}{5}$
- (G) $2\frac{1}{20}$
- (H) $1\frac{19}{20}$
- (J) None of these

3. $24\overline{)1,246}$
- (A) 50 R23
- (B) 52 R16
- (C) 51 R20
- (D) None of these

4.
```
  1.576
+ 2.33
```
- (F) 4.102
- (G) 3.906
- (H) 3.889
- (J) None of these

5.
```
  3,006
- 1,549
```
- (A) 1,457
- (B) 2,007
- (C) 1,896
- (D) None of these

6. $9\overline{)310.5}$
- (F) 36.1
- (G) 35.9
- (H) 34.5
- (J) None of these

7.
```
  1 1/2
+ 2 3/4
```
- (A) $3\frac{1}{2}$
- (B) $4\frac{1}{4}$
- (C) $5\frac{4}{6}$
- (D) None of these

8.
```
  303
+  26
```
- (F) 330
- (G) 328
- (H) 327
- (J) None of these

GO

Sample Test 7: Computation

Directions: Solve each problem. Fill in the circle for the correct answer. Choose "None of these" if the correct answer is not given.

9. 36% + 27% =

Ⓐ 63%

Ⓑ 75%

Ⓒ 61%

Ⓓ None of these

10. 439 ÷ 6 =

Ⓕ 75 R2

Ⓖ 74 R3

Ⓗ 73 R1

Ⓙ None of these

11. 1,999 + 463 + 275 =

Ⓐ 3,982

Ⓑ 2,737

Ⓒ 2,688

Ⓓ None of these

12. 99% ÷ 33 =

Ⓕ 6%

Ⓖ 3%

Ⓗ 4 R1

Ⓙ None of these

13. 4.968
**   + 0.554**

Ⓐ 5.443

Ⓑ 5.524

Ⓒ 5.522

Ⓓ None of these

14. 68.4% − 55.7% =

Ⓕ 12.7%

Ⓖ 13.9%

Ⓗ 11.4%

Ⓙ None of these

15. 14% of 6 =

Ⓐ 0.69

Ⓑ 0.78

Ⓒ 0.84

Ⓓ None of these

16. 3,268
**   × 135**

Ⓕ 441,180

Ⓖ 440,286

Ⓗ 444,223

Ⓙ None of these

17. 5,032 − 3,659 =

Ⓐ 1,377

Ⓑ 1,273

Ⓒ 1,337

Ⓓ None of these

18. 7.03
**   × 6.2**

Ⓕ 43.968

Ⓖ 43.586

Ⓗ 43.685

Ⓙ None of these

GO

Name _____ Date _____

Sample Test 7: Computation

Directions: Solve each problem. Fill in the circle for the correct answer. Choose "None of these" if the correct answer is not given.

19. 3,566
   + 2,409
   - (A) 1,157
   - (B) 6,975
   - (C) 5,975
   - (D) 5,935

20. $541.6 \times 5 =$
   - (F) 2,708
   - (G) 2,788
   - (H) 3,708
   - (J) 2,718

21. $6\frac{7}{12} + \frac{5}{6} =$
   - (A) $7\frac{5}{6}$
   - (B) $7\frac{5}{12}$
   - (C) $7\frac{7}{12}$
   - (D) $6\frac{5}{12}$

22. $18\overline{)594}$
   - (F) 32 R2
   - (G) 23
   - (H) 33
   - (J) 35

23. It rained 18 out of 30 days in April. What percentage of the days did it rain?
   - (A) 18%
   - (B) 12%
   - (C) 60%
   - (D) 68%

24. $\frac{9}{14} - \frac{3}{7} =$
   - (F) $\frac{2}{7}$
   - (G) $\frac{1}{7}$
   - (H) $\frac{5}{14}$
   - (J) $\frac{3}{14}$

25. 6,512
   - 803
   - (A) 5,709
   - (B) 7,315
   - (C) 5,970
   - (D) 5,809

26. Carson bought a coffee mug for his mom's birthday. It cost $8.95. Tax was 7%. What was his total?
   - (F) $9.78
   - (G) $9.58
   - (H) $9.62
   - (J) $9.66

STOP

Lines and Angles

Directions: Fill in the circle for the correct answer to each problem.

1. How many pairs of lines below are parallel?

- (A) one
- (B) two
- (C) three
- (D) four

2. Which statement is true about line segment AB?

A _____ B

- (F) It extends infinitely in both directions.
- (G) It cannot be measured.
- (H) It is the same as line segment BA.
- (J) It is the same as line AB.

3. Two lines that intersect at a right angle are _____.

- (A) similar
- (B) curved
- (C) parallel
- (D) perpendicular

4. Which of the following statements is true about the radius of a circle?

- (F) The radius is the distance around the circle.
- (G) The radius is a line that connects two points on a circle and passes through the center.
- (H) The radius is half the length of the diameter.
- (J) There is only one radius in a circle.

5. The _____ is the intersection of two sides of an angle.

- (A) radius
- (B) circumference
- (C) vertex
- (D) ray

6. Which of these shows a ray?

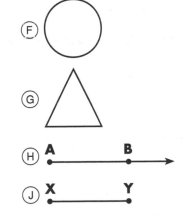

(F)

(G)

(H) A ———————→ B

(J) X ——————— Y

Lines and Angles

Directions: Fill in the circle for the correct answer to each problem.

1. What is the measurement of a straight angle?

Ⓐ 78°

Ⓑ 25°

Ⓒ 90°

Ⓓ 180°

2. Which of the following figures shows at least one right angle?

Ⓕ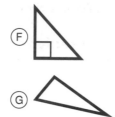

Ⓖ

Ⓗ

Ⓙ

3. Which of these is an obtuse angle?

Ⓐ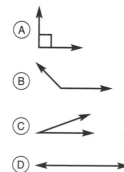

Ⓑ

Ⓒ

Ⓓ

4. What is the name for this type of angle?

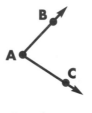

Ⓕ obtuse

Ⓖ straight

Ⓗ right

Ⓙ acute

5. Which of the following is not a correct name for the angle shown?

Ⓐ ∠ A

Ⓑ ∠ C

Ⓒ ∠ CAB

Ⓓ ∠ BAC

Lines and Angles

Directions: Fill in the circle for the correct answer to each problem.

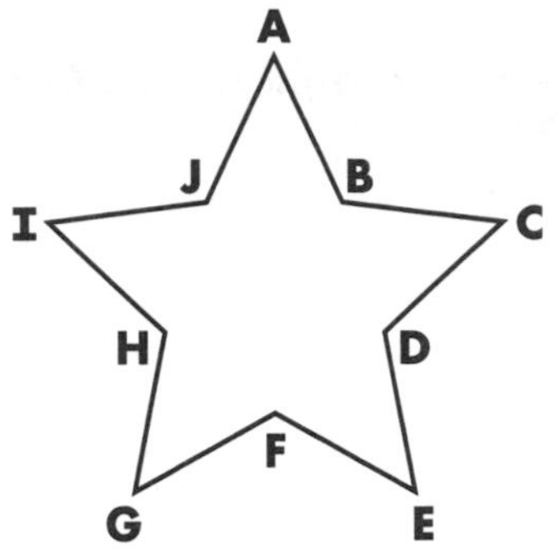

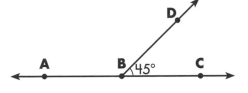

1. **Which angle from the figure above is an acute angle?**

   Ⓐ ∠ IJB

   Ⓑ ∠ HGF

   Ⓒ ∠ CDE

   Ⓓ None of these

2. **Which line segments in the figure above are parallel?**

   Ⓕ $\overline{HG}$ and $\overline{DE}$

   Ⓖ $\overline{IJ}$ and $\overline{BC}$

   Ⓗ $\overline{GF}$ and $\overline{JA}$

   Ⓙ The figure contains no parallel lines.

3. **How many obtuse angles does the figure above contain?**

   Ⓐ 5

   Ⓑ 10

   Ⓒ 15

   Ⓓ The figure contains no obtuse angles.

4. **Which angle measures 45°?**

   Ⓕ ∠ ABD

   Ⓖ ∠ DBC

   Ⓗ ∠ ABC

   Ⓙ None of these

5. **What is the measurement of ∠ DBA?**

   Ⓐ 45°

   Ⓑ 135°

   Ⓒ 180°

   Ⓓ Not enough information

6. **Which of the following is not a ray in the figure above?**

   Ⓕ $\overrightarrow{BA}$

   Ⓖ $\overrightarrow{BC}$

   Ⓗ $\overrightarrow{BD}$

   Ⓙ $\overrightarrow{DB}$

Lines and Angles

Directions: Follow the directions to answer each problem.

1. Draw $\overline{AB}$.

4. $\angle$ IJK is a right angle. Draw $\angle$ IJK.

2. Draw $\overleftrightarrow{CD}$.

5. $\overrightarrow{LM}$ and $\overrightarrow{MN}$ form an acute angle. Draw $\overrightarrow{LM}$ and $\overrightarrow{MN}$.

3. $\overleftrightarrow{EF}$ and $\overleftrightarrow{GH}$ are parallel to each other. Draw $\overleftrightarrow{EF}$ and $\overleftrightarrow{GH}$.

6. What is the name of the angle you drew above?

_____

Shapes and Figures

Directions: Fill in the circle for the correct answer to each problem.

1. Which of these shapes has an area of 20 square units?

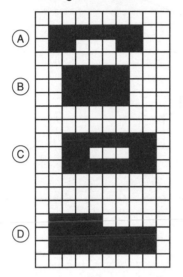

Ⓐ

Ⓑ

Ⓒ

Ⓓ

2. A triangle with no sides of equal length is called _____.

Ⓕ an isosceles triangle

Ⓖ an equilateral triangle

Ⓗ a right triangle

Ⓙ a scalene triangle

3. Which letter is symmetrical?

Ⓐ **J**

Ⓑ **P**

Ⓒ **G**

Ⓓ **T**

4. Which numbered rectangle is similar to rectangle A?

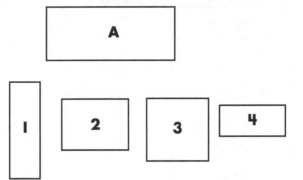

Ⓕ rectangle 1

Ⓖ rectangle 2

Ⓗ rectangle 3

Ⓙ rectangle 4

5. Below is a code. Use the code to figure out what word is spelled by the shapes in the box.

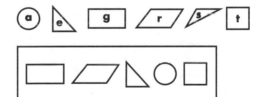

Ⓐ stars

Ⓑ great

Ⓒ greet

Ⓓ treat

6. A quadrilateral with 4 equal sides and 2 pairs of parallel sides is a _____.

Ⓕ rhombus

Ⓖ trapezoid

Ⓗ hexagon

Ⓙ rectangular prism

Name _____ Date _____

Shapes and Figures

Directions: Write the name of each polygon.

Polygon Name	Number of Sides
triangle	3
quadrilateral	4
pentagon	5
hexagon	6
heptagon	7
octagon	8
decagon	10
dodecagon	12

4.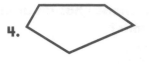

_____

5.

_____

1.

_____

6.

_____

2.

_____

7.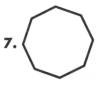

_____

3.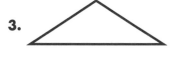

_____

8.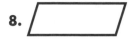

_____

Shapes and Figures

Directions: Write the letter of the polygon name in the blank next to the matching shape.

A. triangle	**D. hexagon**
B. quadrilateral	**E. heptagon**
C. pentagon	**F. octagon**

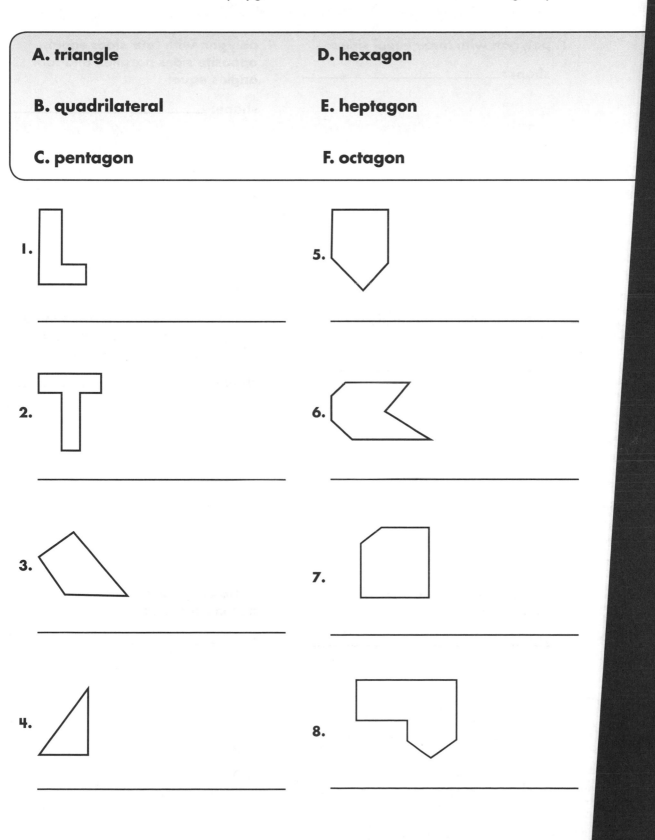

1. _____

2. _____

3. _____

4. _____

5. _____

6. _____

7. _____

8. _____

Shapes and Figures

Directions: Name and draw the described polygon.

1. polygon with three equal sides

shape: _____

4. polygon with four sides equal, opposite sides parallel, and four angles equal

shape: _____

2. polygon with opposite sides equal and four right angles

shape: _____

5. a three-dimensional shape with a polygon for a base and triangles with a common vertex

shape: _____

3. polygon with three sides of different lengths

shape: _____

6. completely curved three-dimensional shape

shape: _____

Shapes and Figures

Directions: Measure the angles and sides of the shapes. Write *congruent* or *similar* below each set of shapes based on your findings.

1. _____

2. _____

3. _____

4. _____

5. _____

6. _____

Congruent shapes have the same measures of angles and sides.

Similar shapes have the same measures of angles, but not of sides.

Shapes and Figures

Directions: Fill in the circle for the correct answer to each problem.

1. **Which line segment seems to be congruent to $\overline{AB}$?**

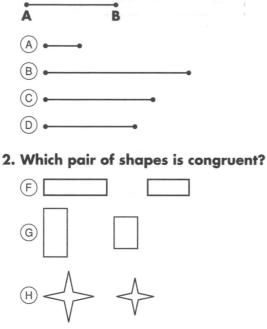

2. **Which pair of shapes is congruent?**

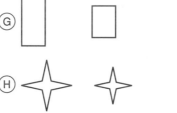

3. **Which shape is similar, but not congruent, to the shape below?**

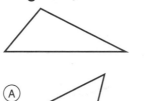

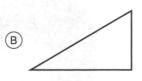

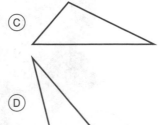

4. **Which pair of shapes is congruent?**

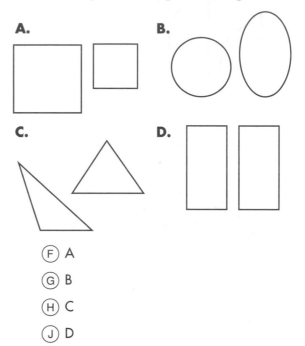

- (F) A
- (G) B
- (H) C
- (J) D

5. **Look at the shape below. Draw a congruent shape.**

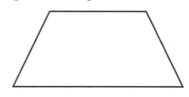

6. **Draw a shape that is similar, but not congruent, to the shape above.**

Name _____ Date _____

3-D Shapes

Directions: Fill in the circle for the correct answer to each problem.

1. **A basketball is shaped like a _____.**

   Ⓐ cylinder

   Ⓑ sphere

   Ⓒ cube

   Ⓓ rectangular prism

2. **Four faces of a pyramid are triangles. What shape is the fifth face?**

   Ⓕ triangle

   Ⓖ circle

   Ⓗ square

   Ⓙ rectangle

3. **How many faces does a cube have?**

   Ⓐ 2

   Ⓑ 4

   Ⓒ 6

   Ⓓ 8

4. **How many vertices does a cube have?**

   Ⓕ 4

   Ⓖ 6

   Ⓗ 8

   Ⓙ 12

5. **Which two shapes have the same number of flat sides?**

   Ⓐ cube and rectangular prism

   Ⓑ sphere and cylinder

   Ⓒ cone and cylinder

   Ⓓ pyramid and cube

6. **Which 2-D shape matches the 3-D shape below?**

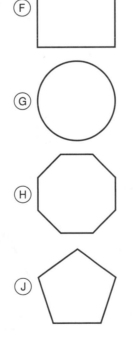

   Ⓕ

   Ⓖ

   Ⓗ

   Ⓙ

Name _____   Date _____

3-D Shapes

Directions: Next to each shape below, write *prism*, *pyramid*, or *neither* to show what type of three-dimensional object it is.

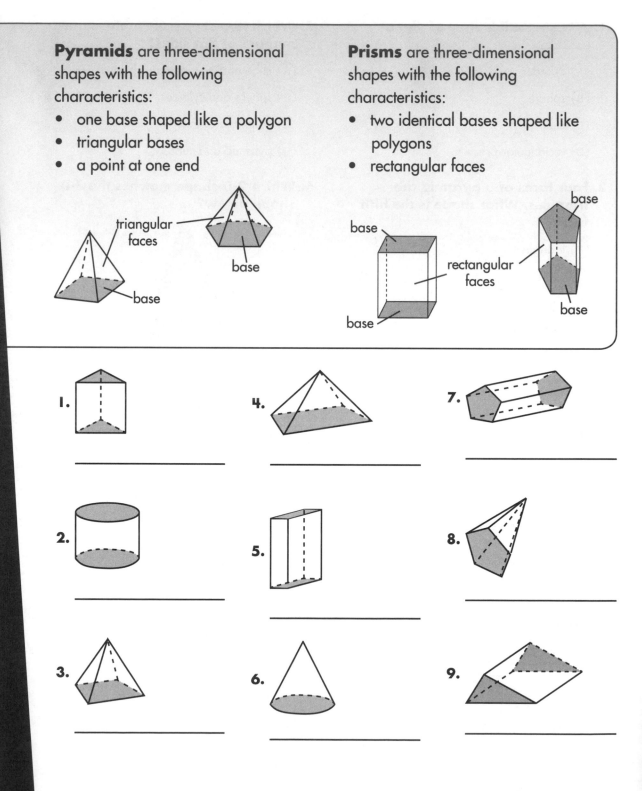

Pyramids are three-dimensional shapes with the following characteristics:
- one base shaped like a polygon
- triangular bases
- a point at one end

Prisms are three-dimensional shapes with the following characteristics:
- two identical bases shaped like polygons
- rectangular faces

1. _____

2. _____

3. _____

4. _____

5. _____

6. _____

7. _____

8. _____

9. _____

3-D Shapes

Directions: Solve each problem. Fill in the circle for the correct answer.

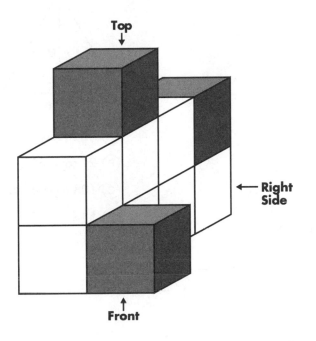

Top ↓

← **Right Side**

↑ **Front**

1. Which of these shows the right side view of the figure above?

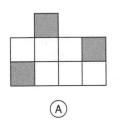
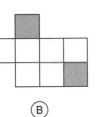
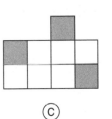
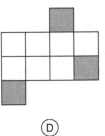

Ⓐ   Ⓑ   Ⓒ   Ⓓ

2. Which of these shows the front view of the figure above?

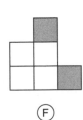
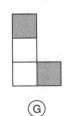
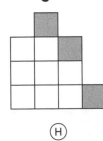
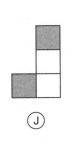

Ⓕ   Ⓖ   Ⓗ   Ⓙ

3. Which of these shows the top view of the figure above?

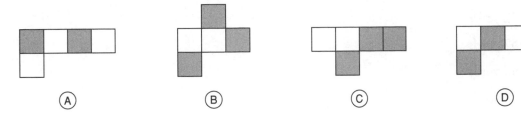

Ⓐ   Ⓑ   Ⓒ   Ⓓ

Perimeter, Area, and Volume

Directions: Find the area of each figure below.

1.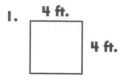
4 ft.
4 ft.

Ⓐ 20 square feet

Ⓑ 8 square feet

Ⓒ 16 square feet

Ⓓ 12 square feet

2.
5 cm
3 cm

Ⓕ 15 square centimeters

Ⓖ 8 square centimeters

Ⓗ 16 square centimeters

Ⓙ 4 square centimeters

3.
9 in.
12 in.

Ⓐ 42 square inches

Ⓑ 21 square inches

Ⓒ 108 square inches

Ⓓ 54 square inches

Directions: Find the perimeter of each figure below.

4.
7 m
6 m

Ⓕ 13 meters

Ⓖ 42 meters

Ⓗ 26 meters

Ⓙ 52 meters

5.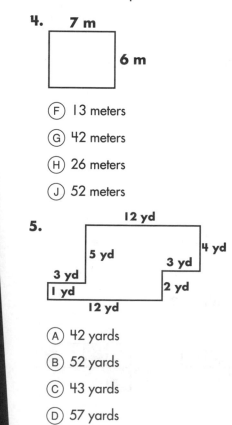
12 yd
5 yd
4 yd
3 yd
3 yd
1 yd
2 yd
12 yd

Ⓐ 42 yards

Ⓑ 52 yards

Ⓒ 43 yards

Ⓓ 57 yards

6. **Look at the circle. What does the line segment AB represent?**

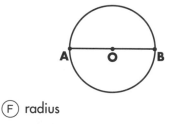

A   O   B

Ⓕ radius

Ⓖ diameter

Ⓗ perimeter

Ⓙ volume

Perimeter, Area, and Volume

Directions: Use the shapes below to develop the correct formulas.

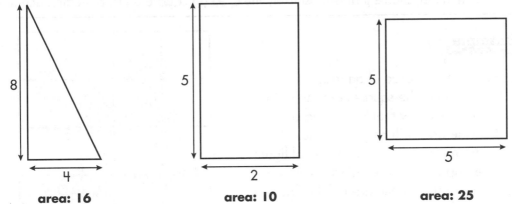

area: 16   area: 10   area: 25

1. Which of the following is the correct formula for finding the area of a right triangle?

- (A) base × height
- (B) $\frac{1}{2}$ base × height
- (C) base + height
- (D) $\frac{1}{2}$ base × $\frac{1}{2}$ height

3. Which of the following is the correct formula for finding the area of a square?

- (A) length^2
- (B) 4 × length
- (C) 2 × length
- (D) $\frac{1}{2}$ length × $\frac{1}{2}$ length

2. Which of the following is the correct formula for finding the area of a rectangle?

- (F) (length × 2) + (width × 2)
- (G) length + width
- (H) length × width
- (J) length^2

Directions: Find the area of the following shapes.

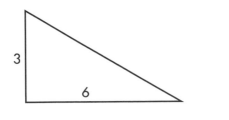

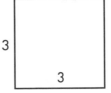

4. area _____

6. area _____

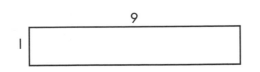

5. area _____

Perimeter, Area, and Volume

Directions: For each of the following figures, estimate the area of the shaded portion. Circle the number choice that is most likely the area (in square units) beneath each figure.

Example

You can estimate the area of an irregular shape by looking at the squares around it. In the example, you know that 4 full squares are covered, so the area will be greater than 4 square units. You also know that the total figure is not larger than 16 square units (4 units × 4 units). You can estimate the area of the figure is between 4 and 16 units.

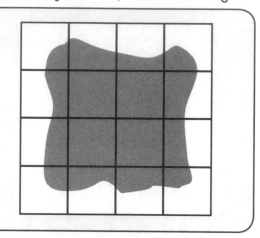

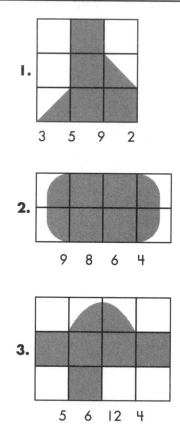

1.

3   5   9   2

2.

9   8   6   4

3.

5   6   12   4

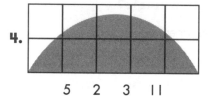

4.

5   2   3   11

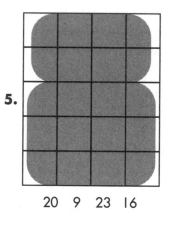

5.

20   9   23   16

Perimeter, Area, and Volume

Directions: Read the description of each shape, and determine its volume.

1. A rectangular prism has a length of 12 inches, a width of 12 inches, and a height of 5 inches. What is the volume?

   (A) 720 cubic inches

   (B) 144 cubic inches

   (C) 60 cubic inches

   (D) 29 cubic inches

2. A rectangular box is 53 centimeters long, 25 centimeters wide, and 15 centimeters high. What is the volume?

   (F) 1,170 cubic centimeters

   (G) 2,120 cubic centimeters

   (H) 19,875 cubic centimeters

   (J) 33,125 cubic centimeters

3. The roof of a building is shaped like a square. The perimeter of the roof measures 160 feet. The building is 60 feet tall. What is the building's volume?

   (A) 9,600 cubic feet

   (B) 96,000 cubic feet

   (C) 384,000 cubic feet

   (D) Not enough information

4. A rectangular shed has a volume of 144 cubic meters. The shed is 12 meters long and 4 meters wide. How tall is the shed?

   (F) 2 meters

   (G) 3 meters

   (H) 4 meters

   (J) Not enough information

5. A pool is 12 yards long, 7 yards wide, and 2 yards deep. How many cubic yards of water can it hold?

   (A) 168 cubic yards

   (B) 504 cubic yards

   (C) 1,512 cubic yards

   (D) 4,536 cubic yards

6. What is the volume of a cube that is 14 inches wide?

   (F) 2,744 cubic inches

   (G) 196 cubic inches

   (H) 1,764 cubic inches

   (J) Not enough information

Directions: The volume of a pyramid with a square base can be found using the following formula: $V = $ (the area of the base × the height) ÷ 3. Determine the volumes of the following pyramids.

7. The area of the pyramid's base is 25 square inches. The pyramid's height is 12 inches. What is the pyramid's volume?

   (A) 900 cubic inches

   (B) 300 cubic inches

   (C) 100 cubic inches

   (D) Not enough information

8. The pyramid's base is 4 feet wide. The pyramid is 6 feet tall. What is the pyramid's volume?

   (F) 288 cubic feet

   (G) 32 cubic feet

   (H) 8 cubic feet

   (J) Not enough information

Using Coordinates

Directions: Use the coordinate grid to answer the questions that follow.

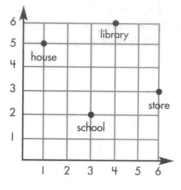

3. What type of movement do the figures in the grid below indicate?

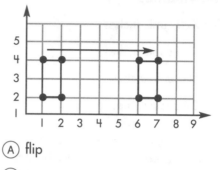

Ⓐ flip

Ⓑ turn

Ⓒ slide

Ⓓ rotate

1. Yvonne left (1, 5) at 8:30. She made a quick stop at (6, 3), and then headed to (3, 2). Later that afternoon, she picked up a few items at (4, 6). Which list shows the places Yvonne went in the correct order?

Ⓐ house, store, library, school

Ⓑ library, school, store, house

Ⓒ house, store, school, library

Ⓓ house, school, store, library

4. What are the coordinates of the four points in the second rectangle?

Ⓕ (6, 2), (7, 2), (7, 4), (6, 4)

Ⓖ (1,2), (2, 2), (2, 4), (1, 4)

Ⓗ (6, 3), (7, 3), (7, 4), (6, 4)

Ⓙ (6, 2), (7, 2), (7, 5), (6, 5)

2. Which sequence of ordered pairs would allow you to move from the school to the library?

Ⓕ (2,3), (3,3), (4,3), (5,3), (6,3), (6,4)

Ⓖ (3,2), (3,3), (3,4), (3,5), (2,5), (1,5)

Ⓗ (3,2), (3,3), (3,4), (3,5), (3,6), (4,6)

Ⓙ (2,3), (2,4), (2,5), (2,6), (3,6), (4,6)

Don't be nervous!

It's important that your sleep well the night before your test.

Using Coordinates

Directions: Write the coordinate pairs for each figure plotted.

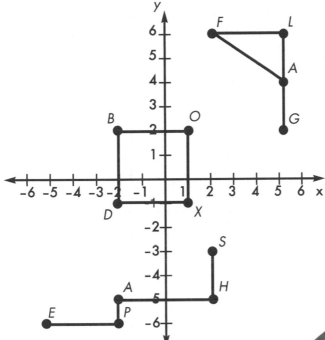

1. FLAG

F = (,   )

L = (,   )

A = (,   )

G = (,   )

2. BOXD

B = (,   )

O = (,   )

X = (,   )

D = (,   )

3. SHAPE

S = (,   )

H = (,   )

A = (,   )

P = (,   )

E = (,   )

The first number in an ordered pair shows the horizontal distance from zero. A **positive** number means to move **right**. A **negative** number means to move **left**.

The second number shows the vertical distance from zero. A **positive** number means to move **up**. A **negative** number means to move **down**.

Using Coordinates

188

Directions: Follow the directions.

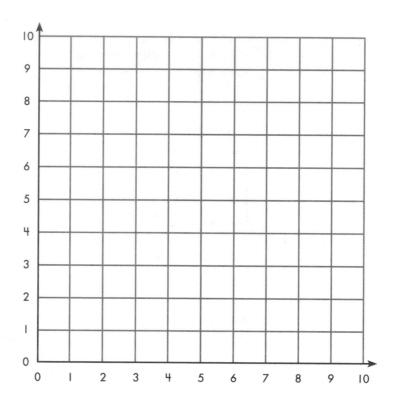

1. Draw a line from (7, 4) to (1, 4).

2. Draw a line from (1, 4) to (7, 10).

3. Draw a line from (7, 10) to (10, 4).

4. Draw a line from (10, 4) to (7, 4).

5. Draw a line from (7, 4) to (7, 2).

6. Draw a line from (7, 2) to (1, 2).

7. Draw a line from (1, 2) to (3, 0).

8. Draw a line from (3, 0) to (8, 0).

9. Draw a line from (8, 0) to (10, 2).

10. Draw a line from (10, 2) to (7, 2).

What object have you drawn in the coordinate grid?

_____

Sample Test 8: Geometry

Directions: Read and work each problem. Choose the correct answer, and mark it.

Example

Two lines that do not intersect and are the same distance apart at every point are said to be

- Ⓐ congruent.
- Ⓑ parallel.
- Ⓒ right angles.
- Ⓓ perpendicular.

Answer: B

---

1. Which two line segments are congruent?

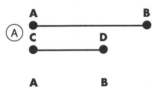

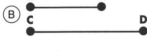

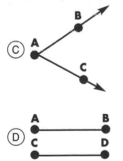

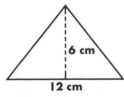

2. What is the area of this triangle?

6 cm
12 cm

- Ⓕ 72 square centimeters
- Ⓖ 48 square centimeters
- Ⓗ 36 square centimeters
- Ⓙ 18 square centimeters

3. What is the volume of this figure?

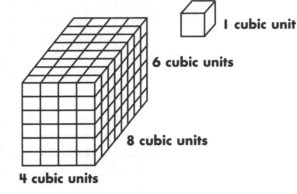

1 cubic unit
6 cubic units
8 cubic units
4 cubic units

- Ⓐ 18 cubic units
- Ⓑ 192 cubic units
- Ⓒ 32 cubic units
- Ⓓ 48 cubic units

4. Glen is planting a flower garden in the shape of a triangle. He has placed 80 meters of fencing around the garden. Two sides of the garden are the same length—25 meters. What is the length of the third side?

- Ⓕ 30 meters
- Ⓖ 40 meters
- Ⓗ 25 meters
- Ⓙ 50 meters

5. Which shape contains the most angles?

- Ⓐ a quadrilateral
- Ⓑ a hexagon
- Ⓒ a pentagon
- Ⓓ an octagon

GO

Sample Test 8: Geometry

Directions: Use this graph to answer the questions that follow.

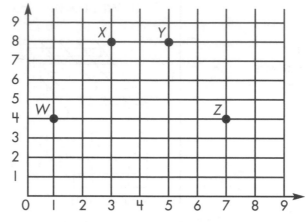

6. If you moved one unit at a time and did not move diagonally, which two of the following points would be the farthest from each other?

(F) W and Y

(G) Y and Z

(H) W and Z

(J) W and X

7. What point is at (5,8)?

(A) W

(B) X

(C) Y

(D) Z

8. How would you have to move to go from point W to point X?

(F) −2 units horizontally, +4 units vertically

(G) −2 units horizontally, −4 units vertically

(H) +2 units horizontally, −4 units vertically

(J) +2 units horizontally, +4 units vertically

9. If you connected point W and X, points X and Y, points Y and Z, and points Z and W, what shape would you have?

(A) a rhombus

(B) a trapezoid

(C) a hexagon

(D) a pentagon

10. Which of these does not show a line symmetry?

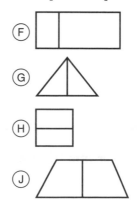

Name _____ Date _____

Sample Test 8: Geometry

Directions: Read each problem. Choose the correct answer, and mark it.

11. Which of the figures below is a sphere?

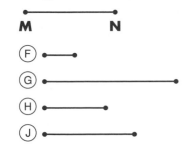

12. Which of these shows the top view of the figure below?

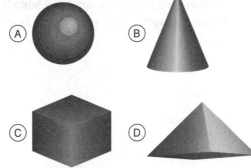

Ⓕ   Ⓖ   Ⓗ   Ⓙ

13. A rectangle has a length of 15 and a width of 5. What is the area?

Ⓐ 20 square units

Ⓑ 75 square units

Ⓒ 3 square units

Ⓓ 40 square units

14. Which line segment seems to be congruent to MN?

M •——————• N

Ⓕ •——•

Ⓖ •——————————•

Ⓗ •————•

Ⓙ •————————•

15. Which two shapes are congruent?

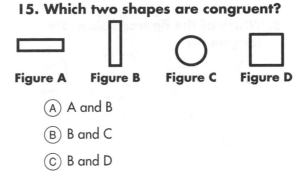

Figure A   Figure B   Figure C   Figure D

Ⓐ A and B

Ⓑ B and C

Ⓒ B and D

Ⓓ A and C

16. Which point is at (1, 4)?

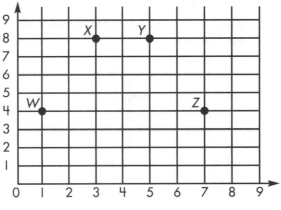

Ⓕ W

Ⓖ X

Ⓗ Y

Ⓙ Z

17. Which points have the same y coordinate?

Ⓐ X and Y; W and Z

Ⓑ X and W; Y and Z

Ⓒ X and Z; Y and W

Ⓓ Y and Z

Sample Test 8: Geometry

Directions: Read and work each problem. Choose the correct answer, and mark it.

18. Which of the figures below are congruent?

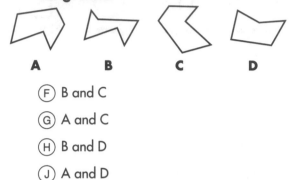

A   **B**   **C**   **D**

(F) B and C

(G) A and C

(H) B and D

(J) A and D

19. What is the approximate area of this shape?

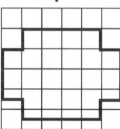

(A) 16 square units

(B) 18 square units

(C) 20 square units

(D) 23 square units

20. What is the area of this rectangle?

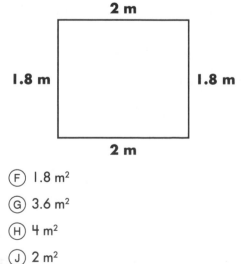

2 m

1.8 m   1.8 m

2 m

(F) 1.8 m²

(G) 3.6 m²

(H) 4 m²

(J) 2 m²

21. A three-dimensional figure with rectangular faces and two identical bases shaped like polygons is a _____.

(A) pyramid

(B) sphere

(C) cylinder

(D) prism

22. What is the measure of a right angle?

(F) 45°

(G) 360°

(H) 180°

(J) 90°

23. How many faces does a cylinder have?

(A) 2

(B) 3

(C) 4

(D) None

24. What is the perimeter of a rectangle with sides 20 mm and 10 mm long?

(F) 30 mm

(G) 50 mm

(H) 60 mm

(J) 200 mm

STOP

Measuring

Directions: Solve each problem. Fill in the circle for the correct answer.

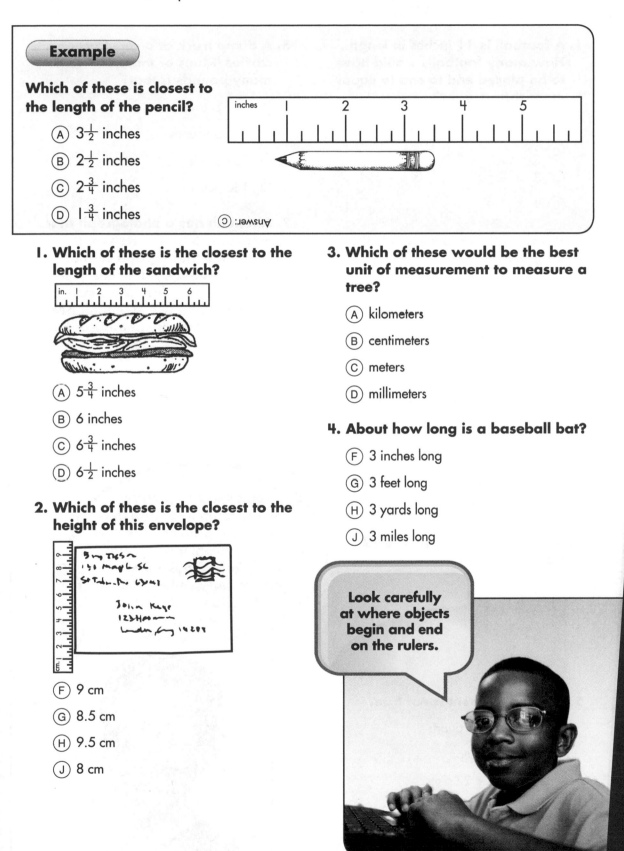

Example

Which of these is closest to the length of the pencil?

(A) $3\frac{1}{2}$ inches

(B) $2\frac{1}{2}$ inches

(C) $2\frac{3}{4}$ inches

(D) $1\frac{3}{4}$ inches

Answer: C

1. Which of these is the closest to the length of the sandwich?

(A) $5\frac{3}{4}$ inches

(B) 6 inches

(C) $6\frac{3}{4}$ inches

(D) $6\frac{1}{2}$ inches

2. Which of these is the closest to the height of this envelope?

(F) 9 cm

(G) 8.5 cm

(H) 9.5 cm

(J) 8 cm

3. Which of these would be the best unit of measurement to measure a tree?

(A) kilometers

(B) centimeters

(C) meters

(D) millimeters

4. About how long is a baseball bat?

(F) 3 inches long

(G) 3 feet long

(H) 3 yards long

(J) 3 miles long

Look carefully at where objects begin and end on the rulers.

Name _____ Date _____

Measuring

Directions: Solve each problem. Fill in the circle for the correct answer.

1. **A football is 11 inches in length. How many footballs would have to be placed end to end to equal more than 1 yard?**

   (A) 1

   (B) 2

   (C) 3

   (D) 4

2. **Which of these measures is the longest?**

   (F) 1 kilometer

   (G) 1 millimeter

   (H) 1 meter

   (J) 1 centimeter

3. **About how long is a city block?**

   (A) 120 meters

   (B) 55 centimeters

   (C) 48 kilometers

   (D) 100 millimeters

4. **What fraction of a yard is 12 inches?**

   (F) $\frac{1}{3}$

   (G) $\frac{1}{4}$

   (H) $\frac{2}{3}$

   (J) $\frac{1}{12}$

5. **Which statement is not true?**

   (A) 2 gallons > 6 quarts

   (B) 3 pints = 6 cups

   (C) 10 quarts < 22 pints

   (D) 5,000 milligrams = 50 grams

6. **A dump truck at a construction site carries 4 tons of material. How many pounds is that?**

   (F) 800 pounds

   (G) 8,000 pounds

   (H) 80 pounds

   (J) 180 pounds

7. **Jeremiah has a photograph that measures 5" x 7." He wants to frame the photograph so that it is surrounded by 3 inches of mat board on all sides. What size picture frame will Jeremiah need to accommodate the photograph and mat?**

   (A) 5" x 7"

   (B) 8" x 10"

   (C) 9" x 11"

   (D) 11" x 13"

Sometimes, you don't have to compute to find the answer to a problem. For this type of problem, it is especially important to look for key words and numbers that will help you find the answer.

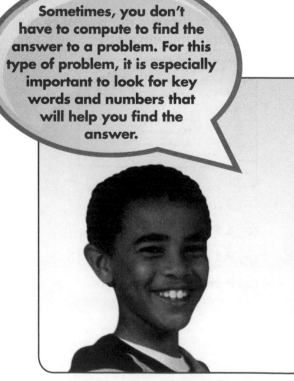

Measuring

Directions: Solve each problem. Fill in the circle for the correct answer.

1. **Which of the following shows the correct order from largest to smallest?**

   (A) centimeter, millimeter, meter, kilometer

   (B) millimeter, centimeter, meter, kilometer

   (C) millimeter, centimeter, kilometer, meter

   (D) kilometer, meter, centimeter, millimeter

2. **If you wanted to measure the length of a canoe, you would most likely use _____.**

   (F) feet

   (G) inches

   (H) centimeters

   (J) kilometers

3. **A child who is 38 inches tall is**

   (A) a little less than 1 yard tall.

   (B) a little more than 1 yard tall.

   (C) almost four feet tall.

   (D) a little more than 4 feet tall.

4. **A map scale shows that 1 inch equals 5 miles. The distance between Falls Valley and Waterside is 3.5 inches. How many miles is it between these two towns?**

   (F) 12 miles

   (G) 15 miles

   (H) 16.5 miles

   (J) 17.5 miles

5. **To measure the weight of a banana, Aaron should use _____.**

   (A) inches

   (B) liters

   (C) gallons

   (D) ounces

6. **Layla plans to run a 5-mile race. How many feet is the race?**

   (F) 5,280 feet

   (G) 26,400 feet

   (H) 10,000 feet

   (J) Not enough information

7. **A millimeter is _____.**

   (A) 10 meters

   (B) $\frac{1}{10}$ of a meter

   (C) $\frac{1}{100}$ of a meter

   (D) $\frac{1}{1,000}$ of a meter

8. **To measure the amount of water in a bathtub, Kylie should use _____.**

   (F) ounces

   (G) feet

   (H) gallons

   (J) pints

MATH 196

Comparing Units of Measurement

Directions: Solve each problem. Fill in the circle for the correct answer.

1. 1 kilogram =
   - (A) 100 milligrams
   - (B) 10 grams
   - (C) 100 grams
   - (D) 1,000 grams

2. **Takashi's book is 30 mm thick. How many centimeters thick is the book?**
   - (F) 0.3 cm
   - (G) 3 cm
   - (H) 33 cm
   - (J) 300 cm

3. **Eric can throw a ball about 2,300 cm. How many meters can he throw the ball?**
   - (A) 2.3 meters
   - (B) 23,000 meters
   - (C) 230 meters
   - (D) 23 meters

4. **A comb weighs about 35 grams. How many milligrams is that?**
   - (F) 3.5 mg
   - (G) 35,000 mg
   - (H) 350 mg
   - (J) 3,500 mg

5. **Olivia is mailing a puzzle that is 34 cm long. Which length of box will be long enough for the puzzle?**
   - (A) 14 inches
   - (B) 12 inches
   - (C) 10 inches
   - (D) 9 inches

6. **A football field is 100 yards long. About how many inches is that?**
   - (F) 800 inches
   - (G) 3,600 inches
   - (H) 33 inches
   - (J) 400 inches

7. 75 mm =
   - (A) 75 m
   - (B) 0.75 m
   - (C) 0.075 m
   - (D) 7.5 m

8. 6 km =
   - (F) 6,000 m
   - (G) 600 m
   - (H) 60 m
   - (J) 6 m

Comparing Units of Measurement

Directions: Use the chart to answer the questions. Fill in the circle for the correct answer.

1 gallon = 4 quarts	1 quart = 2 pints
1 pint = 2 cups	1 cup = 8 ounces

1. A recipe calls for 6 quarts of water. How many gallons is that?

(A) 1 gallon

(B) $1\frac{1}{2}$ gallons

(C) 2 gallons

(D) $2\frac{1}{2}$ gallons

2. A faucet was leaking water at a rate of 3 cups per day. A total of 9 pints of water leaked from the faucet. How many days did the faucet leak before it was repaired?

(F) 2 days

(G) 4 days

(H) 6 days

(J) 9 days

3. 4 gallons =

(A) 40 cups

(B) 8 quarts

(C) 16 pints

(D) 64 cups

4. If one drop of water is equal to 1 milliliter, how many drops of water are in a container holding 3 liters of water?

(F) 30

(G) 300

(H) 3,000

(J) 30,000

5. Fuel is stored in a 12-kiloliter tank. How many liters does the tank hold when it is full?

(A) 1,200 liters

(B) 12,000 liters

(C) 120 liters

(D) 120,000 liters

MATH
198

Comparing Units of Measurement

Directions: The metric system is based on multiples of 10. Use the metric conversion chart to help you answer the questions that follow.

Metric Units of Length

1 centimeter (cm) = 10 millimeters (mm)

1 meter (m) = 100 centimeters (cm)

1 kilometer (km) = 1,000 meters (m)

Metric Units of Capacity

1 liter (L) = 1,000 milliliters (mL)

1 decaliter (daL) = 10 liters (L)

1 hectoliter (hL) = 100 liters (L)

1 kiloliter (kL) = 1,000 liters (L)

Metric Units of Mass

1 gram (g) = 1,000 milligrams (mg)

1 decagram (dag) = 10 grams

1 hectogram (hg) = 100 grams

1 kilogram (kg) = 1,000 grams (g)

1 metric ton (t) = 1,000 kilograms (kg)

1. **Jesse measured her computer screen. It was 40 centimeters wide. How many millimeters is this?**

   _____

2. **Devon has a container that is 24 centimeters long. He found an item that is 186 millimeters long. Will it fit in the container?**

   _____

3. **Jazmin climbed 2.5 meters up a ladder. How many centimeters is this?**

   _____

4. **Jackson's art project is 45 centimeters by 90 centimeters. Will it fit into a box that is 0.5 meter by 1 meter?**

   _____

5. **Which statement is true?**

   (A) 1 kilometer > 800 meters

   (B) 300 centimeters > 3 meters

   (C) $\frac{1}{2}$ kiloliter > 600 L

   (D) 20,000 milligrams = 200 grams

6. **Which of the following equals 2,000 meters?**

   (F) 200 km

   (G) 0.2 km

   (H) 20 km

   (J) 2 km

Comparing Units of Measurement

Directions: Use the metric conversion chart on the previous page to help you answer the questions that follow.

1. 3,000 mL = _____ L

2. 4 daL = _____ L

3. 6 kL = _____ L

4. 10 kL = _____ daL

5. 25 hL = _____ daL

6. 700 mL = _____ L

7. 80 hL = _____ kL

8. 10 kg = _____ g

9. 1 hg = _____ dag

10. 2,000 g = _____ kg

11. 500 g = _____ kg

12. 70 hg = _____ kg

13. 2 g = _____ mg

14. 3 t = _____ kg

Money

Directions: Solve each problem. Fill in the circle for the correct answer.

Example

Regina has $2.33 in coins. She has 6 quarters, 5 dimes, 2 nickels, and the rest in pennies. How many pennies does Regina have?

Ⓐ 12

Ⓑ 33

Ⓒ 17

Ⓓ 23

Answer: Ⓓ

---

1. Scott and Tess have a dog-walking business. They earn $0.75 every 15 minutes for each dog that they walk. If they take 5 dogs on a one-hour walk, how much money will they earn?

Ⓐ $3.75

Ⓑ $11.00

Ⓒ $15.00

Ⓓ $9.00

2. Isabella buys her lunch at school 4 days a week. Lunch costs $2.25 per day. If Isabella pays for two weeks worth of lunches in advance, how much change will she get from a $20 bill?

Ⓕ $2.00

Ⓖ $3.75

Ⓗ $6.50

Ⓙ $11.00

3. Which of these statements is true?

Ⓐ 25 dimes = $2.75

Ⓑ 15 quarters = $4.25

Ⓒ 100 nickels = $5.00

Ⓓ 20 quarters = $6.00

4. Mr. Riga buys two new shirts. Each shirt costs $32.00. The store is having a sale, so Mr. Riga receives a 15% discount. How much money does he save?

Ⓕ $8.60

Ⓖ $9.40

Ⓗ $9.60

Ⓙ $10.20

5. How much was Mr. Riga's total for the shirts in question 4?

Ⓐ $54.40

Ⓑ $54.00

Ⓒ $56.40

Ⓓ $55.00

6. Mr. Riga decides to go back to the store and stock up on shirts for next fall. He buys four more. What is his total savings on the six shirts?

Ⓕ $26.20

Ⓖ $27.80

Ⓗ $28.00

Ⓙ $28.80

Money

Directions: Solve each problem. Fill in the circle for the correct answer.

1. **Marisol buys a new laptop case for $13.26. She pays with one $10 bill and one $5 bill. How much change will she get back?**

   (A) $1.84

   (B) $1.74

   (C) $0.74

   (D) $2.24

2. **Mr. Lepinski goes out for breakfast. His bill totals $8.40. He wants to leave a 20% tip. What tip should he leave?**

   (F) $0.84

   (G) $1.26

   (H) $1.68

   (J) Not enough information

3. **You have coins that total $0.68. What coins do you have?**

   (A) 1 quarter, 3 dimes, 3 nickels, and 3 pennies

   (B) 2 quarters, 1 dime, 1 nickel, and 3 pennies

   (C) 6 dimes, 1 nickel, and 8 pennies

   (D) 3 dimes, 4 nickels, and 28 pennies

4. **Esther and Ethan go to the store to buy ingredients to make a few things for the bake sale. They purchase a bag of flour, a pound of butter, 6 apples, and a bottle of vanilla. Which of the following is the most likely amount they spent?**

   (F) $42.00

   (G) $3.00

   (H) $29.00

   (J) $12.00

5. **Ms. Rogers buys a book for $11.95 and a magazine for $4.50. She receives $0.55 in change. Which combination of bills and coins did she give to the cashier?**

   (A) Three $5 bills, one $1 bill, 2 quarters, and 6 dimes

   (B) One $10 bill, one $5 bill, one $1 bill, and 5 quarters

   (C) One $10 bill, one $5 bill, two $1 bills

   (D) Three $5 bills, one $1 bill, 2 quarters, 5 dimes

6. **Coach Wu is going to buy new t-shirts for the girls' track team. There are 11 girls on the team, and the t-shirts cost $12.48 each. Coach has $125 dollars in the budget for shirts. How much more does he need?**

   (F) $12.28

   (G) $12.88

   (H) $13.08

   (J) $11.28

7. **Vincent has been saving for a new guitar. His grandparents told him that for every dollar he saves, they'll contribute $0.50. Vincent has saved $104. What will Vincent's grandparents contribute?**

   (A) $52

   (B) $50

   (C) $64

   (D) $104

MATH
202

Money

Directions: Use the table below to solve each problem. Fill in the circle for the correct answer.

Frank's Fresh Fruit Stand

Kiwis: $0.94 each	Bananas: $0.49/pound	Apples: $0.78/pound
Oranges: $0.74/pound	Pineapples: $3.15 each	Watermelon: $0.69/pound
Blueberries: $1.79/pint	Strawberries: $2.75/pound	Grapes: $3.65/bag

---

1. Holly bought 2 pounds of strawberries, a 6-pound watermelon, a bag of grapes, and 2 pints of blueberries. What was her total?

   (A) $15.87

   (B) $16.87

   (C) $16.97

   (D) $17.96

2. Mr. and Mrs. Patel bought a pineapple, 3 pounds of oranges, 6 kiwis, and 4 pounds of bananas. They paid with a $20 bill. How much did they receive in change?

   (F) $7.03

   (G) $8.13

   (H) $11.87

   (J) $12.97

3. Luis has three $1 bills, 14 quarters, 8 dimes, and 4 nickels. What is the largest watermelon he can buy?

   (A) a 6-pound watermelon

   (B) an 8-pound watermelon

   (C) a 10-pound watermelon

   (D) a 12-pound watermelon

4. Frank is running a special today. Any customer who spends more than $20 receives 10% off his or her total. How much does Madeline pay for 6 pounds of apples, an 8-pound watermelon, 2 pints of blueberries, a pineapple, 5 kiwis, and 2 bags of grapes?

   (F) $26.03

   (G) $28.93

   (H) $31.83

   (J) $20.90

5. Henry spent exactly $12.80. He bought only grapes and strawberries. How much of each did he buy?

   (A) 3 bags of grapes and 1 pound of strawberries

   (B) 2 bags of grapes and 2 pounds of strawberries

   (C) 1 bag of grapes and 3 pounds of strawberries

   (D) 3 bags of grapes and $\frac{1}{2}$ pound of strawberries

Time and Temperature

Directions: Solve each problem. Fill in the circle for the correct answer.

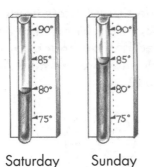

Saturday   Sunday

1. How did the temperature change between Saturday and Sunday? On Sunday, it was

- Ⓐ 5 degrees cooler than Saturday.
- Ⓑ 10 degrees cooler than Saturday.
- Ⓒ 5 degrees warmer than Saturday.
- Ⓓ 10 degrees warmer than Saturday.

2. The graph shows the daily temperature in Holton City. If the pattern continues, what will the temperature be on Friday?

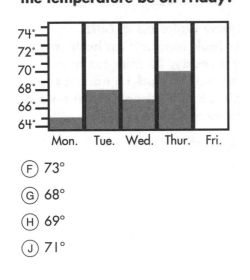

- Ⓕ 73°
- Ⓖ 68°
- Ⓗ 69°
- Ⓙ 71°

3. On the Fahrenheit scale, what is the temperature for the freezing point of water?

- Ⓐ 32°F
- Ⓑ 0°F
- Ⓒ 57°F
- Ⓓ 24°F

4. What time will this clock show in 45 minutes?

- Ⓕ 4:05
- Ⓖ 4:00
- Ⓗ 4:15
- Ⓙ 4:20

5. Baxter begins his guitar lesson at 3:00. His lesson lasts for 45 minutes. Before going home, he plays basketball for 35 minutes. It will take him 20 minutes to walk home. At what time will Baxter arrive at home?

- Ⓐ 4:55
- Ⓑ 4:40
- Ⓒ 5:15
- Ⓓ 5:05

6. What temperature does this thermometer show?

- Ⓕ 87°F
- Ⓖ 82°F
- Ⓗ 80°F
- Ⓙ 78°F

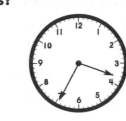

Time and Temperature

Directions: Solve each problem. Fill in the circle for the correct answer.

1. How many seconds are in 4 hours?

   (A) 1,400

   (B) 240

   (C) 24,000

   (D) 14,400

2. What temperature will this thermometer show if the temperature rises 15°?

   (F) 0°F

   (G) 5°F

   (H) 10°F

   (J) 15°F

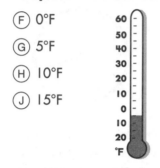

3. The temperature on Monday was 36°. On Tuesday, it was 42°, on Wednesday it was 48°, and on Thursday it was 40°. What was the average temperature for the 4 days?

   (A) 38°

   (B) 40°

   (C) 41.5°

   (D) 44.5°

4. When Cassidy gets home at 4:18, Brie tells her that Aunt Bess called half an hour ago. Which clock shows what time Aunt Bess called?

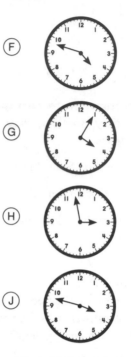

   (F)

   (G)

   (H)

   (J)

5. Drew woke up at 6:45. It took him half an hour to get ready, 20 minutes to eat breakfast, and 15 minutes to ride his bike to school. What time did he arrive?

   (A) 7:45

   (B) 7:50

   (C) 7:25

   (D) 8:05

Estimating Measurement

Directions: Draw a line from the description on the left to the approximate length on the right.

1. length of a pen	0.25 mile
2. length of a paper clip	20,000 feet
3. one lap on a track surrounding a football field	13 centimeters
4. length of a car	1.25 inches
5. elevation of the tallest mountain in Alaska	4 meters

Directions: Solve each problem. Fill in the circle for the correct answer.

6. A hot dog weighs _____.

- (F) a few pounds
- (G) a few ounces
- (H) a few grams
- (J) a few milligrams

Do two answer choices look a lot alike? One of them is probably correct!

7. Aisha wants to run in the Fort Worth 10,000, a 10,000-meter race. The farthest Aisha has ever run before is half that distance. In kilometers, what is the greatest distance Aisha has ever run before?

- (A) 5 km
- (B) 10 km
- (C) 50 km
- (D) 1,000 km

Estimating Measurement

Directions: Read each problem. Fill in the circle for the correct answer.

1. Which measurement is about the same as the width of a piece of twine?

(A) 1 meter

(B) 1 kilometer

(C) 1 centimeter

(D) 1 millimeter

2. About how long is a school bus?

(F) 12 meters

(G) 55 centimeters

(H) 48 kilometers

(J) 100 millimeters

3. About how much does a loaf of bread weigh?

(A) 500 ounces

(B) 500 grams

(C) 500 milligrams

(D) 500 kilograms

4. This fingernail is about 1 cm wide. About how many centimeters long is this paper clip?

(F) 1 cm

(G) 2 cm

(H) 3 cm

(J) 4 cm

About 1 cm

5. About how much paint is there in a bucket of paint?

(A) 4 milliliters

(B) 4 liters

(C) 4 kiloliters

(D) 4 cups

6. How much does a car weigh?

(F) about 2,000 ounces

(G) about 200 pounds

(H) about 2 tons

(J) about 2,000 grams

7. There is a bottle of juice in the Gomez's refrigerator. Most of it is gone, but there is enough left for Ana's breakfast. About how much is left?

(A) 1 gallon

(B) 32 ounces

(C) 8 ounces

(D) $\frac{1}{2}$ liter

Sample Test 9: Measurement

Directions: Solve each problem. Fill in the circle for the correct answer.

Example

3 cups =

- (A) 1 pint
- (B) 24 ounces
- (C) 16 ounces
- (D) 1 quart

Answer: (B)

---

1. This clock shows the time Tina's soccer game ended. It took 15 minutes to help pack up the equipment and then 20 minutes to arrive at the pizza parlor. At what time did Tina and her teammates arrive at the pizza parlor?

- (A) 4:50
- (B) 5:05
- (C) 4:55
- (D) 5:00

2. Which of the following equals 27 cm?

- (F) 270 mm
- (G) 2.7 m
- (H) 270 m
- (J) 2.7 mm

3. A penny weighs about 2.5 grams. How many milligrams does that equal?

- (A) 2.5
- (B) 2,500
- (C) 250
- (D) 25,000

4. Which of these would be the best unit of measurement to measure a ballpoint pen?

- (F) miles
- (G) yards
- (H) inches
- (J) feet

5. Sofia wanted to buy a new basket for her bike. The basket cost $16. Sofia saved $2.50 a week. How many weeks did she need to save to buy the basket?

- (A) 6 weeks
- (B) 7 weeks
- (C) 8 weeks
- (D) 9 weeks

6. Anatole attended a comic book convention. At 11:45, he left to get lunch. He wanted to be back to meet a friend at 1:10. How much time did he have for lunch?

- (F) 1 hour 15 minutes
- (G) 1 hour 10 minutes
- (H) 1 hour 25 minutes
- (J) 1 hour 30 minutes

7. At which of the following temperatures would you be most likely to go to the beach?

- (A) 30°C
- (B) 4°C
- (C) 52°F
- (D) 18°F

GO

Sample Test 9: Measurement

Name _____   Date _____

Directions: Solve each problem. Fill in the circle for the correct answer.

8. **Which of these would be the best unit to measure the dimensions of a room?**

   Ⓕ inches

   Ⓖ yards

   Ⓗ kilometers

   Ⓙ centimeters

9. **Samantha purchased $6\frac{1}{4}$ yards of fabric. How many inches of fabric is that?**

   Ⓐ 264 inches

   Ⓑ 212 inches

   Ⓒ 188 inches

   Ⓓ 225 inches

10. **Which of these statements is not true?**

    Ⓕ 36 quarters = $9.00

    Ⓖ 130 dimes = $13.00

    Ⓗ 85 nickels = $17.00

    Ⓙ 7 quarters = $1.75

11. **How many meters are in 1 kilometer?**

    Ⓐ 10

    Ⓑ 100

    Ⓒ 1,000

    Ⓓ 10,000

12. **Erik's mom asks him to buy 6 pints of blueberries at the farmer's market. The blueberries come in quart containers. How many quarts does Erik need?**

    Ⓕ 3 quarts

    Ⓖ 6 quarts

    Ⓗ 2 quarts

    Ⓙ Not enough information

13. **What time will this clock show in 50 minutes?**

    Ⓐ 2:45

    Ⓑ 2:40

    Ⓒ 1:35

    Ⓓ 2:35

    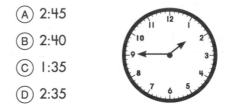

14. **Kylie ran 3 miles on Tuesday. How many feet did she run?**

    Ⓕ 500 feet

    Ⓖ 10,000 feet

    Ⓗ 15,840 feet

    Ⓙ 41,250 feet

15. **Sanjana made a painting that measures 22 inches by 18 inches. Which of the following frames would be large enough for her to use?**

    Ⓐ 22 in. by 16 in.

    Ⓑ 26 in. by 12 in.

    Ⓒ 20 in. by 20 in.

    Ⓓ 24 in. by 20 in.

GO

Ready to Test • Fifth Grade

Sample Test 9: Measurement

Sample Test 9: Measurement

Directions: Read and solve each problem. Fill in the circle for the correct answer.

16. A sheet of notebook paper is about _____ long.

(F) 6 cm

(G) 30 cm

(H) 25 mm

(J) $\frac{1}{2}$ yd.

17. The thermometer below shows the temperature at 9:45 on Tuesday morning. A storm rolled in, and the temperature dropped 7 degrees. By late afternoon, it had increased 14 degrees. What is the temperature now?

(A) 74°F

(B) 69°F

(C) 71°F

(D) 70°F

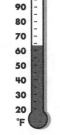

18. Mariah raises chickens on her family's farm. She sells a dozen eggs for $4.00. If she made $92 last weekend, how many eggs did she sell?

(F) 25

(G) 276

(H) 23

(J) 256

19. Antonio has $6.47 in coins. He has 18 quarters, 2 dimes, 37 pennies, and the rest in nickels. How many nickels does Antonio have?

(A) 15

(B) 18

(C) 27

(D) 28

20. The most likely unit for measuring the amount of water in a bathtub is _____.

(F) pints

(G) ounces

(H) gallons

(J) milliliters

21. 6,000 grams = _____ kilograms

(A) 6

(B) 60

(C) 600

(D) 6,000

STOP

Probability

Directions: Solve each problem. Fill in the circle for the correct answer.

Example

In the group of shapes, the odds of picking a square over a triangle are 3 to 1. What are the odds of choosing a circle over a square?

Ⓐ 1 to 5

Ⓑ 3 to 5

Ⓒ 5 to 3

Ⓓ 5 to 1

Answer: C

Use the information in the box to answer the questions that follow.

1. The tiles above are in a bag. If you randomly chose one without looking, which type would you most likely choose?

Ⓐ ▨

Ⓑ ▤

Ⓒ ◼

Ⓓ ⚃

2. Which fraction shows the ratio of ⚃ to ▨?

Ⓕ $\frac{2}{4}$

Ⓖ $\frac{1}{5}$

Ⓗ $\frac{2}{5}$

Ⓙ $\frac{4}{4}$

3. Which spinner would give you the best chance of landing on the number 2?

Ⓐ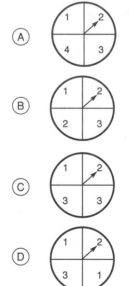

Ⓑ

Ⓒ

Ⓓ

Look for patterns to help you solve the problems.

Name _____ Date _____

Probability

Directions: Read each problem. Fill in the circle for the correct answer.

1. There are 10 silver earrings and 10 gold earrings in a jewelry box. Luisa reaches in without looking. What is the probability that she will pick a gold earring?

   (A) $\frac{1}{2}$

   (B) $\frac{1}{3}$

   (C) $\frac{1}{4}$

   (D) None of these

2. A group of teachers are ordering sandwiches from the deli. They can choose ham, beef, turkey, or bologna on white bread, wheat bread, or rye bread. How many different meat and bread combinations are possible?

   (F) 12

   (G) 16

   (H) 7

   (J) None of these

3. Elliott spun the arrow on a spinner 30 times. The results are shown in the table. Which of these spinners did Elliott most likely spin?

Diamond	Heart	Spade	Total Spins
11	10	9	30

   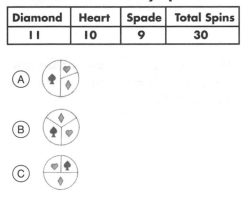

   (A)

   (B)

   (C)

   (D) None of these

4. A healthy snack food company makes chewy fruit shapes of lions, monkeys, elephants, and giraffes in red, green, purple, and yellow. They put the same number of each kind in a package. How many different outcomes are there?

   (F) 4

   (G) 8

   (H) 16

   (J) None of these

Choose "None of these" only if you are sure the right answer is not one of the choices.
Look for key words, numbers, and figures in each problem, and be sure you perform the correct operation.

Probability

Directions: Look at the spinner. Mark the probability that the arrow will land on each of the following numbers

1. an even number

   Ⓐ certain

   Ⓑ likely

   Ⓒ unlikely

   Ⓓ impossible

2. a 2

   Ⓕ certain

   Ⓖ likely

   Ⓗ unlikely

   Ⓙ impossible

3. a number less than 15

   Ⓐ certain

   Ⓑ likely

   Ⓒ unlikely

   Ⓓ impossible

Directions: Look at the spinner. Choose the correct answer to each question.

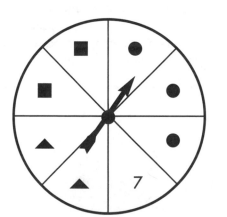

4. How likely is it that the spinner will land on a square compared to how likely it is that the spinner will land on a triangle?

   Ⓕ more likely

   Ⓖ less likely

   Ⓗ equally likely

   Ⓙ Not enough information

5. What is the probability that the spinner will land on a circle?

   Ⓐ $\frac{1}{3}$

   Ⓑ $\frac{3}{8}$

   Ⓒ $\frac{3}{5}$

   Ⓓ $\frac{8}{3}$

6. What is the probability that the spinner will land on a circle or the number 7?

   Ⓕ $\frac{1}{2}$

   Ⓖ $\frac{1}{3}$

   Ⓗ $\frac{3}{1}$

   Ⓙ $\frac{1}{8}$

Probability

Directions: Read each problem. Fill in the circle for the correct answer.

1. One letter is randomly chosen from the word *accident*. What are the chances the letter will be a *c*?

   Ⓐ $\frac{1}{4}$

   Ⓑ $\frac{1}{2}$

   Ⓒ $\frac{1}{8}$

   Ⓓ $\frac{1}{3}$

2. A bookshelf contains 7 science fiction books, 6 nonfiction books, 3 adventures, 4 fairy tales, and 5 mysteries. If you pull a book randomly from the shelf, what is the probability that it will be a mystery?

   Ⓕ $\frac{1}{25}$

   Ⓖ $\frac{5}{20}$

   Ⓗ $\frac{1}{5}$

   Ⓙ $\frac{1}{4}$

3. One letter is randomly chosen from the word *encyclopedia*. Which statement is true?

   Ⓐ The letter *c* is most likely to be chosen.

   Ⓑ The letter *c* and the letter *y* are equally likely to be chosen.

   Ⓒ The letter *e* is more likely to be chosen than the letter *o*.

   Ⓓ The letter *n* and the letter *e* are equally likely to be chosen.

4. A bag contains 15 peanuts, 17 cashews, 12 almonds, and 11 hazelnuts. A random handful of nuts are taken from the bag. The handful contains 2 peanuts, 6 cashews, 3 almonds, and 2 hazelnuts. If one more nut is randomly chosen from the bag, which statement is true?

   Ⓕ A cashew is more likely to be chosen than a peanut.

   Ⓖ An almond or a hazelnut are equally likely to be chosen.

   Ⓗ A peanut or a cashew are equally likely to be chosen.

   Ⓙ A hazelnut is more likely to be chosen than a cashew.

5. There are 52 cards in a deck of cards. Cards can be one of four suits: hearts, diamonds, clubs, or spades. There are 13 cards of each suit. If a random card is drawn from the deck, what is the probability that it will be a heart?

   Ⓐ $\frac{1}{52}$

   Ⓑ $\frac{1}{13}$

   Ⓒ $\frac{1}{4}$

   Ⓓ $\frac{1}{2}$

Probability

Directions: Read each problem. Fill in the circle for the correct answer.

1. If all these chips were put into a bag, what is the probability that you would pick a chip with a letter that comes before **M** in the alphabet?

   (A) $\frac{3}{5}$

   (B) $\frac{3}{8}$

   (C) $\frac{5}{3}$

   (D) $\frac{5}{8}$

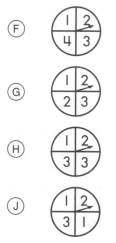

2. For the above chips, what is the probability that you would pick a chip with a vowel?

   (F) $\frac{1}{7}$

   (G) $\frac{1}{8}$

   (H) $\frac{7}{1}$

   (J) $\frac{8}{1}$

3. Which spinner would give you the best chance of landing on the number 6?

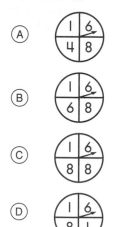

4. Which spinner would give you the best chance of landing on the number 1?

   (F)

   (G)

   (H)

   (J)

5. A bag contains 5 cherry jelly beans, 3 licorice jelly beans, 6 lime jelly beans, and 6 lemon jelly beans. When randomly pulling a jelly bean from the bag, which two flavors are you equally likely to pick?

   (A) cherry and licorice

   (B) licorice and lime

   (C) lime and lemon

   (D) cherry and lime

6. Caroline wants a cherry jelly bean. Without looking, she reaches into the bag and grabs a lime jelly bean. She eats the lime jelly bean anyway. Then she chooses another jelly bean at random. How does her chance of getting a cherry jelly bean this time compare to her chance of grabbing another lime jelly bean?

   (F) better

   (G) worse

   (H) same

   (J) Not enough information

Solving Word Problems

Directions: Solve each problem. Fill in the circle for the correct answer. Fill in the circle for "Not given" if your answer is not listed as a choice.

Example

Tim's mother is a landscaper. On a new home in the neighborhood, she spent $829 for trees, $358 for flowers, and $352 for a fishpond. How much did she spend on the items for the new yard?

Ⓐ $1,600

Ⓑ $1,539

Ⓒ $1,459

Ⓓ Not given

Answer: Ⓑ

---

1. A Ferris wheel was built for the Chicago Fair in 1893. In 1904, it was torn down and sold for scrap. How many years did the Ferris wheel run?

Ⓐ 9 years

Ⓑ 11 years

Ⓒ 10 years

Ⓓ Not given

2. Three friends started a scrapbook business. They charge customers $3.25 per page to make a scrapbook. They spend $1.33 per page on materials. If the friends made a 50-page scrapbook and divided the profits evenly, how much money would each person earn on the project?

Ⓕ $96.00

Ⓖ $54.16

Ⓗ $32.00

Ⓙ Not given

3. Bert estimates that he will pay about $1,400 a year for his car expenses. He makes $35 every Saturday. How many Saturdays will he need to work to cover his car expenses for one year?

Ⓐ 35 Saturdays

Ⓑ 40 Saturdays

Ⓒ 50 Saturdays

Ⓓ Not given

4. On Monday, Ramona read for 20 minutes. She increased her amount of reading time by two minutes a day, every day for 21 days. For how many minutes did Ramona read on the last Sunday during this time?

Ⓕ 60 minutes

Ⓖ 56 minutes

Ⓗ 64 minutes

Ⓙ Not given

Cover the answer choices, and read the question. Think about your answer before you look at the choices.

Solving Word Problems

Directions: Use the information in the box to answer the questions that follow. Fill in the circle for "Not given" if your answer is not listed as a choice.

$A = (D - C) \div 2$
$B = A + C$
$C = D \div 2$
D = The difference between 20 and 4

1. What is the value of A?

Ⓐ 4

Ⓑ 5

Ⓒ 6

Ⓓ Not given

2. What is the value of B?

Ⓕ 9

Ⓖ 11

Ⓗ 12

Ⓙ Not given

Directions: Use the information in the box to answer the questions that follow. Fill in the circle for "Not given" if your answer is not listed as a choice.

Xavier is twice the age of Yvonne.
Yvonne is three years younger than Zane.
Zane is two years older than Alisa.
Alisa is 6 years old.

3. How many years older is Xavier than Zane?

Ⓐ 1 year

Ⓑ 2 years

Ⓒ 3 years

Ⓓ Not given

4. Who is the youngest?

Ⓕ Yvonne

Ⓖ Alisa

Ⓗ Zane

Ⓙ Not given

5. There are 5 stuffed animals on a shelf. The giraffe is before the dog. There are two animals between the dog and the bear. The cat is next to the bear, and the zebra is last. Which sequence shows the order the animals are in?

Ⓐ giraffe, dog, cat, bear, zebra

Ⓑ bear, cat, giraffe, dog, zebra

Ⓒ dog, giraffe, cat, bear, zebra

Ⓓ Not given

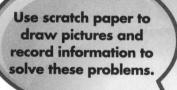

Use scratch paper to draw pictures and record information to solve these problems.

Name _____ Date _____

Solving Word Problems

Directions: Read and solve each problem. Fill in the circle for the correct answer.

1. Two numbers have a product of 108 and a quotient of 12. What are the two numbers?

   (A) 9, 12

   (B) 7, 16

   (C) 36, 3

   (D) 54, 6

2. Several uninvited ants arrived at a picnic. Including ants and people, there are 9 guests at the picnic with a total of 30 legs. Each ant has 6 legs. How many ants are at the picnic?

   (F) 9 ants

   (G) 6 ants

   (H) 4 ants

   (J) 3 ants

3. Mr. Grace found three programs that he wanted to buy for the classroom. *Math Busters* was $21.80. *Spelling Practice* was $16.85. *Reading Classics* was $13.65. He spent a total of $35.45. Which programs did he buy?

   (A) *Math Busters* and *Spelling Practice*

   (B) *Math Busters* and *Reading Classics*

   (C) *Spelling Practice* and *Reading Classics*

   (D) None of these

4. Carla has 6 hockey cards. Cole and Carla have 16 hockey cards altogether. Malia and Cole have 25 hockey cards altogether. How many hockey cards does Malia have?

   (F) 6 hockey cards

   (G) 9 hockey cards

   (H) 15 hockey cards

   (J) 20 hockey cards

5. The number of people watching a hockey game is 900 when rounded to the nearest hundred and 850 when rounded to the nearest ten. Which of these could be the number of people watching the game?

   (A) 847 people

   (B) 849 people

   (C) 856 people

   (D) 852 people

6. Mickey's Card Shop receives a shipment of trading cards each month. There are 8 hockey cards in a pack, 12 packs in a box, and 16 boxes in a shipping crate. Which is the total number of hockey cards in the shipping crate?

   (F) 1,536 hockey cards

   (G) 672 hockey cards

   (H) 1,436 hockey cards

   (J) 662 hockey cards

7. After the hockey game, each of these players bought a juice box from a machine that takes both coins and bills. Each juice box costs 70 cents. Luke used only dimes. Jacques used only quarters. Pierre used only half-dollars. Roland used a dollar bill. Which two players got the same amount of change?

   (A) Luke and Jacques

   (B) Jacques and Pierre

   (C) Pierre and Roland

   (D) Roland and Luke

Solving Word Problems

Directions: Read and solve each problem. Fill in the circle for the correct answer.

1. Monica ate $\frac{1}{8}$ of her sandwich for lunch. Sam ate $\frac{2}{3}$ of his apple. Deepak drank all of his milk. How much of her milk did Monica drink?

   (A) $\frac{1}{85}$ of the milk

   (B) $\frac{2}{3}$ of the milk

   (C) all of the milk

   (D) Not enough information

2. There were 258 cans of soup on the grocery store shelf in the morning. At 1:00, there were 156 cans of soup on the shelf. By the time the store closed at 7:00, several more cans of soup had been sold. How many cans of soup did the store sell in the entire day?

   (F) 102 cans

   (G) 288 cans

   (H) 414 cans

   (J) Not enough information

3. Sasha went to the park at 9:30 A.M. She played for 45 minutes and then started soccer practice. She had soccer practice for 90 minutes. At what time did soccer practice end?

   (A) 10:45 A.M.

   (B) 11:15 A.M.

   (C) 11:45 A.M.

   (D) Not enough information

4. Lexi must find the area of a square with one side that is 12 inches long. How can she figure it out?

   (F) She can add all the sides together.

   (G) She can multiply two sides together.

   (H) She can divide two sides by each other.

   (J) She cannot figure out the area with the information she has.

5. Naomi works at the hardware store. Her hourly wage is $7.50. How much money is Naomi paid for one week's work? Which piece of information will help you solve this problem?

   (A) the number of hours she works each day

   (B) the number of days she works each week

   (C) the number of hours she works each week

   (D) the address of the hardware store

6. At the school store, José bought 2 pencils for $0.10 each, a notebook for $0.65, and a bottle of water for $0.60. To find out how much change he will get, you need to know _____.

   (F) how much 2 notebooks cost

   (G) how much money he gave the salesperson

   (H) how much money he saved by buying one notebook

   (J) how much money he has

Solving Word Problems

Directions: Read and solve each problem. Fill in the circle for the correct answer.

1. The Florida State Fair is held every year in Tampa. At one of the state fairs, there were 48 Girl Scouts marching in the parade. There were 6 girls in each row. Which equation would you use to find how many rows of Girl Scouts were marching in the parade?

   Ⓐ $48 + 6 = n$

   Ⓑ $n \times 6 = 48$

   Ⓒ $48 - n = 6$

   Ⓓ $48 \times 6 = n$

2. The human heart pumps about 24 liters of blood in 5 minutes. You want to know about how many liters of blood are pumped in 1 minute. Which math problem will help you find the answer?

   Ⓕ $24 \div 5 = \square$

   Ⓖ $24 \times 5 = \square$

   Ⓗ $24 + 5 = \square$

   Ⓙ $24 - 5 = \square$

3. A flea can jump 130 times its own height. If you could do the same thing, and your height is 54 inches, how high could you jump? Which math problem could help you find the answer?

   Ⓐ $130 + 54 = \square$

   Ⓑ $130 - 54 = \square$

   Ⓒ $130 \div 54 = \square$

   Ⓓ $130 \times 54 = \square$

4. Lila collects football cards. She puts them into stacks of 9 cards each. She has 36 stacks of cards. She wants to know how many cards she has in all. Which computation shows how to find the correct answer?

   Ⓕ $36 + 9 = 45$

   Ⓖ $36 \times 9 = 324$

   Ⓗ $36 \div 9 = 4$

   Ⓙ $36 - 9 = 27$

5. Kenya has 72 books in her collection. She wants to put only 8 books on each of her shelves. Which expression could she use to figure out how many shelves she will need for her books?

   Ⓐ $72 + 8 = s$

   Ⓑ $72 - 8 = s$

   Ⓒ $72 \div 8 = s$

   Ⓓ $s \div 8 = 72$

6. Mario drove 350 miles in 7 hours and used 17.5 gallons of gas. How can you determine his speed?

   Ⓕ $350 \times 7 \div 17.5$

   Ⓖ $350 \div 17.5$

   Ⓗ 17.5×7

   Ⓙ $350 \div 7$

Solving Word Problems

Directions: Read and solve each problem. Fill in the circle for the correct answer.

1. Dylan wears a uniform to school. He has a choice of a blue shirt, a white shirt, or a maroon shirt. He can wear navy pants, khaki pants, or khaki shorts. How many possible outfits can Dylan choose from?

   (A) 3

   (B) 6

   (C) 9

   (D) 12

2. A group of friends is standing in line at a movie theater. Sadie is in line behind Dominic. Dominic is not standing next to Matt. Vinh is between two girls. Becca is in front of Matt. Which list shows the correct order of the friends?

   (F) Sadie, Vinh, Matt, Becca, Dominic

   (G) Dominic, Sadie, Vinh, Matt, Becca

   (H) Dominic, Sadie, Vinh, Becca, Matt

   (J) Matt, Becca, Vinh, Sadie, Dominic

3. Mr. Shulevitz owns an art gallery. Last week, he sold $375 worth of photos and $1,268 worth of paintings. He keeps 40% of the sales for the artwork and gives 60% to the artists. How much money did Mr. Shulevitz make last week?

   (A) $1,643.00

   (B) $657.20

   (C) $985.80

   (D) $687.28

4. In question 4, how much did the artists make last week?

   (F) $657.20

   (G) $864.66

   (H) $1,268.00

   (J) $985.80

5. How much more did the artists earn than Mr. Shulevitz?

   (A) $300.26

   (B) $348.60

   (C) $328.60

   (D) $280.62

6. At the school cafeteria, an average of 68 cartons of milk are sold each day at lunch. One quarter as many boxes of orange juice are sold as milk cartons. Three times as many boxes of fruit punch are sold as orange juice. How many boxes of fruit punch are sold each day?

   (F) 68

   (G) 17

   (H) 51

   (J) 34

7. Mrs. Halliwell made a quilt for her daughter's bed. The quilt measures 60 inches by 80 inches. How much fabric will she need to make the backing for the quilt?

   (A) 4,800 square inches

   (B) 280 square inches

   (C) 480 square inches

   (D) 2,800 square inches

Solving Word Problems

Directions: Use the following recipe to answer the questions that follow

---

Morning Glory Muffins

2 cups all-purpose flour
1 cup sugar
2 teaspoons baking soda
2 teaspoons cinnamon
$\frac{1}{4}$ teaspoon salt
2 cups shredded carrots
$\frac{1}{2}$ cup dried cranberries
or blueberries
$\frac{1}{2}$ cup chopped walnuts
$\frac{1}{2}$ cup unsweetened flaked
coconut
$\frac{1}{4}$ cup applesauce
1 apple, cut into small pieces
2 eggs
$\frac{2}{3}$ cup vegetable oil
2 teaspoons vanilla extract

---

1. **Irina wants to triple the recipe for a family reunion. How much oil will she need?**

   (A) 3 cups

   (B) $1\frac{1}{3}$ cups

   (C) 2 cups

   (D) $2\frac{1}{3}$ cups

2. **How many tablespoons of shredded carrots are in the recipe?**

   (F) 32 tablespoons

   (G) 18 tablespoons

   (H) 16 tablespoons

   (J) 48 tablespoons

3. **William wants to use $\frac{1}{3}$ less sugar than the recipe calls for. How much sugar will he use?**

   (A) $\frac{1}{3}$ cup

   (B) $1\frac{1}{6}$ cup

   (C) $\frac{2}{3}$ cup

   (D) $\frac{5}{6}$ cup

4. **Casey is allergic to walnuts. Instead, she plans to substitute pecans and almonds. How much should she use of each?**

   (F) $\frac{1}{8}$ cup

   (G) $\frac{1}{2}$ cup

   (H) $\frac{1}{4}$ cup

   (J) $\frac{1}{3}$ cup

Name _____ Date _____

Solving Word Problems

Directions: Read and solve each problem. Fill in the circle for the correct answer.

1. It takes 3 bakers at the Down Home Bake Shop 4 hours to make the morning bread and rolls. How long would it take if there were 6 bakers?

   Ⓐ 3.5 hours

   Ⓑ 2 hours

   Ⓒ 2.5 hours

   Ⓓ 1 hour 45 minutes

2. Shyla collected 14 pounds of cans from her neighbors for her school recycling project. Annie collected $16\frac{1}{4}$ pounds, and Darius collected $17\frac{2}{3}$ pounds. How much did they collect altogether?

   Ⓕ $37\frac{11}{12}$ pounds

   Ⓖ 47 pounds

   Ⓗ $47\frac{11}{12}$ pounds

   Ⓙ $42\frac{7}{12}$ pounds

3. An airplane can hold 224 passengers. It is only 75% full. How many more passengers can get on the plane?

   Ⓐ 56

   Ⓑ 168

   Ⓒ 72

   Ⓓ Not enough information

4. Which number sentence shows the first step in solving question 3?

   Ⓕ $224 \div 0.75 = p$

   Ⓖ $224 \times 0.75 = p$

   Ⓗ $224 \times 75 = p$

   Ⓙ $224 + 75 = p$

5. Rocky's Sporting Goods gets in a shipment of 2,016 baseball gloves. They have 18 equal orders for the gloves. How many gloves are in each order?

   Ⓐ 88 gloves

   Ⓑ 106 gloves

   Ⓒ 118 gloves

   Ⓓ 112 gloves

6. Jake made a birdhouse that he wants to send to his aunt. It is 13 inches tall and 7 inches wide. Which of the following boxes is likely to be large enough?

   Ⓕ 96 cubic inches

   Ⓖ 80 cubic inches

   Ⓗ 72 cubic inches

   Ⓙ 64 cubic inches

If you have enough time, review both questions and answers. When you are in a hurry, it is easy to miss something!

Chapter 10: Applications

Organizing and Displaying Data

Directions: Solve each problem. Fill in the circle for the correct answer.

> ### Example
>
> There were 4 schools that participated in a district fundraiser. The schools raised a total of $2,500. The graph below shows the percentages that each school contributed to the total amount raised. Use the information in the graph to answer the question.
>
> **How much money did Willow School contribute to the fundraiser?**
>
> (A) $750
>
> (B) $250
>
> (C) $625
>
> (D) $875
>
>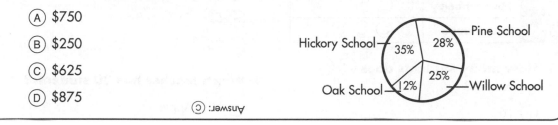
>
> Answer: C

Directions: Use the graph to answer the questions that follow.

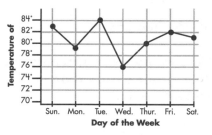

1. What is the difference between the highest temperature and the lowest temperature shown?

(A) 1°

(B) 10°

(C) 8°

(D) 12°

2. Which day has the median temperature of the week?

(F) Tuesday

(G) Saturday

(H) Friday

(J) Wednesday

Directions: Use the table to answer the questions below.

Summer Sale		
	Regular Price	Sale Price
Shorts	$15.99	$13.99
Shirts	$12.99	$11.00
Shoes	$45.99	$39.09

3. Lydia bought 3 pairs of shorts, 4 shirts, and a pair of shoes for the advertised sale prices. Before tax, how much did she spend?

(A) $87.35

(B) $145.92

(C) $63.68

(D) $125.06

4. How much money did Lydia save on her purchase because of the sale?

(F) $20.86

(G) $25.32

(H) $18.58

(J) $21.73

Organizing and Displaying Data

Directions: There are five classes in the fifth grade at Tropicana School. A different teacher teaches each class. The number of students in each class is represented by the pictograph below. Each ☺ stands for 8 students. Use the following chart to answer the questions that follow.

Class	Teacher	Number of Students
5-1	Miss Apple	☺ ☺ ☺ ◖
5-2	Mr. Kiwi	☺ ☺ ☺ ◕
5-3	Ms. Melon	☺ ☺ ☺ ◿
5-4	Mr. Cranberry	☺ ☺ ◖
5-5	Miss Mango	☺ ☺ ☺ ☺

1. How many students does ☺ ☺ represent?

Ⓐ 16

Ⓑ 8

Ⓒ 4

Ⓓ 2

2. How many students does ☺ ◖ represent?

Ⓕ 16

Ⓖ 8

Ⓗ 12

Ⓙ 2

3. How many students does ☺ ◿ represent?

Ⓐ 2

Ⓑ 10

Ⓒ 6

Ⓓ 8

4. How many students are in Mr. Cranberry's class and Miss Mango's class combined?

Ⓕ 7

Ⓖ 13

Ⓗ 52

Ⓙ 25

5. Which teacher has 30 students?

Ⓐ Miss Apple

Ⓑ Mr. Kiwi

Ⓒ Ms. Melon

Ⓓ Mr. Cranberry

6. How many more students are in Miss Apple's class than in Ms. Melon's class?

Ⓕ 1

Ⓖ 2

Ⓗ 3

Ⓙ 4

7. Mr. Kiwi divides his students into 5 equal teams. How many students are on each team?

Ⓐ 8

Ⓑ 5

Ⓒ 6

Ⓓ 4

Organizing and Displaying Data

Directions: Gina asked 250 students about their favorite types of restaurants. Her results are shown in the chart below. Use the chart to answer the questions.

Restaurant Type	Number
Italian	85
Diner	32
Mexican	45
Fast Food	70
Chinese	18

1. What is the range of the data above? _____

2. In order to use the graph below to show Gina's data, each tick mark on the vertical axis will need to represent _____ people. Put a scale on the vertical axis.

3. Label the vertical axis.

4. Complete the bar graph using the data from the table.

Restaurant Preferences

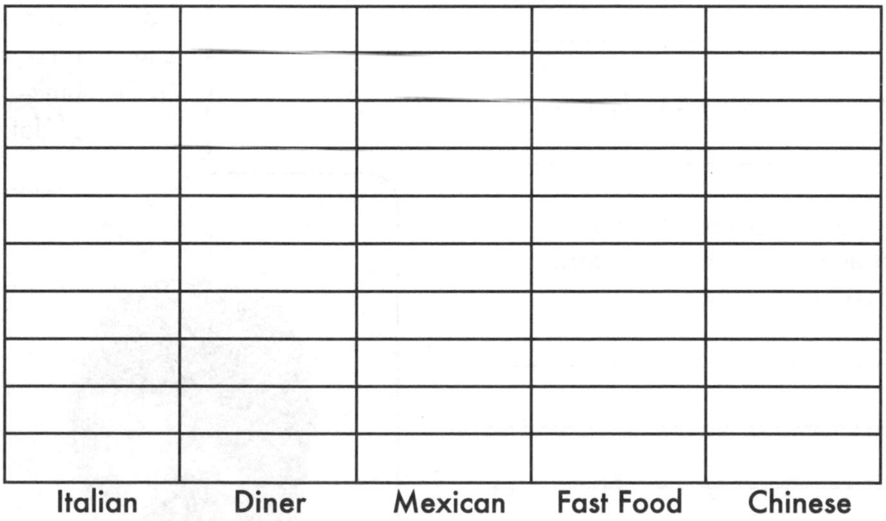

Italian   Diner   Mexican   Fast Food   Chinese

5. If Gina stood outside a local Italian restaurant and asked people about their favorite restaurants, how do you think the data would be different? Explain.

_____

_____

Organizing and Displaying Data

Directions: The fifth-grade class at Martin Luther King, Jr. Middle School collects items to donate to a local homeless shelter. The chart below shows an inventory of items collected. Use the chart to answer the questions.

Items	Last Year	This Year
Snack foods	21	32
Paper goods	28	42
Instant foods	22	38
Canned goods	42	63
Infant clothing	42	40

1. Find the average number of items collected each year.

Last Year: _____

This Year: _____

2. What was the difference in the mean number of items collected?

_____

3 Which item showed the greatest increase from last year to this year?

_____

Which items showed a decrease?

_____

4. Which year showed the most variation in the types of items collected? Explain.

_____

_____

_____

5. Based on this data, what can the class predict will happen with the collection next year?

_____

_____

_____

_____

The **mean**, or average, of a set of data is the sum of the data divided by the number of pieces of data.

Name ______________________ Date ______________

Organizing and Displaying Data

Directions: Use the pictograph below to answer the questions that follow.

Number of Students at Highview School

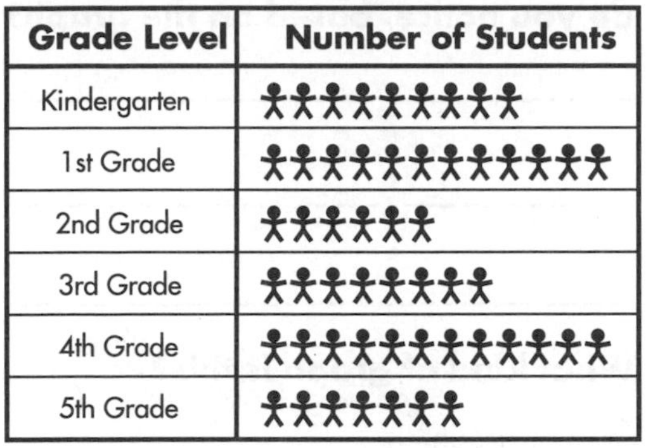
Grade Level
Number of Students
Kindergarten
1st Grade
2nd Grade
3rd Grade
4th Grade
5th Grade

Key: 🯅 = 5 students

1. How many Highview students are fifth graders?

Ⓐ 30 students

Ⓑ 35 students

Ⓒ 40 students

Ⓓ 60 students

2. How many more first graders are there than second graders?

Ⓕ 30

Ⓖ 35

Ⓗ 40

Ⓙ 25

3. What is the total number of third, fourth, and fifth graders?

Ⓐ 125 students

Ⓑ 150 students

Ⓒ 135 students

Ⓓ 115 students

Directions: Anthony did an experiment to see how the flight of a paper airplane would be affected by changing the angle of the airplane's wings. Use the graph below to answer the questions that follow.

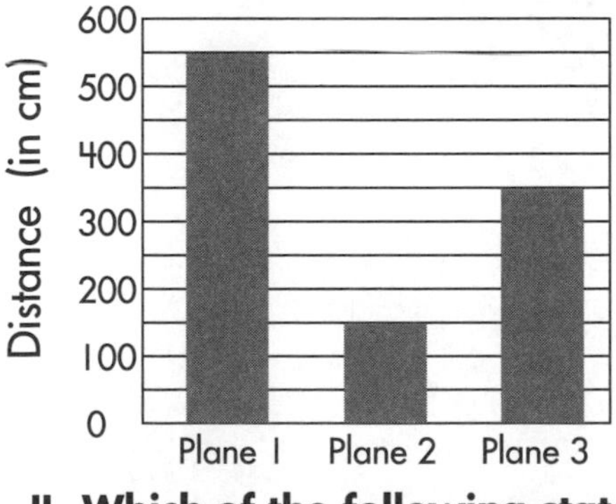
600
500
400
300
200
100
0
Distance (in cm)
Plane 1
Plane 2
Plane 3

4. Which of the following statements is true?

Ⓕ Plane 1 flew more than 3 times as far as Plane 2.

Ⓖ Plane 3 flew exactly 2 times as far as Plane 2.

Ⓗ Plane 1 flew exactly 2 times as far as Plane 3.

Ⓙ Plane 3 flew farther than Planes 1 and 2.

5. What is the combined distance the three planes flew?

Ⓐ 900 cm

Ⓑ 950 cm

Ⓒ 1,050 cm

Ⓓ 1,200 cm

MATH
228

Organizing and Displaying Data

Directions: Use the graph below to answer the questions that follow.

Number of People Who Immigrated to the U.S.	
1820–1840	⚬
1841–1860	
1861–1880	
1881–1900	
1901–1920	

⚬ = 1,000,000 immigrants

1. During which years did the greatest number of people immigrate?

(A) 1841–1860

(B) 1861–1880

(C) 1881–1900

(D) 1901–1920

2. How many more people immigrated between 1881 and 1900 than between 1861 and 1880?

(F) 4 million

(G) 4.5 million

(H) 6 million

(J) 6.5 million

3. Which of the following statements is not true?

(A) There were the fewest immigrants from 1820–1840.

(B) There were 4.5 million immigrants from 1841–1860.

(C) There were the same number of immigrants from 1841–1860 as there were from 1861–1880.

(D) The number of immigrants did not decrease during any of the years listed in the graph.

4. What sort of trend in immigration do you notice, based on the graph?

_____

_____

_____

5. What kind of graph is this?

(A) bar graph

(B) pie chart

(C) line graph

(D) pictograph

6. Which of the following represents half a million people?

(F)

(G)

(H)

(J)

Sample Test 10: Applications

Directions: Solve each problem. Fill in the circle for the correct answer.

1. Lincoln School is hosting a dinner for its honor students. There will be 50 students at the dinner. If 4 chairs fit around one table, how many tables will be needed for the students?

   Ⓐ 12
   Ⓑ 13
   Ⓒ 14
   Ⓓ 15

2. The figure below is a sketch showing the cafeteria at Lincoln School. If you walked completely around the cafeteria, about how far would you go?

   Ⓕ 100 ft.
   Ⓖ 80 ft.
   Ⓗ 120 ft.
   Ⓙ 400 ft.

   20 ft.

3. Midori was paid $204 for 3 days of work. She worked 8 hours each day. What was her rate?

   Ⓐ $8.50 per hour
   Ⓑ $8.50 per day
   Ⓒ $25.50 per day
   Ⓓ $68 per hour

4. Which computation shows how to find the correct answer for question 3?

   Ⓕ $204 \div 3$
   Ⓖ $204 \div 8$
   Ⓗ $(204 \div 3) \times 8$
   Ⓙ $204 \div (3 \times 8)$

Directions: A survey on favorite colors was taken at Rosa's school. The graph below shows the results of the survey. Study the graph, then answer the questions.

5. How many students chose blue as their favorite color?

   Ⓐ 8
   Ⓑ 50
   Ⓒ 24
   Ⓓ 40

6. How many more students prefer red over yellow?

   Ⓕ 4
   Ⓖ 12
   Ⓗ 20
   Ⓙ 35

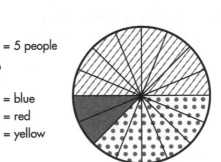

= 5 people

▨ = blue
⊡ = red
▦ = yellow

Sample Test 10: Applications

Directions: Solve each problem. Fill in the circle for the correct answer.

7. **Mrs. Hammersmith's fifth-grade class took a science test. There are 32 students in the class. The class scored a total of 2,848 points on the test. What was the average score?**

   (A) 89

   (B) 92

   (C) 73

   (D) 87

8. **On Monday, Austin took 20 minutes to wash the dishes. On Tuesday, Selena took $\frac{1}{4}$ hour to wash the dishes. On Wednesday, Huan took $\frac{2}{5}$ hour to wash the dishes. On Thursday, Emma took $\frac{1}{5}$ hour to wash the dishes. Which person took the least amount of time to wash the dishes?**

   (F) Austin

   (G) Selena

   (H) Huan

   (J) Emma

Directions: Use the graph to answer the questions that follow.

9. **On average, about how many people attended each game?**

   (A) 12,000

   (B) 26,000

   (C) 22,000

   (D) 18,000

10. **How many more people attended the Jan. 6 game than the Jan. 12 game?**

    (F) 10,000

    (G) 8,000

    (H) 5,000

    (J) 2,000

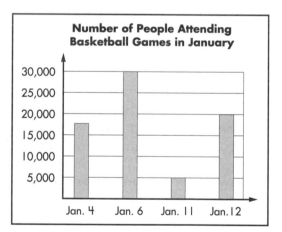

Number of People Attending Basketball Games in January

Name _____   Date _____

Sample Test 10: Applications

Directions: Solve each problem. Fill in the circle for the correct answer.

11. The art teacher is paid $15 per hour. She works for 6 hours a day. Which number sentence shows how to find the amount she earns in one day?

(A) $15 + 6 = \square$

(B) $15 - 6 = \square$

(C) $15 \times 6 = \square$

(D) $15 \div 6 = \square$

12. What is the mean of this data?
31, 54, 34, 31, 56

(F) 31

(G) 34

(H) 41.2

(J) 51.5

13. A bag contains 7 red marbles, 5 green marbles, 3 white marbles, and 2 gold marbles. What is the probability of picking a red marble?

(A) $\frac{7}{10}$

(B) $\frac{7}{17}$

(C) $\frac{7}{8}$

(D) $\frac{7}{9}$

14. What is the probability of picking a white or green marble?

(F) $\frac{8}{8}$

(G) $\frac{3}{8}$

(H) $\frac{5}{8}$

(J) $\frac{8}{17}$

Directions: The graph below shows the cost of a ticket to the movies in five different cities. Use the graph to answer the questions below

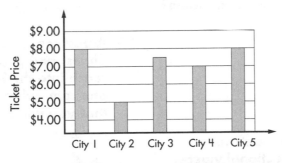

15. Which cities have the same ticket price?

(A) cities 1 and 3

(B) cities 3 and 5

(C) cities 1 and 5

(D) cities 4 and 5

16. What is the difference between the price of a ticket in cities 1 and 2?

(F) $2.00

(G) $3.00

(H) $4.00

(J) $5.00

Sample Test 10: Applications

Ready to Test • Fifth Grade

Name _____

Date _____

Sample Test 10: Applications

Directions: Solve each problem. Fill in the circle for the correct answer.

17. Taizo read for 30 minutes on Monday, 47 minutes on Tuesday, 64 minutes on Wednesday, and 81 minutes on Thursday. Which statement describes Taizo's pattern for reading?

(A) Add 15 minutes each day.

(B) Subtract 17 minutes each day.

(C) Add 12 minutes each day.

(D) Add 17 minutes each day.

18. Gavin flips a coin 10 times and gets 8 heads and 2 tails. What would he expect the next flip to result in?

(F) heads

(G) tails

19. On a baseball diamond, it is 90 feet between each base, and there are 4 bases. Suppose a runner hits a double and has reached second base. How much farther does the runner have to go to reach home?

(A) 90 ft.

(B) 180 ft.

(C) 270 ft.

(D) 360 ft.

20. The Spanish Club wants to buy a set of instructional videos. Each video costs $12.50. What information will they need to determine how much money they must raise to buy the entire set of videos?

(F) the number of students in the school

(G) how long each video is

(H) the number of videos in the set

(J) how many students there are in the Spanish Club

21. Natalie is building her strength for the swimming season. She can now lift 75 pounds. She wants to increase the weight she can lift by 5 pounds a week for 6 weeks. At the end of 6 weeks, how much weight should she be able to lift?

(A) 105 pounds

(B) 30 pounds

(C) 92 pounds

(D) 80 pounds

22. An auto mechanic earns $19 an hour. She works 8 hours a day. Which number sentence shows how to find how much she earns in a day?

(F) $19 + 8 = \square$

(G) $19 - 8 = \square$

(H) $19 \times 8 = \square$

(J) $19 \div 8 = \square$

23. A bag contains 10 nickels, 7 dimes, and 5 quarters. If you reach into the bag and take out one coin, what is the probability that you will choose a nickel?

(A) $\frac{5}{11}$

(B) $\frac{5}{22}$

(C) $\frac{10}{12}$

(D) $\frac{10}{23}$

Practice Test 3: Math
Part 1: Concepts

Directions: Read each problem. Fill in the circle for the correct answer.

1. **Which group of decimals is ordered from least to greatest?**

   (A) 3.332, 3.321, 3.295, 3.287, 3.111

   (B) 3.424, 3.425, 3.339, 3.383, 3.214

   (C) 3.109, 3.107, 3.278, 3.229, 3.344

   (D) 3.132, 3.234, 3.262, 3.391, 3.406

2. **Which of these is even and cannot be evenly divided by 6?**

   (F) 28

   (G) 30

   (H) 35

   (J) 42

3. **$\sqrt{64}$ =**

   (A) 12

   (B) 9

   (C) 8

   (D) 7

4. **One hundred fourteen thousand, two hundred =**

   (F) 1,014,200

   (G) 11,420

   (H) 114,002

   (J) 114,200

5. **Three students collected cans of food for a local food drive. The first student collected 78 cans, the second student collected 66 cans, and the third student collected 63 cans. If they rounded the number of cans to the nearest ten and added them together, what number would they get?**

   (A) 206

   (B) 210

   (C) 200

   (D) 190

6. **Forty-two thousand, six hundred seventy-seven =**

   (F) 420,677

   (G) 40,267

   (H) 24,767

   (J) 42,677

7. **Which of these is true?**

   (A) $\frac{5}{8} > \frac{6}{9}$

   (B) $\frac{2}{3} < \frac{3}{4}$

   (C) $\frac{5}{10} = \frac{9}{11}$

   (D) $\frac{4}{5} > \frac{5}{4}$

GO ▶

MATH
234

Practice Test 3: Math
Part 1: Concepts

Directions: Read each problem. Fill in the circle for the correct answer.

8. 49 =

  (F) 7^2

  (G) 6^2

  (H) 7^7

  (J) 8^5

9. **What are all of the factors of the product of 8 times 3?**

  (A) 2, 4, 6, 8, 10, 12

  (B) 1, 2, 4, 8, 12

  (C) 1, 2, 3, 4, 6, 8, 12, 24

  (D) 1, 2, 3, 4, 5, 6, 7, 8

10. **Which number sentence goes in the same fact family as 6 × 3 = □?**

  (F) 3 × □ = 6

  (G) □ ÷ 3 = 6

  (H) 3 + □ = 6

  (J) □ − 3 = 6

11. **Suppose you replaced the number 5 in 50,692 with an 8. How much larger would the new number be?**

  (A) 50,000

  (B) 10,000

  (C) 30,000

  (D) 3,000

12. **Which of these is a prime number?**

  (F) 75

  (G) 25

  (H) 13

  (J) 21

13. **What number should go in both boxes to make these number sentences true?**
□ − 9 = 27
6 × 6 = □

  (A) 36

  (B) 30

  (C) 42

  (D) 39

14. **On the number line below, which letter is closest to 3.8?**

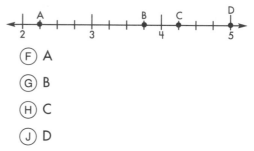

  (F) A

  (G) B

  (H) C

  (J) D

15. **What symbol should go in both boxes to make this number sentence true?**
48 □ 6 = 8 □ 1

  (A) +

  (B) −

  (C) ×

  (D) ÷

16. **Look at the table below. The numbers in row A follow a rule to create the numbers in row B. What is the missing number in row B?**

A	3	5	7	9	11
B	5	9	13	□	21

  (F) 15

  (G) 17

  (H) 11

  (J) 19

Practice Test 3: Math
Part 1: Concepts

Directions: Read each problem. Fill in the circle for the correct answer.

17. What is an odd number that is less than 7,983 and more than 6,735?

(A) 6,659

(B) 7,989

(C) 7,827

(D) 6,573

18. The sum of 287 and 421 is closest to _____.

(F) 600

(G) 800

(H) 700

(J) 500

19. Which of these is another way to write 0.20?

(A) $\frac{10}{20}$

(B) $\frac{1}{5}$

(C) 25%

(D) $\frac{2}{5}$

20. How would you rewrite this expression using the distributive property?
5(8 + 9) =

(F) $5 \times 9 + 8$

(G) $5 \times 8 + 9$

(H) $5 + 8 \times 5 + 9$

(J) $5 \times 8 + 5 \times 9$

21. What does the 2 in 204,369 mean?

(A) 200,000

(B) 20,000

(C) 2,000

(D) 200

22. Which of the following is true?

(F) 3.26 < 3.21

(G) $\frac{5}{8} > \frac{7}{12}$

(H) $6 = \frac{35}{5}$

(J) $\frac{3}{8} > \frac{1}{2}$

23. What are all of the factors of the product of 8 and 5?

(A) 1, 2, 3, 5, 8, 20, 40

(B) 2, 4, 5, 8, 10, 20, 40

(C) 1, 2, 4, 5, 8, 10, 20

(D) 1, 2, 4, 5, 8, 10, 20, 40

24. How would you write this decimal as a fraction in simplest form?
13.45

(F) $13\frac{45}{100}$

(G) $13\frac{9}{10}$

(H) $13\frac{1}{3}$

(J) $13\frac{9}{20}$

25. Extend the number pattern.
5.55, 5.65, 5.75, 5.85, _____

(A) 5.90

(B) 5.95

(C) 6.85

(D) 6.95

Name _____   Date _____

Practice Test 3: Math
Part 1: Concepts

Directions: Solve each problem. Fill in the circle for the correct answer.

26. What number makes this number sentence true?
$22 \times \square = 132$

- (F) 8
- (G) 6
- (H) 12
- (J) 14

27. Which of these Roman numerals comes between 15 and 20?

- (A) XVI
- (B) XXIX
- (C) XXI
- (D) VI

28. Which of the following equations does not belong to the same family or group as the equation $f \times 7 = 56$?

- (F) $56 \div f = 8$
- (G) $56 \div f = 4$
- (H) $56 \div 8 = f$
- (J) $7 \times f = 56$

29. Which of these is 4,322,504?

- (A) four hundred thirty-two thousands, five hundred four
- (B) forty-three hundred, twenty-two thousand, five hundred four
- (C) four million, three hundred twenty-two thousand, five hundred forty
- (D) four million, three hundred twenty-two thousand, five hundred four

30. Which statement is true about the value of k in the equation $512 \div 128 = k$?

- (F) It is less than 4.
- (G) It is equal to 5.
- (H) It is between 3 and 5.
- (J) It is greater than 4.

31. $1,580 \ \square \ 34 = 1,546$
Which operation sign belongs in the box?

- (A) +
- (B) −
- (C) ×
- (D) ÷

32. These squares show groups of numbers that are related by the same rule. What number is missing from the second square?

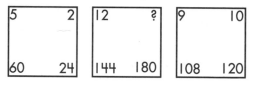

5	2
60	24

12	?
144	180

9	10
108	120

- (F) 14
- (G) 12
- (H) 15
- (J) 16

STOP

Practice Test 3: Math
Part 2: Computation

Directions: Solve each problem. Fill in the circle for the correct answer. Choose "None of these" if the correct answer is not given.

237

1. 9 × 3.5 =

Ⓐ 27.15

Ⓑ 30.9

Ⓒ 32.5

Ⓓ None of these

2. 23.54
   − 0.26

Ⓕ 22.83

Ⓖ 23.28

Ⓗ 23.82

Ⓙ None of these

3. 574 + 44 + 3,996 =

Ⓐ 4,614

Ⓑ 5,321

Ⓒ 4,782

Ⓓ None of these

4. 58)‾348‾

Ⓕ 8

Ⓖ 4

Ⓗ 12

Ⓙ None of these

5. 7,302
   +6,528

Ⓐ 138,210

Ⓑ 13,830

Ⓒ 14,388

Ⓓ None of these

6. $\frac{1}{4}$ × 36 =

Ⓕ 8

Ⓖ 12

Ⓗ 9

Ⓙ None of these

7. 3)‾47‾

Ⓐ 14

Ⓑ 16 R1

Ⓒ 15 R2

Ⓓ None of these

8. 10,030 − 2,856 =

Ⓕ 7,174

Ⓖ 6,741

Ⓗ 8,224

Ⓙ None of these

9. $4\frac{5}{6} - \frac{2}{3}$ =

Ⓐ $4\frac{1}{3}$

Ⓑ $3\frac{2}{3}$

Ⓒ $3\frac{4}{6}$

Ⓓ None of these

10. 2,468 ÷ 6 =

Ⓕ 410 R4

Ⓖ 411 R2

Ⓗ 411 R5

Ⓙ None of these

Practice Test 3: Math
Part 2: Computation

Directions: Solve each problem. Fill in the circle for the correct answer. Choose "None of these" if the correct answer is not given.

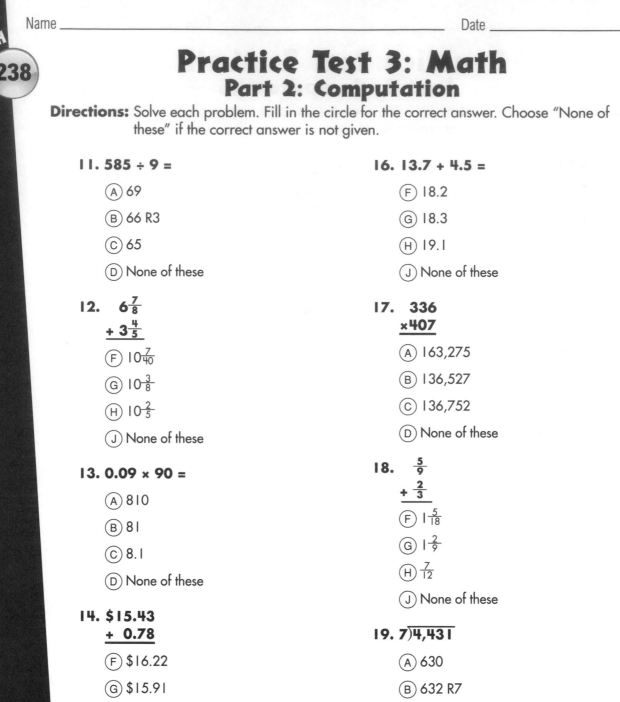

11. 585 ÷ 9 =

    Ⓐ 69

    Ⓑ 66 R3

    Ⓒ 65

    Ⓓ None of these

12. $6\frac{7}{8}$
    $+ 3\frac{4}{5}$

    Ⓕ $10\frac{7}{40}$

    Ⓖ $10\frac{3}{8}$

    Ⓗ $10\frac{2}{5}$

    Ⓙ None of these

13. 0.09 × 90 =

    Ⓐ 810

    Ⓑ 81

    Ⓒ 8.1

    Ⓓ None of these

14. $15.43
    + 0.78

    Ⓕ $16.22

    Ⓖ $15.91

    Ⓗ $16.38

    Ⓙ None of these

15.   28
    566
      4
  +1,927

    Ⓐ 2,763

    Ⓑ 3,968

    Ⓒ 2,525

    Ⓓ None of these

16. 13.7 + 4.5 =

    Ⓕ 18.2

    Ⓖ 18.3

    Ⓗ 19.1

    Ⓙ None of these

17.   336
   ×407

    Ⓐ 163,275

    Ⓑ 136,527

    Ⓒ 136,752

    Ⓓ None of these

18. $\frac{5}{9}$
   $+ \frac{2}{3}$

    Ⓕ $1\frac{5}{18}$

    Ⓖ $1\frac{2}{9}$

    Ⓗ $\frac{7}{12}$

    Ⓙ None of these

19. $7\overline{)4,431}$

    Ⓐ 630

    Ⓑ 632 R7

    Ⓒ 631 R9

    Ⓓ None of these

GO

Practice Test 3: Math
Part 2: Computation

Directions: Solve each problem. Fill in the circle for the correct answer

20. $3\frac{4}{15}$
    $+ \frac{6}{15}$

    (F) $3\frac{1}{5}$

    (G) $3\frac{2}{15}$

    (H) $3\frac{2}{3}$

    (J) None of these

21. $\frac{3}{8}$
    $+ \frac{2}{10}$

    (A) $\frac{5}{2}$

    (B) $\frac{23}{40}$

    (C) $\frac{7}{10}$

    (D) None of these

22. $3.96 \times 5 =$

    (F) 19.8

    (G) 18.9

    (H) 19.30

    (J) 19.98

23. $\frac{4}{9} - \frac{1}{6}$

    (A) $\frac{5}{6}$

    (B) $\frac{7}{18}$

    (C) $\frac{5}{9}$

    (D) $\frac{5}{18}$

24. 22,509
    $-$ 4,382

    (F) 18,277

    (G) 17,127

    (H) 18,127

    (J) 19,017

25. $450 \div \square = 15$

    (A) 30

    (B) 15

    (C) 45

    (D) 10

26. When a box is 100% full of books, the total weight of the books is 62 pounds. When the box is only 20% full, approximately how much does it weigh?

    (F) 12.8 lb.

    (G) 49.6 lb.

    (H) 11.6 lb.

    (J) 12.4 lb.

27. $7\overline{)128.8}$

    (A) 17.4

    (B) 18.8

    (C) 18.4

    (D) 19

28. $\$36.25 - \$4.04 =$

    (F) $32.12

    (G) $32.02

    (H) $32.22

    (J) $32.21

GO

Name _____ Date _____

Practice Test 3: Math
Part 2: Computation

Directions: Solve each problem. Fill in the circle for the correct answer.

29. 421
905
+287

(A) 1,633

(B) 1,316

(C) 1,613

(D) 1,936

30. 85% ÷ 5 =

(F) 14%

(G) 25%

(H) 19%

(J) 17%

31. 98.9% − 42.21% =

(A) 56.96%

(B) 56.69%

(C) 55.69 %

(D) 57.08%

32. Find 128 × 13.

(F) 141

(G) 1,646

(H) 1,664

(J) 115

33. 33% of 16 =

(A) 5.28

(B) 5

(C) 5.3

(D) 5.22

34. 8 × ☐ × 5 = 360

(F) 7

(G) 9

(H) 6

(J) 13

35. $6\frac{7}{18}$
$-2\frac{5}{6}$

(A) $2\frac{5}{9}$

(B) $3\frac{5}{9}$

(C) $3\frac{4}{16}$

(D) $4\frac{1}{9}$

36. 46
×18

(F) 888

(G) 64

(H) 920

(J) 828

37. 12)‾170‾

(A) 14 R2

(B) 14

(C) 13 R2

(D) 13

38. $102.44 × 18 =

(F) $1,482.92

(G) $1,842.91

(H) $1,843.92

(J) $1,840.02

Practice Test 3: Math
Part 3: Applications

Directions: Solve each problem. Fill in the circle for the correct answer.

1. This clock shows the time that a family arrived at a campground. It took the family 3.25 hours to drive from their home to a restaurant. They took 0.75 hours to eat lunch and then drove for another 2.5 hours to the campground. At what time did the family leave their home?

Ⓐ 9:15

Ⓑ 8:45

Ⓒ 8:30

Ⓓ 9:00

2. A factory shipped 848 cars to 8 cities. Each city received the same number of cars. How many cars were shipped to each city?

Ⓕ 112

Ⓖ 108

Ⓗ 101

Ⓙ 106

3. Maria is making a video recording for a family history project. She plans to record 30 minutes of live action herself. Her parents have agreed to provide her with twice as much taped footage from the past as the live action she plans to shoot. Her grandparents have given her a recording they had made for their 50th wedding anniversary. That video runs $\frac{3}{4}$ the length of time of the footage Maria's parents will give her. How long will Maria's recording be after she puts all of the pieces together?

Ⓐ 2 hours 30 minutes

Ⓑ 2 hours 15 minutes

Ⓒ 3 hours 5 minutes

Ⓓ 3 hours 45 minutes

4. What is the best way to describe the figure below?

Ⓕ parallel lines

Ⓖ perpendicular lines

Ⓗ obtuse angles

Ⓙ acute angles

GO

MATH
242

Practice Test 3: Math
Part 3: Applications

Directions: Solve each problem. Fill in the circle for the correct answer.

5. Brian made a fruit salad. He included 6 cups of raspberries, 4 cups of grapes, 3 cups of chopped pears, and 1 cup of sliced bananas. What is the ratio of raspberries to bananas?

- (A) 4 to 6
- (B) 6 to 2
- (C) 1 to 3
- (D) 6 to 1

6. A rectangular prism is 4 units wide, 10 units long, and 3 units high. What is its volume?

- (F) 17 cubic units
- (G) 120 cubic units
- (H) 102 cubic units
- (J) 60 cubic units

7. What number sentence shows the perimeter of the square below?

- (A) $4 + 25 = \square$
- (B) $252 = \square$
- (C) $4 \times 25 = \square$
- (D) $25 \times 25 \times 25 \times 25 = \square$

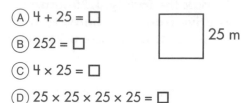

25 m

8. For the first 26 weeks of this year, Kendra watched 546 hours of television. In the next 13 weeks, she cut her television time in half. During the last 13 weeks of the year, she cut that time in half again. By the end of the year, what was the average amount of television that Kendra watched per day?

- (F) 55 minutes
- (G) 2 hours 37 minutes
- (H) 1 hour 30 minutes
- (J) 45 minutes

Directions: The graph below shows the number of books that were donated to a children's hospital each week for a month. Use the graph to answer the question below.

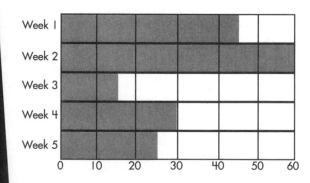

9. Which of the following statements is true?

- (A) There were twice as many books collected in week 2 as in week 1.
- (B) The number of books collected in weeks 3 and 4 is equal to the number of books collected in week 2.
- (C) There were twice as many books collected in week 1 as in week 4.
- (D) There were 3 times the number of books collected in week 1 as in week 3.

GO ▶

Practice Test 3: Math
Part 3: Applications

Directions: Solve each problem. Fill in the circle for the correct answer.

10. Noah's age is an even number less than 14. He is one half his sister's age. His sister's age is between 17 and 23. How old is Noah?

(F) 8
(G) 9
(H) 10
(J) 11

11. What is the average length of a side of the figure below?

(A) 9 cm
(B) 12 cm
(C) 8 cm
(D) 10 cm

12 cm

6 cm

12. In the figure below, the distance between each letter is the same. Which statement about the figure is false?

L   M   N   O   P

(F) Distance LP = 4 times Distance MN
(G) Distance NP = Distance MO
(H) Distance LN = 2 times Distance OP
(J) Distance MP = Distance LN

13. Which of these is the shortest distance?

(A) 2 miles
(B) 3 kilometers
(C) 14 meters
(D) 500 yards

Directions: Three schools are collecting aluminum cans as part of the school district's recycling effort. Use the graph below to answer the questions that follow.

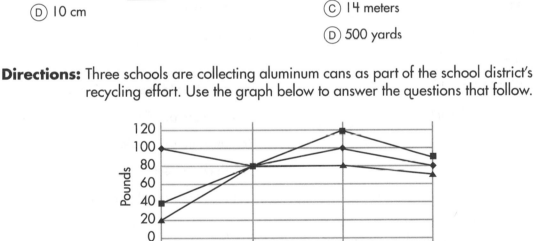

◆ Western Hills   ■ South Middle   ▲ Willow East

14. Which week saw each school collect the same weight of cans?

(F) week 1
(G) week 2
(H) week 3
(J) week 4

15. If aluminum cans are currently worth $0.53 per pound at the local recycling station, how much did the three schools earn in total?

(A) $425.30
(B) $433.70
(C) $469.40
(D) $498.20

Practice Test 3: Math
Part 3: Applications

Directions: Solve each problem. Fill in the circle for the correct answer.

16. Juan and Levi have been working on a computer project, and they want to protect their work. They decide to use the sum of all the prime numbers between 0 and 30 as the password. What is their password?

(F) 130

(G) 129

(H) 112

(J) 123

17. What is the number sentence for determining the volume of a rectangular prism that measures 3 units long, 5 units wide, and 8 units high?

(A) $3 \times 5 \times 8 = \square$

(B) $3 + 5 + 8 = \square$

(C) $(3 \times 5) + 8 = \square$

(D) $(3 + 5) \times 8 = \square$

18. A package weighs 18 kilograms. The contents weigh 16.25 kilograms. How much does the container weigh?

(F) 1.5 kg

(G) 2.25 kg

(H) 1,750 g

(J) 175 g

19. Andrea bought 4 packs of stickers for $3.45 each. If she gave the clerk $20, how much change did she receive?

(A) $5.20

(B) $8.20

(C) $7.20

(D) $6.20

20. How can the yard lines on a football field be described?

(F) They are parallel.

(G) They are perpendicular.

(H) They intersect.

(J) They have an infinite length.

Directions: Use the graph to answer the question that follows.

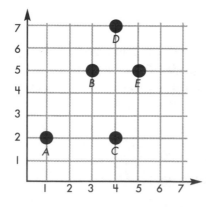

21. What are the coordinates for point D?

(A) (4, 2)

(B) (4, 7)

(C) (5, 5)

(D) (7, 4)

Practice Test 3: Math
Part 3: Applications

Directions: Solve each problem. Fill in the circle for the correct answer.

22. It takes Amelia 35 minutes to mow the front yard and 20 minutes to mow the backyard. If she began at 3:30, what time will she be done?

- (F) 4:15
- (G) 4:25
- (H) 4:20
- (J) 4:35

23. If a machine can cap 120 bottles in one minute, how many bottles can it cap in 10 seconds?

- (A) 10
- (B) 2
- (C) 20
- (D) 12

Directions: Use the information in the box to answer the questions that follow.

$A = (D - 10) \div 7$
$B = A + C$
$C = D - 2$
$D = $ The product of 6 and 4

24. What is the value of A?

- (F) 4
- (G) 2
- (H) 6
- (J) 12

25. What is the value of B?

- (A) 10
- (B) 18
- (C) 20
- (D) 24

26. What is the value of C?

- (F) 22
- (G) 6
- (H) 12
- (J) 18

27. What is the value of C + D?

- (A) 44
- (B) 22
- (C) 42
- (D) 38

GO

Practice Test 3: Math
Part 3: Applications
Directions: Solve each problem. Fill in the circle for the correct answer.

28. A desk normally costs $129. It is on sale for $99. How much would you save if you bought two desks on sale?

(F) $30
(G) $129
(H) $99
(J) $60

29. You helped your mom plant 40 tulip bulbs in the fall. In the spring, 10 of the tulips did not come up at all, and $\frac{1}{3}$ of the rest had yellow flowers. How many tulips had yellow flowers?

(A) 13
(B) 10
(C) 23
(D) 30

30. There are 52 weeks in a year. Jenna works 46 weeks each year. During each week, she works 32 hours. How many hours does Jenna work in a year?

(F) 1,472
(G) 76,544
(H) 1,664
(J) 2,392

31. Sergio spent $3.80 on heavy-duty string for his project. He bought 20 feet of string. How much was the price per foot?

(A) $1.90
(B) $1.70
(C) $0.19
(D) $0.38

32. Evaluate $5g + 2h$, if $g = 1$ and $h = 9$.

(F) 13
(G) 28
(H) 23
(J) 7

33. Evaluate $3b - 2a + 4c$, if $a = 4$, $b = 3$, and $c = 2$.

(A) 25
(B) 38
(C) 9
(D) 13

34. How do you find the perimeter of a rectangle?

(F) square the length of one side
(G) subtract the length of the shortest side from the length of the longest side
(H) multiply the base times the height
(J) add the length on all sides

page 9
1. A
2. H
3. C
4. F
5. B
6. J
7. A
8. H

page 10
1. A
2. J
3. B
4. F
5. C
6. H
7. C

page 11
1. A
2. J
3. A
4. H
5. B
6. F
7. D

page 12
1. B
2. F
3. C
4. J
5. A
6. G
7. B
8. J

page 13
1. D
2. H
3. A
4. G

page 14
1. C
2. J
3. D
4. F
5. B
6. G
7. C

page 15
1. B
2. F

3. B
4. J
5. C
6. J

page 16
1. C
2. F
3. D
4. J
5. B
6. F
7. C
8. H

page 17
1. B
2. J
3. A
4. F
5. C

page 18
1. C
2. G
3. A
4. J
5. D
6. F
7. D
8. H
9. A
10. H

page 19
1. B
2. H
3. C
4. F
5. A
6. J
7. C
8. H
9. D
10. F

page 20
1. A
2. H
3. B
4. F
5. D
6. G
7. C
8. F

page 21
9. D
10. H
11. A
12. H
13. B
14. F
15. B
16. J
17. A
18. G

page 22
19. D
20. G
21. A
22. J
23. C
24. G
25. A
26. H

page 23
27. C
28. G
29. D
30. F
31. C
32. F
33. D
34. G

page 24
1. B
2. H
3. D
4. F

page 25
1. C
2. J
3. A
4. F

page 26
1. A
2. J
3. C
4. J

page 27
1. B
2. J
3. B
4. H
5. D

6. G

page 28
1. what you spend your money on
2. items you subtract from your income
3. items you add to your income
4. relationship between debits and credits; the amount you have available to spend

page 29
1. B
2. G
3. A
4. J
5. C
6. F

page 30
1. D
2. F
3. B
4. J

page 31
1. B
2. H
3. D
4. H

page 32
1. A
2. H
3. A
4. J

page 33
1. B
2. H
3. D
4. Answers will vary. Possible answer: Sofia will explain what happened and pay for the repairs to her mom's camera.

page 34
1. myth
2. science fiction
3. realistic fiction
4. nonfiction

page 36
Hibernation

Includes facts

Made up or fantasized

Main purpose is to inform

Main purpose is to entertain

Organized into setting, characters, problem, goal, events, and resolution

Organized according to the purpose the authors wish to achieve (steps to achieve a goal; explain why something happens; attempt to make an argument, etc.)

Waterland

Includes facts

Made up or fantasized
Main purpose is to inform

Main purpose is to entertain

Organized into setting, characters, problem, goal, events, and resolution

Organized according to the purpose the authors wish to achieve (steps to achieve a goal; explain why something happens; attempt to make an argument, etc

page 37
1. A
2. The lines in the passage rhyme.
3. Possible answers:
A. squirrel, adoring

B. rabbit, practical
4. Answers will vary. Possible answer: the value of knowing where you belong

page 39
1. B
2. F
3. D
4. J
5. B
6. H

page 41
1. A
2. H
3. B
4. H
5. B
6. F

page 43
1. B
2. H
3. A
4. J
5. C
6. F

page 44
1. B
2. J
3. C
4. G

page 46
1. C
2. F
3. D
4. H
5. A
6. H

page 48
1. D
2. G
3. D
4. H
5. A
6. G

page 50
1. A
2. F

3. C
4. J
5. B
6. H

page 51
1. textbook
2. newspaper
3. biography
4. instruction manual
5. A
6. G

page 52
1. first passage: journal
   second passage: newspaper article
2. Ben Hanson wrote the first passage. second passage appeared in a newspaper.
3. Answers will vary.
Possible answers: Both passages tell that (a) Ben missed the word *cannibal*; (b) a girl named Rebecca won the spelling bee; (c) Ben won a dictionary.
4. Answers will vary.
Possible answers: (a) Only the diary entry tells how nervous Ben was at first; (b) only the newspaper entry tells Rebecca's last name; (c) only the newspaper article tells how many words Ben spelled correctly.

page 53
1. B
2. G
3. A
4. Answers will vary.

page 54
1. B

2. G
3. A
4. J

page 56
5. C
6. J
7. A
8. J
9. C
10. H

page 58
11. A
12. H
13. B
14. J
15. A
16. J

page 60
17. B
18. G
19. A
20. J
21. B
22. H

page 61
1. D
2. F
3. A
4. J
5. C
6. G
7. A
8. J

page 62
9. C
10. F
11. D
12. G
13. D
14. H
15. A

page 63
16. G
17. C
18. F
19. A
20. J
21. B

page 64
1. D

2. H
3. A
4. G

page 66
5. B
6. F
7. B
8. J
9. C
10. F

page 68
11. C
12. G
13. D
14. F
15. C
16. G

page 69
17. B
18. J
19. C
20. F

page 70
21. C
22. F
23. C
24. J
25. B

page 71
1. B
2. H
3. A
4. J
5. B
6. F

page 72
1. A
2. H
3. B
4. G
5. C
6. F
7. B

page 73
1. B
2. J
3. D
4. G
5. C

page 74
1. D
2. F
3. B
4. H
5. B
6. J
7. A
8. J

page 75
1. D
2. G
3. A
4. G
5. A
6. J
7. C

page 76
1. B
2. F
3. D
4. F
5. C
6. J
7. A
8. F

page 77
1. C
2. F
3. D
4. F
5. C
6. H
7. B
8. J
9. B

page 78
1. B
2. H
3. A
4. F
5. C
6. G

page 79
7. D
8. G
9. D
10. F
11. B
12. H
13. C

page 80
14. G
15. C
16. J
17. B
18. F

page 81
19. A
20. J
21. A
22. H
23. B
24. F
25. C
26. G
27. D

page 82
1. D
2. G
3. A
4. G
5. D
6. F
7. D
8. H

page 83
1. B
2. H
3. B
4. J
5. B

page 84
1. B
2. J
3. B
4. F
5. D
6. F
7. A
8. J
9. B
10. H

page 85
1. A
2. F
3. C
4. F

page 86
1. led
2. where
3. due
4. it's
5. there
6. here
7. you're
8. read
9. sent

page 87
1. B
2. H
3. A
4. G
5. D
6. H

page 88
1. D
2. F
3. A
4. G

page 89
1. D
2. F

page 90
1. **IN**   You are on a deserted island: no town, no people—just you and those crazy, noisy seagulls. What are you going to do?
2. **none**   Toward the castle she fled. She begged the gatekeeper for entrance. He did not hear her cries. Past the stone walls she scurried, the hounds in pursuit.
3. **none**   Maggie bit her lip. No use crying about it. She pulled her math homework out of the sink and just stared at her little sister.
4. **IN**   The music is playing those lovely tunes, but you're not listening. You can't. You have too many important things to plan. What should you buy for Teddy? Who should you invite to the party?

5. **EX** Columbus stood on the deck of the ship. Land was on the horizon. Land! Not the edge of the world, not dragons to devour the ship, but the land that would make his fortune . . . his and Spain's.

6. **EX** I think Mama forgot me. Otherwise, she would come and find me. Oh, no! Mama said not to go see the toys because I'd get lost. Mama is going to be mad at me!

7. **IM** Do not stop reading until you reach the end of this story. What you are about to read is so amazing that you simply *must* hear about it now. So settle back and get ready for the most incredible tale you've ever heard.

page 91
1. C
2. I can ride faster than you can. Let's race to the stop sign.
3. I'm thirsty. Does anyone have some bottled water?
4. We need to be careful on the bike trail. In-line skaters can appear out of nowhere.
5. C
6. Answers will vary, but the sentence should be complete.
7. Answers will vary, but the sentence should be complete.
8. Answers will vary, but the

sentence should be complete.
9. Answers will vary, but the sentence should be complete.

page 92
1. B
2. J
3. A

page 93
1. D
2. H
3. B

page 94
1. B
2. H
3. A

page 95
1. D
2. G
3. C
4. F

page 96
1. A
2. J
3. B

page 97
1. D
2. G
3. C
4. F
5. B
6. J

P98 1. D
2. G
3. C
4. J
5. C
6. H
7. C

page 99
1. D
2. H
3. B
4. H
5. D
6. G
7. A
8. J

page 100
1. B
2. H

page 101
1. A
2. G

3. D
4. G
5. A
6. H
7. B
8. J

page 102
9. D
10. I love the playground. It has great swings.
11. When I swing too high, I get sick. Do you?
12. C
13. Answers will vary, but the sentence should be complete.
14. Answers will vary, but the sentence should be complete.
15. Answers will vary, but the sentence should be complete.

page 103
16. F
17. D
18. F
19. B

page 104
20. F
21. B
22. J
23. A
24. H
25. A

page 105
1. Answers will vary but should include three memorable experiences.
2. Answers will vary but should describe the students' chosen experiences.
3. Answers will vary but should describe the three most

important things the students would want to relate about their chosen experiences.

page 106
Answers will vary. In the first paragraph, students should choose three things that need improvement in their community. In the second paragraph, they should give reasons why these things should be improved. In the concluding paragraph, students should explain what they could personally do to make these improvements.

page 107
Answers will vary, but students' paragraphs should explain an activity using a logical order of directions and sufficient detail.

page 108
1. Answers will vary. Possible answer: popcorn
2. Answers will vary. Possible answer: diving into cool water
3. Answers will vary. Possible answer: a child's painting
4. Answers will vary. Possible answer: a spring breeze

Answers will vary, but the paragraph should include two metaphors.

page 109
1. To persuade or convince people that part of Beatty Park should be turned into a dog

park

2. Dogs are the most popular pets for people. Owners have not had a place for their pets to socialize since the last dog park closed. Beatty Park is within walking distance for most people. Making a new dog park would make the residents (and dogs) of Lydenville very happy.

3. Answers will vary, but students' paragraphs should include details to support their position.

page 110
Answers will vary, but students' paragraphs should include a main idea and details that support the main idea

page 111
Answers will vary, but students' paragraphs should be clearly written and include details, descriptions, and feelings.

page 112
1. C
2. F
3. D
4. H
5. B
6. G
7. D
8. H
9. B

page 113
10. J
11. B
12. H
13. A

14. F
15. C
16. F

page 114
17. B
18. F
19. C
20. J

page 115
21. B
22. H
23. A
24. J
25. B
26. J
27. B
28. F
29. D
30. J

page 116
31. B
32. F
33. A
34. F
35. C
36. J
37. B
38. J
39. C

page 117
1. D
2. H
3. B
4. J
5. B
6. J

page 118
7. C
8. G
9. D
10. F
11. C

page 119
12. J
13. B
14. H

page 120
15. D
16. H
17. D

18. F

page 121
1. B
2. F
3. D
4. G

page 122
5. B
6. F
7. C
8. J
9. D
10. H
11. B

page 123
Answers will vary. Students' paragraphs should describe their favorite way to spend a day and include details that express their feelings.

page 124
1. D
2. H
3. B
4. G
5. A

page 125
1. –2, 4, –9, 3, –7, –4, 6, –6
2. porpoise, clouds, flag, sail of boat, buoy, bird
3. eel, jellyfish, octopus, porpoise, buoy, bird, clouds
4. J
5. D

page 126
1. C
2. F
3. D
4. F
5. C
6. G

page 127
1. C
2. F

3. C
4. H
5. B
6. J
7. B
8. G

page 128
1. A
2. G
3. D
4. H
5. C
6. G
7. D
8. H

page 129
1. C
2. J
3. D
4. G
5. C

page 130
1. C
2. H
3. B
4. F
5. D
6. F

page 131
1. C
2. J
3. C
4. F
5. B
6. J
7. A
8. G

page 132
1. D
2. H
3. A
4. F
5. C
6. J
7. A
8. J

page 133
1. >
2. <
3. >

4. =
5. >
6. =
7. >
8. =
9. >
10. >
11. =
12. <
13. <
14. >
15. <
16. =
17. >
18. >

page 134
1. D
2. G
3. A
4. J
5. B
6. H

page 135
1. C
2. G
3. A
4. H
5. D
6. F
7. B
8. J
9. D
10. G

page 136
1. B
2. J
3. B
4. H

page 137
1. D
2. H
3. A
4. H
5. B
6. G

page 138
1. C
2. J
3. B
4. H
5. B

6. H

page 139
1. 5.75
2. 2.4
3. 3.33
4. 0.38
5. 3.29
6. 9.11
7. $9\frac{1}{4}$
8. $\frac{3}{5}$
9. $4\frac{3}{25}$
10. $5\frac{7}{10}$
11. $100\frac{3}{4}$
12. $22\frac{3}{20}$

page 140
1. B
2. G
3. D
4. G
5. C

page 141
1. $2 \times 6 + 2 \times 3$
   $2 \times 9 = 12 + 6$
   $18 = 18$
2. $(3 \times 4) + (3 \times 3)$
   $21 = (4 + 3)3$
   $21 = 21$
3. $4 \times 9 - 4 \times 1$
   $4 \times 8 = 36 - 4$
   $32 = 32$
4. $(9 \times 2) - (3 \times 2)$
   $12 = (9 - 3)2$
   $12 = 12$
5. $2 \times 15 - 2 \times 3$
   $12 \times 2 = 30 - 6$
   $24 = 24$
6. $7 \times 8 + 5 \times 8$
   $12 \times 8 = 56 + 40$
   $96 = 96$
7. $(5 \times 5) - (3 \times 5)$
   $10 = (5 - 3)5$
   $10 = 10$
8. $(3 \times 5) + (3 \times 6)$
   $3 \times 11 = 15 + 18$
   $33 = 33$
9. $(2 \times 4) + (3 \times 4)$
   $20 = 8 + 12$
   $20 = 20$
10. $3 \times 8 + 3 \times 3$
   $3 \times 11 = 24 + 9$
   $33 = 33$

page 142
1. C
2. J
3. D
4. G
5. A
6. J

page 143
1. 5th–15; 6th–21;
   7th–28; 8th–36
2. The pattern
   grows by
   successive
   integers: +2,
   +3, +4, +5, +6,
   etc.
3. 55
4. 5th–12; 6th–14;
   7th–16; 8th–18
5. The number of
   guests increases
   by two for each
   table added.
6. 22

page 144
1. A
2. F
3. C
4. J
5. B
6. G

page 145
1. B
2. H
3. D
4. G
5. C
6. J

page 146
1. C
2. J
3. A
4. H
5. C
6. F
7. B

page 147
8. F
9. C

10. J
11. C
12. H
13. A
14. G
15. A
16. H

page 148
17. A
18. G
19. C
20. J
21. B
22. F

page 149
23. B
24. J
25. C
26. H
27. A
28. G
29. C
30. G

page 150
1. C
2. F
3. B
4. J
5. A
6. J
7. C
8. F

page 151
1. A
2. J
3. C
4. G
5. C
6. J
7. B
8. J

page 152
1. D
2. F
3. C
4. F
5. C
6. G
7. A
8. H

page 153
1. B
2. F
3. D
4. G
5. A
6. H
7. A
8. H

page 154
1. B
2. F
3. D
4. F
5. D
6. G
7. C
8. H

page 155
1. C
2. G
3. C
4. J
5. A
6. H

page 156
1. C
2. F
3. D
4. G
5. C
6. J
7. C
8. G
9. B
10. F

page 157
1. $11\frac{9}{16}$
2. $11\frac{5}{36}$
3. $13\frac{5}{8}$
4. $3\frac{3}{10}$
5. $11\frac{17}{25}$
6. $21\frac{13}{72}$
7. $\frac{8}{25}$
8. $7\frac{1}{4}$
9. $82\frac{1}{2}$
10. $11\frac{2}{7}$
11. $4\frac{1}{3}$
12. $10\frac{35}{58}$

page 158

1. A
2. J
3. C
4. F
5. B
6. J

page 159
1. C
2. G
3. D
4. F
5. B
6. J
7. B
8. H

page 160
1. $7\frac{1}{9}$
2. $43\frac{1}{20}$
3. $3\frac{5}{24}$
4. $\frac{13}{32}$
5. $1\frac{5}{21}$
6. $\frac{6}{49}$
7. $31\frac{46}{55}$
8. $27\frac{2}{5}$
9. $111\frac{7}{12}$
10. $3\frac{13}{35}$
11. $1\frac{13}{16}$
12. $16\frac{7}{18}$

page 161
1. C
2. G
3. D
4. J
5. C
6. H

page 162
1. B
2. F
3. B
4. F
5. D
6. F
7. C
8. H
9. B
10. J

page 163
1. A
2. G

3. A
4. H
5. D
6. G

page 164
1. $150.36
2. 3.27
3. 2.48
4. 5,255.12
5. 9.15
6. 2.31
7. 236.7
8. 2.74
9. 21.76
10. 46

page 165
1. B
2. H
3. B
4. J
5. A
6. F

page 166
1. C
2. H
3. D
4. G
5. A
6. H
7. B
8. J

page 167
9. A
10. H
11. B
12. G
13. C
14. F
15. C
16. F
17. D
18. G

page 168
19. C
20. F
21. B
22. H
23. C
24. J
25. A
26. G

page 169
1. C
2. H
3. D
4. H
5. C
6. H

page 170
1. D
2. F
3. B
4. J
5. B

page 171
1. B
2. J
3. A
4. G
5. B
6. J

page 172
1.

A   B

2.

C   D

3.

E   F
G   H

4.

I
J   K

5.

L
M   N

6. ∠LMN

page 173
1. D
2. J
3. D
4. J
5. B
6. F

page 174
1. pentagon
2. decagon
3. triangle
4. pentagon
5. dodecagon
6. hexagon
7. octagon
8. quadrilateral (parallelogram)

page 175
1. D
2. F
3. B
4. A
5. C
6. E
7. C
8. E

page 176
Students should have drawn each figure next to its name.
1. triangle
2. rectangle
3. scalene triangle
4. square
5. pyramid
6. sphere

page 177
1. congruent
2. congruent
3. congruent
4. similar
5. congruent
6. similar

page 178
1. D
2. J
3. A
4. J
5. See student work.
6. See student work.

page 179
1. B
2. H
3. C
4. H
5. A
6. G

page 180
1. prism
2. neither
3. pyramid
4. pyramid
5. prism
6. neither
7. prism
8. pyramid
9. prism

page 181
1. A
2. G
3. D

page 182
1. C
2. F
3. D
4. H
5. A
6. G

page 183
1. B
2. H
3. A
4. 9
5. 9
6. 9

page 184
1. 5
2. 6
3. 6
4. 5
5. 16

page 185
1. A
2. H
3. B
4. G
5. A
6. F
7. C
8. G

page 186
1. C
2. H
3. C
4. F

page 187
1. (2, 6); (5, 6); (5, 4); (5, 2)
2. (−2, 2); (1, 2); (1, −1); (−2, −1)
3. (2, −3); (2, −5); (−2, −5); (−2, −6); (−5, −6)

page 188

a sailboat

page 189
1. D
2. H
3. B
4. F
5. D

page 190
6. F
7. C
8. J
9. B
10. F

page 191
11. A
12. G
13. B
14. J
15. A
16. F
17. A

page 192
18. G
19. D
20. G
21. D
22. J
23. A
24. H

page 193
1. B
2. J
3. C
4. G

page 194
1. D

2. F
3. A
4. F
5. D
6. G
7. B

page 195
1. D
2. F
3. B
4. J
5. D
6. G
7. D
8. H

page 196
1. D
2. G
3. D
4. G
5. A
6. G
7. C
8. F

page 197
1. B
2. H
3. D
4. H
5. B

page 198
1. 400 mm
2. yes
3. 250 cm
4. yes
5. A
6. J

page 199
1. 3 L
2. 40 L
3. 6,000 L
4. 1,000 daL
5. 250 daL
6. 0.7 L
7. 8 kL
8. 10,000 g
9. 10 dag
10. 2 kg
11. 0.5 kg
12. 7 kg
13. 2,000 mg

14. 3,000 kg

page 200
1. C
2. F
3. C
4. H
5. A
6. J

page 201
1. B
2. H
3. B
4. J
5. C
6. F
7. A

page 202
1. B
2. F
3. C
4. F
5. B

page 203
1. C
2. H
3. A
4. J
5. B
6. G

page 204
1. D
2. H
3. C
4. J
5. B

page 205
1. 13 centimeters
2. 1.25 inches
3. 0.25 miles
4. 4 meters
5. 20,000 feet
6. G
7. A

page 206
1. D
2. F
3. B
4. H
5. B
6. H

7. C

page 207
1. D
2. F
3. B
4. H
5. B
6. H
7. A

page 208
8. G
9. D
10. H
11. C
12. F
13. D
14. H
15. D

page 209
16. G
17. C
18. G
19. D
20. H
21. A

page 210
1. B
2. F
3. B

page 211
1. A
2. F
3. B
4. H

page 212
1. C
2. J
3. A
4. H
5. B
6. F

page 213
1. A
2. H
3. C
4. G
5. C

page 214
1. D

2. G
3. B
4. J
5. C
6. H

page 215
1. B
2. H
3. B
4. F

page 216
1. A
2. H
3. B
4. F
5. B

page 217
1. C
2. J
3. B
4. H
5. D
6. F
7. C

page 218
1. D
2. J
3. C
4. G
5. C
6. G

page 219
1. B
2. F
3. D
4. G
5. C
6. J

page 220
1. C
2. H
3. B
4. J
5. C
6. H
7. A

page 221
1. C
2. F
3. C

4. H

page 222
1. B
2. H
3. A
4. G
5. D
6. F

page 223
1. C
2. G
3. D
4. F

page 224
1. A
2. H
3. B
4. H
5. B
6. G
7. C

page 225
1. 67
2. 10
3. Number of People
4. The vertical axis should be labeled: 0, 10, 20, 30, 40, 50, 60, 70, 80, 90, 100. The bars on the bar graph should reflect the numbers shown in the chart.
5. Answers will vary. Possible answer: Gina probably would have received more than 85 votes for Italian because people who are eating at an Italian restaurant probably enjoy Italian food.

page 226
1. 31 items; 43 items
2. 12 items
3. greatest increase: canned goods; decrease: infant

clothing

4. There was more variation this year. The difference between the low and high amounts collected per item (the range) was 31. Last year, it was 21.

5. Based on this set of data, the class can predict that next year's collection will increase slightly over this year's collection.

page 227
1. B
2. F
3. C
4. F
5. C

page 228
1. D
2. F
3. C
4. An increasing number of people immigrated during each range of years in the graph.
5. D
6. H

page 229
1. B
2. F
3. A
4. J
5. D
6. H

page 230
7. A
8. J
9. D
10. F

page 231
11. C
12. H
13. B
14. J

15. C
16. G

page 232
17. D
18. F
19. B
20. H
21. A
22. H
23. A

page 233
1. D
2. F
3. C
4. J
5. B
6. J
7. B

page 234
8. F
9. C
10. G
11. C
12. H
13. A
14. G
15. D
16. G

page 235
17. C
18. H
19. B
20. J
21. A
22. G
23. D
24. J
25. B

page 236
26. G
27. A
28. G
29. D
30. H
31. B
32. H

page 237
1. D
2. G
3. A

4. J
5. B
6. H
7. C
8. F
9. D
10. G

page 238
11. C
12. J
13. C
14. J
15. C
16. F
17. C
18. G
19. D

page 239
20. H
21. B
22. F
23. D
24. H
25. A
26. J
27. C
28. J

page 240
29. C
30. J
31. B
32. H
33. A
34. G
35. B
36. J
37. A
38. H

page 241
1. B
2. J
3. B
4. G

page 242
5. D
6. G
7. C
8. H
9. D

page 243

10. H
11. A
12. J
13. C
14. G
15. D

page 244
16. G
17. A
18. H
19. D
20. F
21. B

page 245
22. G
23. C
24. G
25. C
26. J
27. C

page 246
28. J
29. B
30. F
31. C
32. H
33. C
34. J